ADVANCE PRAISE FOR FALLOPIAN RHAPSODY: THE STORY OF THE LUNACHICKS

"Their name alone is a stroke of genius, and bless them for keeping the faith in Rock alive. Now *Fallopian Rhapsody* confirms the myth, and after I read the book, I lost weight, my hair got thicker, my nails grew strong enough to climb trees, and my sex life soared to unbelievable heights."

Debbie Harry of Blondie, author of *Face It*

"This book contains the realest, funniest, most heart-wrenching writing about being in a band I've ever read. The first Lunachicks record, *Babysitters on Acid*, gave me permission to be my full self as a singer (though NO ONE can touch Theo Kogan's voice EVER), and now this book has confirmed what I already knew. The Lunachicks, as people, are as hilarious, complicated, and undeniable as their songs."

Kathleen Hanna of The Julie Ruin, Le Tigre, and Bikini Kill

"As a rebellious New York City teenager deeply involved in the underground music scene, I cannot stress the magnitude and impact the Lunachicks had on not just me, not just female musicians, but the New York City scene as a whole. They were torch bearers for all of us, giving us permission and inspiration to be as wild as we could possibly imagine and just go for it. It was an absolute side-splitting and heartbreaking joy to read all these personal stories and know what was really going on behind all that black eyeliner. Thanks for kicking that door open so the rest of us could run in."

Jessica Pimentel of *Orange Is the New Black*

"Was anyone ever as powerful as teen girls in the 1990s NYC? This sexy, funny, totally bonkers band memoir took me right back to that dangerous DIY era in all its filth and freedom. *Fallopian Rhapsody* is a valuable addition to the literary canons of obnoxious punk rock, TV-raised Generation X, and messy, creative female friendships that last a lifetime."

Ada Calhoun, author of *St. Marks Is Dead* and *Why We Can't Sleep*

"For me, the Lunachicks embodied the Lower East Side of the '90s. Gritty, glammy, over-the-top punk rock and rollers, this was a band that you had to see to believe. Out of the thousands of concerts I've seen, the first time I saw the Lunachicks stands out to me as the most 'What the f**k did I just witness?' moment of my concertgoing life. *Fallopian Rhapsody* is a must-read for fans of the CBGB-era rock scene that was New York City and brings to life the unique swagger and controlled (or sometimes not so controlled) chaos that was the Lunachicks. Both poignant and hilarious, it's a book that when finished makes you ponder, 'What the f**k did I just read?'"

Chris Santos, cofounder of Beauty & Essex and judge on *Chopped*

"*Fallopian Rhapsody* is a whirlwind ride through untold punk rock history on the wheels of a cross-country tour with the Lunachicks, from illuminated stories on the catastrophic dynamics between bandmates as sisters to the necessary details on the drugs and assholes who attempted to break them. Often told in first person, *Fallopian Rhapsody* is a tell-all tale on existing fabulously, outside of every potential box. It's a time capsule that brings light to the sound, action, filth, decadence, and nasty-woman rapture of seminal NYC punks, the Lunachicks."

Cristy Road Carrera of *Next World Tarot*, *Spit and Passion*, Choked Up, and The Homewreckers

FALLOPIAN RHAPSODY

FALLOPIAN RHAPSODY

THE STORY OF THE LUNACHICKS

THE LUNACHICKS WITH JEANNE FURY

hachette
BOOKS

New York

Hachette Books
Hachette Book Group
1290 Avenue of the Americas
New York, NY 10104
HachetteBooks.com
Twitter.com/HachetteBooks
Instagram.com/HachetteBooks

First Edition: June 2021

Published by Hachette Books, an imprint of Perseus Books, LLC, a subsidiary of Hachette Book Group, Inc. The Hachette Books name and logo is a trademark of the Hachette Book Group.

The Hachette Speakers Bureau provides a wide range of authors for speaking events. To find out more, go to www.hachettespeakersbureau.com or call (866) 376-6591.

The publisher is not responsible for websites (or their content) that are not owned by the publisher.

Print book interior design by Amy Quinn

Library of Congress Cataloging-in-Publication Data
Names: Lunachicks (Musical group) author. | Fury, Jeanne, author.
Title: Fallopian rhapsody : the story of The Lunachicks / The Lunachicks with Jeanne Fury.
Description: First edition. | New York City : Hachette Books, 2021.
Identifiers: LCCN 2020053786 | ISBN 9780306874482 (trade paperback) | ISBN 9780306874475 (ebook)
Subjects: LCSH: Lunachicks (Musical group) | Women punk rock musicians--United States--Biography. | Punk rock musicians--United States--Biography.
Classification: LCC ML421.L85 L85 2021 | DDC 782.42166/092/2 [B]--dc23
LC record available at https://lccn.loc.gov/2020053786

ISBNs: 978-0-306-87448-2 (trade paperback original); 978-0-306-87447-5 (e-book)

Printed in the United States of America

LSC-C

Printing 1, 2021

This book is dedicated to
friendship, sisterhood,
and rock 'n' roll.
Onetwothreefour!

CONTENTS

A NOTE FROM THE COAUTHOR

It was 1995, and I was a moody little shit lodged in the hemorrhoidal clench of suburban New Jersey. I was predictably histrionic, but I guess I had reason to be: neurobiological fuckery and routine bouts of intestinal turbulence hijacked my life beginning at age twelve. I thought my troubles would have eased at least a little by high school. They hadn't. By the time I was a senior, I hated almost everything and everyone.

Vulgar, dark punk rock made by terrifying, delinquent women was part of my self-prescribed treatment plan. Music offered me scarce semblances of grace in between trips to the toilet and prolonged episodes of self-loathing. The record store was a proverbial pharmacy where I sought antidotes to the gloom that stubbornly clung to my bones. One Saturday afternoon while I was flipping through the *L* section of plastic CD cases, I came across *Jerk of All Trades* by the Lunachicks. The cover showed a blonde lady with eyes like tarantulas and wearing a waitress outfit. Her body appeared to be mid-stroke. The title was displayed ransom note–style, and *Lunachicks* was written in dripping red letters across a giant bone. The back cover was a band photo. To my delight, the Lunachicks were all girls. This mattered. Sisters doin' everything for themselves was a big deal. With their clown makeup, tattoos, feather boas, leopard-print rags, and drag-queen hair, they were reform-school escapees posing as a circus sideshow gang. They looked goofy, mean, and like they would devour their enemies whole. Together, they possessed the kind of self-assured power I could only dream about.

The first few seconds of the opening song, "Drop Dead," charged at me like buffaloes on methamphetamines. Then the singing started. No screaming or sneering or shrieking—it was singing. The oddball voice was operatic, comical, and utterly bananas. And holy shit, the lyrics: "Don't you fuck with us / We will follow you onto the bus / Fart right in your face / And look out because / Should've worn Tussy like your mama said / Then maybe you wouldn't be dead / We can be worster!" Somehow, in that moment, the Lunachicks made me feel less defective as a young woman. My heart thudded, and I was suddenly a thousand feet tall.

It became very apparent very quickly: though the Lunachicks looked demented, none of this was actually a joke. Not only were they comedic geniuses, but they also had killer chops and obvious songwriting smarts. But what truly reverberated deep down was the realization that the Lunachicks were subversive feminist masterminds. They took every damaging female stereotype, turned them inside out, and mashed them into my eyeballs and ear holes with equal parts hostility and jubilation. Despite their penchant for retaliatory flatulence, they were in complete control of their faculties. Never was that more apparent than during their live shows, which were combinations of performance art, stand-up comedy, and sweaty, visceral punk rock. It was a kick in the ass and a pie in the face—or a pie in the ass and a kick in the face. Both analogies are appropriate.

Fate led me to cross paths with these awesome women, and I can say without reserve that the bond between Theo, Syd, and Gina is genuine in a way that strikes me as unusual and also beautiful. They've been in each other's lives for decades not because of financial or creative obligation, but because they love each other and enjoy each other's company. I've spent enough time interviewing and profiling bands to learn that this is something of an anomaly. There's a reason Metallica travels in separate buses.

The Lunachicks' story isn't just about a punk band. It's also about friends who will never leave each other's sides and the implications their sisterhood has had on the people they endeavor to be in this world. It's just one of the many reasons that from now till whenever, the Lunachicks will forever be worster.

Jeanne Fury

DROP YOUR FUCKING PANTS RIGHT NOW

We thought it was business as usual. The five of us were stumbling sweaty and half-naked around a cruddy, airless dressing room trying to dry off after rocking the crowd's ass sideways. The floor was strewn with bits of stage clothes: leopard-print tights, some enormous old-lady bras, tutus, knee socks, what have you. Our makeup was reduced to watery skid marks across our flushed faces. All we could think of was cooling down so we wouldn't faint or shit ourselves or both.

Theo wrestled a giant blonde wig from her head while joining Gina, Sindi, and Squid in peeling off as many articles of clothing as quickly as possible and drying off with bar towels. The unofficial after-show look was basically tutus and ta-tas. We were trying out a new drummer, Chip, who was a great musician, but we weren't yet sure if the fit would work on a personal level. Chip seemed unfazed by this not-sexy, very sweaty, and definitely smelly routine we'd performed countless times around the world. A promising sign. Tonight, May 20, 1993, it was in Southend, which is like the Staten Island or Jersey Shore of England. In that moment, as we ran around the club's dressing room in various states of nakedness, something was very, incredibly off. Every one of us felt it.

Chip walked up to the mirror that was curiously built into the wall, stared at it, and walked out of the room to see a line of guys slinking out

1

of an adjoining office. Sindi called it: two-way mirror. Whoever was next door had a four-by-five-foot clear open view into our dressing room, and they were watching us dress and undress all night.

No. Fucking. Way.

Chip picked up a chair and hurled it into the mirror, smashing it to shards. We threw on whatever clothes were closest to us, which happened to be our stage stuff, and bolted out into the club to confront the last guy leaving the office, who happened to be the owner. We surrounded the dumb schmuck in a circle like a pack of wolves, except we were wearing crooked bras and tutus, and had pigtails in our hair and blackout on our front teeth. We went off.

THEO: We were five clowns in tutus. I imagine from his per-spective it was like we got larger and more looming, frightful, and trippy with every moment—like inflatable lawn ornaments on acid.

SQUID: Chip grabbed a barstool and held it over this guy's head. He was trying to be like, "Buh buh I'm sorry!!" I'm ripping the guy to fucking shreds, turkey-necking right up close in his face, screaming, "DROP YOUR FUCKING PANTS RIGHT NOW!!!!!" We were seething, threatening the guy's fucking life. He dropped his pants.

CHIP: I kind of straight-armed about ten pints of beer off the bar. Then I realized they couldn't do anything to us—we had an advantage—so I went back into a storage room that was filled with expensive stage lighting and amps and sound equipment, and as the owner of the place watched, I just stood there staring at him and picked up piece by piece and smashed it on the floor. Good times, good times.

SINDI: We started breaking shit and would've demolished the place had we not had an experienced tour manager who we trusted and who was able to rein us in and convince us that even though we kinda had the right to do this, we didn't really. Even if somebody fucks you over like this, you can't actually burn down the building because you will still get in trouble. But we did the best we could.

THEO: We were on fire—blindly enraged and fearless. After his pants came down, we dispersed, and there was a general smashing of everything. I remember destroying whatever else was left in the room in a fit of wild cackling and then getting the fuck out of there.

GINA: After the whole thing was over, we were all back in the dressing room and Squid goes, "That's it, Chip, you're joining our band." We hadn't yet decided as a group, but it was so apparent to all of us that Squid just went ahead and said it. And we were like, "Yeah, well, of course." Chip was one of us.

CHIP: I was very proud when they asked me to join the band after that.

We were hoping to get the hell out of Southend without further incident, but our publicist had other plans. She was delighted by this little scandal and ran with the story. She called every trashy tabloid and told them what had happened. And those English sure do love their *Daily Mirror* and *Sun*—they've got like five different versions of *National Enquirer*. The next day, we were on the front page or second page of all the tabloids. Our publicist was thrilled. Us, not so much.

Look, all we ever wanted as crazy kids from New York City, hopelessly devoted to rock 'n' roll, was to play in a kick-ass band—and we did!—but, wow, did that humble pursuit come with a whole lotta bullshit. It wasn't in our nature to stand there, play our instruments, and shrug off the harassment and dismissal. It's not in our DNA. Sorry, no way. If someone fucked with us, we went after them arm in arm and ruined their stupid life.

Our secret? We did it together, as a gang of sisters who always had each other's back, come hell or high-water pants. Our thirteen-year-long career was the centerpiece of a friendship that began when we were teenagers. We traveled the world, played sold-out tours, and inspired girls to form bands; we also juggled internal strife, cheated death on a few occasions, and learned that there is nothing more potent than the power of friendship. As long as we had each other, we were unstoppable.

We were gonna do exactly what we wanted, do it our way, and have a butt-load of fun, even if that meant literally scaring the pants off a few dudes in the process.

CHAPTER 1

FEMME-PIRE STATE OF MIND

It's all New York City's fault. There is no other place on earth that could have spawned the Lunachicks. Our most formative years were spent running wild in this creative and cultural mecca, absorbing its diversity and letting all its weirdness rush through our blood like a virus. New York City turned us out, in every aspect you can imagine and plenty more you can't. We are absolutely a product of our environment, equal parts filthy, funny, and flamboyant.

We didn't have the traditional high school experience that gets played out in every PG-13 movie. We were really lucky. Growing up surrounded by so much dirt and creativity made us restless. After a while, it wasn't enough to be onlookers; we had to be active participants. As artists and musicians, we had a symbiotic relationship with our surroundings; we gave and we took. True love and codependence.

Back in the '70s and '80s, New York City was shitty and gritty and dangerous and fun. Living here certainly made our awkward teenage years more endurable than if we lived anywhere else. Because our outside environment was as twisted and freaky as we felt on the inside, we felt less out of place than we would have if we'd grown up in some manicured, white-picket-fence nightmare. We were born weirdos, and New York offered no resistance to that. We thrived here.

In hindsight, our New York was a fucking hellscape. The AIDS and crack epidemics were heating up. Crime was rampant. Perverts were everywhere. The city was about as hospitable as a turd to the face. And yet, we loved it. Chalk it up to being young and not knowing any better. It's not like we assumed kids in Ohio or Kansas jumped over dirty needles and dodged flashers and mounds of dog shit on their way to school every morning the way we did—we knew our city had its peculiar charms—but it also never occurred to us that New York should be a safer, cleaner place for us to grow up in. We just accepted and loved the city in all its foul, terrifying glory exactly the way it was.

We didn't grow up with cultural subsets of kids, like the jocks or the preps or the nerds. In our New York, everybody was a little strange. Many of our favorite bands and biggest influences were proudly, defiantly "other": the NY Dolls, the Damned, the Cramps, the Misfits, Jayne County—they all sought to infiltrate people's comfort zones and plant their flag like a hot fart in a crowded subway.

Speaking of public transit, the blessed thing about growing up here is that we didn't need a car. The subway made it possible for us to take ourselves to a show or a museum or Coney Island, all in one day. That right there encouraged us to be independent at a young age. We didn't need to rely on other people to create experiences for us. Most kids don't have that kind of luxury and freedom to go wherever they want whenever they want.

That freedom came at a price. For teenagers in 1980s NYC, daily life was a veritable obstacle course of creeps and assholes. We traveled in a pack, like baby hyenas. Because we were punks, we were natural targets for just about everyone, so we had to travel in groups. Your crew needed to be tough—the girls were always much tougher than the boys—and you had to defend yourself or, at the minimum, talk big and run fast.

Kids would sing-scream "Freaks Come Out at Night" by Whodini at us, or they'd scream, "Frrrrreeeeeaaaks!!" Or they'd call us Cyndi Lauper or Boy George or Madonna, which we took to be an insult because those people were on MTV and the radio—pop music, not punk. Kids would yank our hair; one of our friends even got her green hair chopped off by a mob of teens on the subway. You really needed your girls at shows. The bigger girls would make a circle around the smaller girls and stick their elbows out and deliver some well-calculated warning shots. We always looked out for each other.

The punk kids were few and far between. The safe haven for people like us was the Lower East Side and St. Marks Place in the East Village, where the other weirdos congregated. But the comings and goings were treacherous, to say the least. For all its coolness back then, parts of those neighborhoods were bleak as fuck. Bombed-out and burned buildings and empty lots were common. The same goes for the waterfront in Williamsburg, Brooklyn, which was a pure wreckage of corroded iron structures that were fun to explore and full of rusty nails, piss, graffiti, and general danger.

To get to the Lower East Side from Brooklyn, where most of us lived and where we spent the bulk of our time, we had to take the subway through downtown Brooklyn, which was not a very tolerant place for young honkeys with blue hair. Our little crew would get on the subway, clutching our cassette players (everybody carried a boombox back then), and we'd all hold our breath when pulling into the stations. The doors would open, and we'd look down so as not to make eye contact with anybody. If you could get past Fulton Street without getting jumped, you were home free to Second Avenue, the LES.

On the Lower East Side, nobody paid us any mind—except when they did. Cut to a skinhead who saw Theo and friends walking down Second Ave and shouted, "Nuke 'em all, whatever they are!" But we usually didn't feel as ostracized or get called names on the street or get shit thrown at us or feel threatened. Of course, we'd have to eventually take the subway back to Brooklyn, usually at three or four in the morning. More than once, we were mugged, had knives pulled on us, and saw guys jerk off at us. So much of that shit was always happening to the point where it was more of an inconvenience than acts of violence.

We were putting ourselves in all kinds of dangerous places all the time, sometimes intentionally. We used to drop acid and go to Times Square, just to freak out and be freaked out. It was a playground for us. Sometimes we'd drop acid, ride the subway all the way up to the Bronx, and then walk all the way back to Brooklyn just for kicks.

GINA: I was a big acid head. I'll never forget my first time. Freshman year, I was fourteen and had new friends who took me down to Washington Square Park to score some acid. I was like, "I can't do LSD! That's bad! I read *Go Ask Alice*!" But they were like, "Oh, you're gonna love it." Peer pressure, they talked me into it. We scored acid, and we took it. Hours went by, nothing happened. So then our friend says, "Screw this, we're gonna go talk to my dad." This kid's dad was a crazy brainiac hippie computer guy who worked for IBM and whose brother was an acid producer. He had all this windowpane acid, which is really intense, strong acid. This kid explained to his dad that we tried to score acid in the park but it was fake, and can't we please have some of his. The dad was all, "Uh, I dunno if I can do that ... How old is she?" he said, pointing to me. "I'm sixteen!" I lied. He goes, "You don't look sixteen!" After an hour of beating him down, he finally gave us some. We took it. I never tripped that hard since. It was fucking crazy. We wandered the streets all night out of our minds encountering all walks of city nightlife. It became my new favorite thing.

THEO: When we were fifteen, Squid and I were tripping on acid on New Year's Eve while riding the subway back to Brooklyn at four in the morning. We were sitting there and saw the blur of a body go by. Then another guy ran behind the first guy—carrying a fuckin' butcher knife.

SQUID: The only reason I knew it was real and I wasn't hallucinating was because Theo saw the same thing. Another time, Gina and I had a school assignment at the Bronx Zoo, so we split a tab of Doonesbury blotter. We figured we were being extra-responsible by doing this, as opposed to taking one tab each per usual. By the time we got to the Bronx Zoo, we were spiraling.

The bird exhibit blew our mind. One of the questions of our assignment was "Why don't the birds fly out of the exhibit?" And as soon as I finished reading that question, I looked up, and a bird flew right out of the exhibit.

GINA: We went into the World of Darkness—a long cave where all the nocturnal animals are kept—and I panicked because I didn't think we were ever going to find our way out. I had to talk to a guard to keep from freaking out.

THEO: One of the rules of taking acid is that you never look in a mirror, although I often looked anyway, truth be told. It bugged me out to see my eyeballs swirling like the Cheshire cat, but it didn't make me lose it. During one summer in high school, Squid came to visit my grand-parents' house on Fire Island, a nearby vacation spot for city people. We did acid, and late at night we were in the bathroom together, and out of the corner of my eye, I could see Squid's head turning toward the mir-ror. Oh no. I didn't want her to freak out when she saw her tripping reflection, so I tackled her to the floor. It felt like a slow-motion quarterback takedown: "Noooooooooo!!!" *boom* We hit the floor like tangled lov-ers escaping a hand-grenade explosion. In my mind, it was very heroic, very dramatic. Then we laughed until we peed on ourselves. Another time out there, Gina and I stayed at the house of her mom's friend Bob Resnik, a former speechwriter for Nixon. The two of us ate mush-rooms, then tripped our brains out during dinner. All the food looked extra shiny and cartoonish. Fun fact: my grandfather helped in some secret socialist underground organization to get Nixon out of office.

We'd go to Playland, a super-sleazy arcade in Times Square, late at night, surrounded by porno, pimps, and prostitutes. We'd wear skimpy clothes and platforms and go running around like it was no big deal. We shouldn't have been anywhere near Playland at midnight in *any* outfit! But we truly believed we were invincible, or else we wouldn't have attempted any of this shit. Plus, we were streetwise enough to not be dumb. We were dumb, but not *that* dumb. Well, most of the time. We did so much risky shit, but somehow we lived through it.

We made a lot of trips to CBGB and the Pyramid Club in the East Village, and to Danceteria on West Twenty-First Street, where there were four floors, three of which had different music. The drinking age was eighteen, so all you had to do was look eighteen, which was pretty easy when you're fourteen, blind with bravado, and filled with attitude. It's not like any of the clubs gave a shit either. All us kids went to Forty-Second Street to get fake IDs. You had to pick an occupation in order to get your ID.

SQUID: I picked secretary. I looked eleven years old, but I put on red lipstick.

THEO: Mine just said *employee*.

GINA: Mine just said *asthmatic*.

Danceteria closed in 1986 (amid an unsubstantiated rumor that some underage kid fell down the elevator shaft), but for a while, it was the coolest club, with so many different subsets of arty weirdos hanging around. One night, you could see the goth band 45 Grave, or the glam punks Sic Fucks, or the '50s band the Coasters, or you might be hanging out in the same room as Madonna. Occasionally, some of us would get wasted and spit ice cubes at people from the roof of the club. We were assholes. It was a thrill just to be out on the scene.

We'd make our own fun. We'd grab a radio and a bottle of Olde English and sit in piles of garbage on the street like they were beanbag chairs. One popular spot was our friend's house in Brooklyn, nicknamed the Bucket of Blood because the walls were painted red, where we'd get really fucked up and hit the streets to play ring 'n' run. Another favorite hangout was our older friends' apartment, called the Kretin House, which was at the foot of the Manhattan side of the Williamsburg Bridge on the Lower East Side. Being with each other, drinking, smoking pot, listening to the Misfits, making grilled cheese—those were exciting times for teenagers! We'd fall asleep in a cluster, like a lump of hamsters, and wake up in the morning with our hair all messy and our bodies crisscrossed over each other . . . it was so dirty and fun.

Some nights, we'd hang out in a graveyard—the *'yahd*—in Bensonhurst with our metalhead friends. Yep, we had some big plans back then: go to Bensonhurst and drink forties in the graveyard. One kid we'd run into out there was an Orthodox Jew, nicknamed the Heavy Metal Yid, who wore all the Orthodox clothes—the undergarments, a white button-down shirt, black chino pants, and a yarmulke—but he'd roll up his crisp white sleeves and reveal a bunch of Satanic tattoos. We'd see him pushing a shopping cart, and he'd be like, "I'm going to see Slayah!"

THEO: I did it in that graveyard.

GINA: I did it in the pool at Tompkins Square Park.

SQUID: I did it on my homeroom teacher's desk. Not with my homeroom teacher.

Growing up in New York City, random encounters with famous (or soon-to-be-famous or infamous) people were common. We'd see Andy Warhol uptown near our high school, Danny DeVito on the subways, and Iman strolling up Eighth Street. This was our normal.

SINDI: In the very early days of the band, Squid and I were walking in midtown Manhattan one day for some unknown reason when suddenly, "Ohmygod, it's Alice Cooper!" Luckily, we had a rough rehearsal demo tape stuffed in one of our pockets—as well as loads of confidence—so we pounced on him, introduced ourselves, and gave him the tape. He was super-nice and even chitchatted with us and gave us a little pep talk. God only knows what was on that tape. We love you, Alice!

GINA: My friend's mom, Jaki, took me as her guest to a Jack LaLanne gym in lower Manhattan. As I climbed onto the StairMaster, I noticed the woman on the adjacent machine was fit and dressed in full Olivia Newton-John "Physical" attire. "Oh, Gina, this is Wendy," Jaki said, introducing me to the woman. My jaw hit the ground. "Wendy" was Wendy O. fucking Williams of the Plasmatics—punk rock icon! Yeah, that happened. She was so friendly and sweet. W. O. W.

THEO: When I was fifteen, my mom dragged me to an aerobics class in SoHo that Madonna just so happened to be at. There I was, hungover, huffing and puffing and trying to keep up with the steps, while Madonna was in the very front, making love to herself in the mirror and doing everything better than everyone else. I was hoping to evaporate into the smoke that was leaking out of my unwashed pores. Please kill me.

GINA: Matt Dillon started hanging around the CBGB's hardcore matinees to study for an upcoming role as a punk rocker. He invited me and my little crew up to his loft to drink beer. We got hammered. He had a nice place. I learned that he was an Aquarius. I don't think the movie ever came out.

THEO: He showed up at a punk show in a brand-new MC jacket, pulled out a joint, and shared it with me and my friend Amber. He seemed to be trying kinda hard, yet he was so open and generous.

We already thought we were hot shit, so knowing our hometown was also where so much culture was happening and where the cool people came to live or hang out just reinforced our belief that we were predestined for great-ish-ness.

The year we played our first show, 1988, the homicide rate in New York City was the highest it had ever been at that point, but we couldn't tell the difference in crime from one year to the next. It seemed like horrible, nightmarish shit was happening all the time. We weren't exactly desensitized to it, because it freaked us out for sure, but we thought that's just what life was like.

In August of that year, the Tompkins Square Riot happened in the East Village. The gentrifying residents didn't like the fact that a large group of homeless people, plus a bunch of punks and junkies, had taken over the park, so the mayor tried to institute a curfew. People planned a resistance, and so the cops came in and beat the shit out of them.

> **GINA:** I was there, but I didn't know there was going to be a riot; I was at the park to hang out! My friends and I were really wasted, acting stupid and having fun, totally oblivious, and then all of a sudden it was full-on chaos: cops, barricades, fire, people running. We were like, "Time to go. Now."

Mayhem, heinous crimes, and perversions of justice were kind of par for the course. If you grew up here back then, tragedy was common. As young girls, self-preservation was always on our minds because it was constantly taught to us: you are a target, and there are bad, sick people out there who want to hurt you. It was drilled into us at an early age: watch your back!

> **THEO:** I was very young when Son of Sam was on his rampage, and was afraid he would get me. When I was eight, my sister and I were almost abducted by a creep in a car on our way home for lunch, but even at that young age I was smart enough to run down a street he couldn't drive down, and we escaped. In ninth grade, on the way up to school in Harlem, I had my crotch groped on a crowded C train. I thought it was someone's umbrella, but it was a

man's hand. I screamed and pushed the hand away, but it
was so packed it was hard to even tell who did it. Although I felt invincible as a teen, I never really felt
100 percent safe. It's a paradox.

By age fourteen, we'd been bullied in schoolyards, mistaken for prostitutes, and propositioned by Hasidic men; we'd fought off pervy creeps on
the subways and seen enough men tugging their cocks at us to last a million lifetimes. As a result, we have an old-school, ready-to-fight mentality
that will never go away.

One Halloween night, we had to run for our lives in platform shoes
through the East Village because a bunch of kids were chasing us down.
That was Halloween tradition—kids from the neighborhood would beat
you up, or throw eggs at you, or beat you with a sock full of flour. We
were in skimpy little costumes, glammed up. The kids were chasing us
east, and in those years, the farther east you went, the scarier the neighborhood was. As we got older, we'd venture farther and farther: Avenue A, with an occasional visit to Avenue B, then Avenue C. Anyway,
we were running through Tompkins Square Park, from Avenue B to C,
knowing we were headed into uncharted territory. Coming out of the
other side of the park was like going through the gates of Narnia, like going through the wardrobe. So fucking scary! We ran into a bar for safety.
The bartender took one look at us kids and was like, "You can't be in
here!" and we were whimpering, "Please let us stay! They're gonna kill
us!" And he said, "Okay, fine. Want a margarita?"

SQUID: I remember thinking as I was running in those silver
glitter platforms, "Lesson learned: only wear shoes you
can run for your life in."

GINA: To this day, I don't go out casually walking around in
high heels. I have a mentality that's left over from
those old days.

THEO: I learned to run really well in heels when I was
go-go-ing, but that was a few years later.

While we didn't exactly curtail our thrill-seeking in light of the abundance of crime that was all around us all the time our whole lives, it's not like we were particularly brave. Again, that's just the way New York was, and we accepted it as such.

For the most part, our parents attempted to guide—and occasionally control—us, but we paid them little mind. Helicopter parenting didn't exist when we were kids. It was common for us to take the subway by ourselves at eleven, and by twelve we rode it daily to school. We had minimal supervision (or we were really good liars).

GINA: My mom was hardly ever home on weekends. One time there were about a dozen stinky punk rockers crashed out on my bedroom floor when my mom came by to grab more clothes to bring to her boyfriend's place. She poked her head in my room, and I could hear her say to her boyfriend, "No, I don't think Gina's home." What?! My room was packed with sleeping teenagers and reeked of bong water! I think she was in denial and didn't want to deal.

SQUID: Another time, we went to Gina's to grab something and found our friends passed out on the floor. We weren't even there! How'd they get in?? It was a total flophouse.

GINA: I did whatever I wanted, for better or worse. Theo and Squid were at my house one weekend, and we drank so much that the next day Theo's dad had to come get her because she had alcohol poisoning. He was so mad at me.

THEO: I actually regret that, and I don't have many regrets. I was supposed to go to see a ballet with my grandma, and I was too sick. We were drinking straight gin. I don't know what I thought I was doing, I had no tolerance for booze. But next I was doing tequila shots, which I had never done in my life. I drank way, way too much. I was vomiting the rest of the night and into the next morning. I ruined the whole day with my grandma.

Squid's parents were also often MIA, so we spent plenty of time hanging out at her place. Her parents were like the Charlie Brown teacher voice: *womp-womp-womp-womp.* You never saw them; they had an occasional peripheral presence, but they were never around. Or maybe they were home but weren't paying any attention. We would sit in her room and smoke cigarettes and drink. And whenever we slept over at Squid's house, we were "allowed" to stay out till three in the morning. Her parents didn't yell at us.

THEO: I practically lived at Squid's house throughout high school. I was able to get away with everything she got away with at her house, unlike at my own. Plus, her parents liked me. Maybe I was a good influence? Hard to say.

SQUID: I remember my dad being like, "You have to be home at . . ." and me just being like, "Nah! Not doing that" and walking out on him. My poor dad.

GINA: That was shocking to me—"You're allowed to say that??!"

SINDI: One time, I was sitting at Squid's giant kitchen table with her giant dad while waiting for her to finish whatever she was doing so we could head out for the night. She was wearing teensy-weensy leather shorts. Her dad and I were pleading with her to put on some more clothes. He said to me, "Can't you make her change?" And I said, "Can't *you* make her change??" He was concerned for his daughter's safety, and I was imagining the beatings I would be forced to dish out to defend her ass.

SQUID: I had just gotten these leather shorts when I ate mushrooms and went to see Cheech & Chong's *Nice Dreams* in a packed movie theater in Times Square with Sindi and her boyfriend. I was in a seat in the middle of the row, and I felt a "blurp" in my guts. Mushroom stomach. Glug, glug. Oh shit, great. I needed a toilet, but I was tripping so hard, everyone's face was melting. I thought,

"If I leave my seat and go into this sea of black, I'm not going to find my way back EVER." So I held it in and held it in, clenching. On the drive back to Brooklyn, I thought they were dropping me off first, but just as my bowels started to autopilot relax, I saw my corner come and go. Gaaaah! "What? Aren't you coming over?" OKAY FINE. We got to their house, and every second was torture. Finally, five stairs and ten feet from their front door, I felt a warm drip on the back of my thigh. All I could think was, "It's happening." Anyway, I got one wear out of those shorts. Had to throw them out.

Our parents were so *not* attuned to what our teenage lives were like, and it's not as if they got any more clued in as we got older and became touring musicians. Each of us would get asked the same question from random family members: "So how's the singing group going?" They came from a generation that couldn't fathom women decimating the stage as drummers or guitarists. When it came to contemporary music, the only reference in their minds was girls singing sweetly in sparkly dresses, not bashing a drum set apart or blowing out eardrums with their Marshall stacks.

SQUID: I was half out the front door, leaving the house, bags packed, bass in hand, headed to the airport for our first tour in Europe. My parents seemed confused. Not sure how closely they had been paying attention up to that point. It may have been crystallizing—"Uhhh, is there a phone number? Of someone? Or a name? We can call? Just in the case that we never see you again?"

Sindi's mom and Theo's parents were the only ones who were even remotely hip, but Theo's parents were also the strictest, probably because they had a clue.

THEO: To her credit, my mom was an unabashed activist and feminist, and I learned a lot from her how to be strong and stand up for myself. Back in the early '60s, she hitchhiked across Europe and went to a Rolling Stones concert. She bleached her hair and wore a blonde fall (a hairpiece, like a half wig), also known as a bump, to enhance her glamorous look. She had a leather miniskirt that looked more like a belt when I saw it on a hanger, and she knew how much she got harassed. So when I started going out on my own in skimpy skirts and the like, instead of my mom saying, "I used to do this and I am going to explain to you how the way you get treated sucks," she had the exact opposite reaction: "No, you can't do that!!" This was the way parents dealt with their kids back then. Kids weren't owed an explanation. It was just a "do what I say not what I did" situation.

SQUID: One time, Theo was fighting with her mom and we went outside to get away from her. Theo wanted some space. She kicked one of the metal garbage cans on the porch—just kicked it out of frustration, not like kicked it over or anything—and her mom came out onto the porch after us and started whisper-screaming at Theo (you know, neighbors). She was so mad that Theo kicked the can. I couldn't believe she was tearing into Theo for having feelings and trying to blow off some steam. Jeezus, let the girl have a moment. I thought her head was gonna pop off like an exploding melon. Nobody monitored me like that. My parents just ignored me as if it were an art form. Not only was Theo in trouble for doing whatever she did in the first place, but on top of that, she was in trouble for being upset about it! I was appalled. How dare they not let her act like an asshole!

THEO: My parents kept trying to reel me in, to no avail, and each hook they tried to put in me made me pull away harder. When I expressed my feelings or went against the family grain, my feelings of rage were clipped instantly. "Okay, now we're going to sit down to dinner." I'd sit there at the table, quietly seething directly after a fight with them. My quickness to say, "I'll be the singer!!" and be the front person for the band was likely because subconsciously, or even unconsciously, I knew, deep down, if I didn't start screaming out loud, I was gonna kill myself or light the house on fire. I kinda hid this from everyone and attempted to shrink myself for safety. I was a good student, I wanted to do well. But when my attempts to be "myself" and claim my autonomy weren't met with a thumbs-up, I began hiding everything I could from my parents and did what I wanted. I tried the best I could to stay out of their line of vision. I did get caught and I did get grounded, which only fueled the fire and teenage angst. The need to be SEEN was huge for me, so being center stage seemed like a way to get that done. My dad was in his own head playing music, and in some ways we "got" each other, but we did not see eye to eye during this time. I have extremely fond memories of childhood, I promise, but during my teens, emotionally, yeah, not so much. Emotionally, we took care of ourselves. For affection and understanding, I reached for my sister and my friends.

SQUID: My parents were so square, clueless. Completely out to lunch. I remember sitting at the table and shoving pancakes up my nose, just to see what they would (or wouldn't) do. When I was five, I grabbed a packet of macaroni-and-cheese powder while my mom was boiling the water, and instead of taking it away or raising her voice, she softly whispered, "No ... don't ... " Well, undisturbed, I went about eating all the powdered cheese, sat in my high chair, and immediately puked all over the table. Maybe that was her plan?

THEO: Years later, when we were on tour, we stayed at Squid's mom's house in Portland. As we were getting ready for bed, Squid sneaked into her mom's bedroom and whispered to me, "Come here!" She very slowly opened a drawer in her mom's nightstand, and it was like pencil-pencil-pencil, paper-paper-paper, eraser-eraser-eraser all neatly arranged in lines. Nail files stacked. A single tissue perfectly folded into fourths. I had never seen anything like it in my life—cue horror movie music. We were like, "Aaaaaaaggggghghhh!!!" In the bathroom, there were little bottles all perfectly arranged. I'd go in there and turn one slightly so it was facing the wrong way. Our song "Mom" is inspired by Squid's and my mom: "Won't leave the house till it's all in place / You know a mess is a human disgrace."

SQUID: My mom grew up in Virginia in the '50s and wore white gloves like a proper Southern lady should, the type that is better off seen and not heard. She had this trifecta of being Southern, Jewish, and having a raging bitch for a mother. As a matter of survival, she mastered the art of being agreeable, acceptable, and invisible. Like a stealth ninja, she seemed to maneuver so as to be un-detectable—avoiding unwanted attention, making waves, or causing offense. But every now and then, my mom would hit a wall. I remember my parents arguing and hearing my mom push back, "I don't think that's true!" We were shocked. The one moment I saw my mom really lose it was during the Anita Hill testimony at Clarence Thomas's confirmation hearings. My mother is a professor with a doctorate in English, the first in her family to go to college. She saw education as the way out of her famil-ial hellhole. She was furious when Thomas was confirmed to the Supreme Court. I was half paying attention to the hearings, but mostly what I remember was my mom, incensed that Anita Hill, a fellow professor, a highly educated lawyer, wasn't being taken seriously. All that schooling, all those degrees on the wall, that was supposed to earn you the respect, the credibility, equality, and dignity. But it didn't. That shitbag Thomas got away with everything, and they destroyed her. And then called her a bitch and a liar because she didn't cry on the stand and fall to pieces like a "real victim" should. My agreeable Southern belle mother was quietly cultivating a private slow-boil feminist revolt.

For me, though, the damage was done. Years of exposure to her passiveness and indifference left me feeling anxious and unprotected as a child, needing to scream and fight, argue and push my way through life at every turn, defiant, hardheaded, and driven to make shit happen all on my own and ready to employ asshole superpowers to vaporize anyone foolish enough to get in my way.

GINA: From adolescence on, there wasn't a whole lot of parenting going on in my life. I was the youngest child; my oldest sister, Nonda, was already in college, and my sister Ren was in full-on teenager mode doing everything she could to be out of the house. My dad was a typically passionate Italian who could get quite explosive, and both my sisters, Nonda (being the first child) especially, had to deal with the brunt of it. But my dad left when I was ten, so his supervision of me was only peripheral. My mom was still reeling from the divorce years later when I was a teenager. Then she got herself a boyfriend. I think she was done being a mom and was ready to live her own life finally. She was of the '50s era, hailing from a small university town in Kansas. She had that Midwestern sweetness, and she was stunning. But underneath her demure demeanor was a fierce, intelligent, independent (and hilarious) woman who was dying to get the hell out of Dodge. My dad, the dark and charming Italian visiting-student from the Bronx, was her way out. She fled with him back to New York City. But after twenty-three years of marriage and kids, she wanted to have a career. She wanted to put her incredible talents as an artist to use. Marriage, kids, and homemaking were always in her generation's forecast, so she never had the privilege that I did to develop her talents. She wanted to live her own life, to heal from her divorce, and be with her new boyfriend. So every weekend and some days during the week, she was at his house. Every weekend, I basically had my own apartment.

SQUID: Gina's and my mom hit that road in their marriages where they were fed up, like, "Fuck this." We were the amplified versions of their quiet "fuck this" sentiment.

In a traditional sense, we raised each other, with Sindi sitting at the head of the proverbial table. We certainly listened to each other more than we listened to any grown-up, that's for sure. Our families didn't understand us, but we understood us. We were our pride and joy, and so we had this need to somehow be superheroes and protect one another, which made us feel like an invincible sisterhood. There was no deep fear that we had to overcome, especially as teenagers who traveled in a herd. That's the thing about being a teenager: you feel bulletproof, especially when you're with your best friends. For better or for worse, we weren't inclined to feel victimized and weren't actually afraid of anything because we didn't believe there would be any consequences, even though we knew full well the risks our beautiful, menacing city imposed on us every single day.

Our adolescent defiance could've registered on the Richter scale. Our attitude at that age was "Fuck everything, I'm going to do what I want.

Let's goooooooo!" We just wanted to get the fuck out of the house and spend time with each other, doing whatever. Because "whatever" was undoubtedly more fun than sitting at home, rotting from boredom, and occasionally being asked to pick up after ourselves or take out the trash. And this city *was* a fuckin' thrill and molded us in its image. We wanted to be in the middle of the seedy shit, testing the waters, wading further and further out. Risky business, it was. Even as we got older, the adventure of self-discovery, born from the good fortune of being New York City kids, was in every note we ever played, every dopey outfit we ever wore, every last stitch of our being.

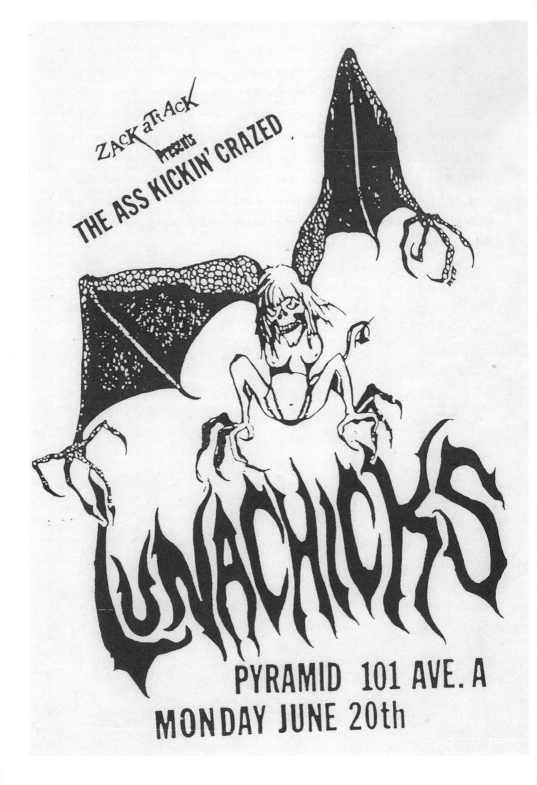

ZACK aTTACK presents
THE ASS KICKIN' CRAZED

LUNACHICKS

PYRAMID 101 AVE. A
MONDAY JUNE 20th

CHAPTER 2

THEO KOGAN, CLOWN PRINCESS

I was born in a crossfire hurricane in the mountains of Quito, Ecuador. I am not Ecuadorian, and there wasn't actually a hurricane when I was born, but that's how I like to see it.

It was December of 1969, and my parents were there because my dad got a grant to play cello in an orchestra. My parents were the artsy type. My mom saved up money from waitressing and then took a year off college and hitchhiked her way around Europe. After they married, they lived together in Cologne, Germany, because my dad played in an orchestra there. They were harassed and robbed by gypsies, experimented with some psychedelics, hung out with other musicians and artists, and lived a very hippie-boho lifestyle.

My mom gave birth to me in a hospital where no one spoke English. She couldn't get me out on her own, so the doctors performed a C-section, which back then was a long vertical slice from the sternum on down. I was yanked out of her guts. The first six months of my life were spent on a mountain in Quito, where my parents had two cats, one of which got in my crib and tried to sit on my head and suffocate me. (My relationship with cats improved greatly as life went on.)

I was born jaundiced and wasn't totally thriving, from what I understand, so six months after I was born, my parents decided they were ready to go back home. We lived with my maternal grandparents in Flatbush, Brooklyn. I am part of the fourth generation of human mutts born from Russian/Ukrainian/Romanian/Polish immigrants who got on a boat and came to America with nothing but holes in their pockets. It was old-world living in that house all together: my grandparents, my aunt (who was thirteen), my maternal great-grandmother, my parents, me, and soon my sister, Zoë, who is seventeen months younger than me.

My paternal grandparents are Eastern European Slavic Jewish mutts. For Jews in America (as in Europe), the arts were very important, and so my father and his brother and sister all played instruments growing up; my uncle and aunt were and still are professional musicians. My aunt is in the National Symphony, and my uncle was a tympanist but now plays with jazz bands.

I grew up with music all around me and am the product of well-educated musicians. My dad is a genius with a brain for computers and music. In addition to playing cello, he conducted regional symphonies and later on created computer programs for businesses. For a couple of years, he taught kids' music classes in our apartment on Ocean Ave, where we lived after we moved out of my grandparents' house. My mom was a secretary and later became an art director at *Diversion* magazine before going back to school to become a social worker/therapist. She sang opera on the side when we were in grade school, which entailed lots of practicing around the house. When she practiced, Zoë and I would look at each other, plug our ears, and scream. We used to fall asleep in the car to all the classical music. I still can't believe my parents drove long distances listening to it without falling asleep. Zoë and I got dragged to all of their concerts where we'd get shushed for being silly before ultimately passing out trying to sit still through those performances that to us felt soooooooooooo loooooooooooong.

I much preferred rock 'n' roll and disco. I loved the stories in Rolling Stones and Beatles songs—they were so good for little kids, really. "Octopus's Garden"! "Yellow Submarine"! The whole *Sgt. Pepper* album took me on a fantasy ride. Some songs were sad, some made me daydream, and some made me laugh. The Beatles' "Run for Your Life" was particularly special to me. One of my unwelcome nicknames in third grade was Ostrich. I was one of the tallest kids in the class and had a long neck, and I would do funny walks inspired by Monty Python's Ministry of Silly Walks. Some of the boys in my class gave me this nickname, and I hated it. But as a result, when the Beatles sang, "Run for your life if you can, little girl / Hide your head in the sand, little girl," I envisioned myself as an ostrich with my head in the sand. It was also funny to imagine a girl actually putting her head in the sand.

Music took me on journeys; I got inside of the song and learned all the words. Being very visual, I imagined that when I put on a record, even on our plastic red-and-white Fisher-Price turntable, the band on the record was in a studio somewhere a zillion miles away and performed the songs live each time I played it. I played songs over and over and over till I was sick of them. I felt a little guilty for the imagined band in the imagined studio having to play the song over and over, but I couldn't help myself.

I loved how music made me feel. My early female musical influences were Debbie Harry, Donna Summer, Chaka Kahn, Joan Jett, Chrissie Hynde, Rickie Lee Jones, and '60s girl groups that my mom was really into. One of the first albums I bought myself was *Crimes of Passion* by Pat Benatar. I had the self-titled Donna Summer album that I played a lot. The song "State of Independence" made me crazy, it was so cool. I was introduced to Blondie's *Parallel Lines* by my friend whose parents smoked pot and had a really cool apartment with a neon-light sculpture of a figure smoking on the living room wall. "Heart of Glass" got me. I made a cassette tape of it playing over and over and over. I loved that Debbie Harry said *ass*, and have mentioned this in countless interviews throughout my life.

My sister and I would do dramatic dance performances and long-winded puppet shows for our parents—our captive audience. My parents said the first act of these puppet shows was always great, and then it undoubtedly went downhill. By act two and a half, they'd be like, "Ohhh-kay, that's enough" and tried to shut us down. And we'd say, "Noooooo! We are not done! We're having so much fun!" Lucky for us, our paternal grandma loved to watch our dance performances and was constantly gifting us tutus and costumes she got at rummage sales. She and her sisters were all dancers and would dance together at parties. They all had gnarled-up toes from wearing too-small shoes and dancing on their tippy-toes for hours on end.

I was a born ham who craved attention. I started dance classes in preschool, and as the years went on I did ballet, tap, and modern. My parents and my paternal grandparents frequently took me and my sister to see dance performances all across the city, including at the Brooklyn Academy of Music and sometimes Lincoln Center. When I watched ballet, I would transcend time. I became entranced completely; I was at one with the entire performance. Watching the ballerinas do solos in the spotlight, I was euphoric. I wanted to be the prima ballerina. It was a deep yearning. After a performance ended, I was blissfully high. This feeling stayed with me. During the ride home, I was still there. During dinner, I was still there. Doing homework and brushing my teeth and taking my bath, I was still there. I would talk about it with my parents and grandparents, reliving it. And when I lay down for sleep, I closed my eyes and was transported right back there. I saw myself alone in the spotlight, wearing a rhinestone-encrusted tutu and crown. I could almost feel the spotlight, like the warm summer sun, and I'd revel in the deliciousness of the audience's adoration. It was a feeling I never quite felt anywhere else. It was this pink, hazy blanket of perfection and pure acceptance and some kind of otherworldly love, and it was mine, all mine.

It's no surprise I was always into fashion, clothes, makeup, tattoos, and big hair. I would spend hours drawing outfits in books that I was meant to write in. My uncle had a girlfriend with a colorful butterfly tattoo on her foot, and upon seeing that in 1977, I knew that I was absolutely, definitely going to get tattooed when I got older. When my dad clocked my first tattoos, he said, "You always wanted one." He got me in so many ways.

My mom was tall, hot, and slim with a great sense of style. She had a sexy, tight pair of blue jeans with a Rolling Stones tongue patch that she sewed on the ass. The jeans also had an owl patch with gold sequins on it. I loved them and later took the patches and sewed them on the ass of my own jeans. Like mothah, like daughtah. I gravitated to tough girls. Olivia Newton-John in *Grease* was the shit. When *Grease* came out, I wasn't allowed to see it, therefore I became completely obsessed with the album. I had the movie booklet and the record and would have my Barbie dolls act out everything I thought might have happened in the movie. *Oh, those pants are tight!* It was so exciting in that it let me express my budding prepubescent sexuality.

I was smitten with the Tuscadero sisters, Pinky and Leather, from the TV show *Happy Days*. Leather was played by the rock star Suzi Quatro. They were two biker chicks, and Pinky dated Fonzie. I imagined that I was her. I really, really went there. (But we all know I was really Leather on the inside.) When I got dressed, I would stand in front of the mirror and become her in my mind. I would also change my outfit up to three times before going to school. And this was in second grade! My dad would always say, "This is not a fashion show." He just didn't understand that it most definitely was.

I had what I thought was a Barbie that was two feet tall. Maybe it was a knockoff, but that doll made me want to be an Amazon, like Wonder Woman, gigantic and glamorous. I had the Growing Up Skipper doll whose boobs grew or deflated when you cranked her arm forward or back. I ended up cutting her open to see what made her work. I was also enamored with wigs. I loved passing by the wig store and pictured myself in a long brown or long red wig. Let's face it, without knowing, I wanted to be a drag queen.

Notwithstanding my taste for fast women and giant dolls, I was always pretty well behaved. My parents would apparently say, "Calmly, Theo" all the time. As in, "Calmly, Theo, put the book on the shelf," or "Calmly, Theo, come to the table for dinner." One day I asked my mom if my name was actually Calmly Theo.

I've always loved to make people laugh—that is when I feel really full and like my best self. I had a gift for physical comedy. All the things I liked and were drawn to at a very early age were funny: Carol Burnett, Bugs Bunny, Sherman Hemsley as George Jefferson, Dr. Seuss, Eloise, and the Marx Brothers—I did a great Harpo imitation. Seventies shows like *What's Happening!!* and *Good Times* were all a part of making me, me. Lucille Ball is my absolute hero. In school I was the class clown, which was unusual for a girl, but it felt completely natural to me. I wanted to be a clown and run off with the circus. In support, my parents took me to a clown class twice but the teacher was a flake and didn't show up either time. I was heartbroken.

As a student, if I had a hard time with the teacher, I went home and cried to my parents, but I did not act out in school. I loved my first-grade teacher, but she left and was replaced with a substitute for the rest of the year who hated me for reasons unknown. She harassed me to no end while I was learning to read even though I already knew how. If I fucked up one word while reading aloud, I'd have to start over, even if I was on the very last page of the book. It was sadistic. One kid in the class used to freak out and throw chairs. I don't blame him one bit. It was fairly common to see that amount of acting out back then.

Thankfully, I always had creative outlets. During grade school, I drew, danced, and would jam at the piano a lot. I loved spacing out with the echo pedal. I wound up picking the flute for band in third grade and became pretty good at it. I had a very cool music teacher that year. One afternoon, he let me into the music room and I played everything I wanted for hours, all by myself. I played the trumpet, saxophone, trombone—I loved it all, especially the trumpet, how my lips blew up and buzzed as I played. As a teen, I had my uncle's old Gretsch drum set for a while, which I loooooved. I was good at the drums. It was in my blood.

Music, art, and dance were the constants in my life, even when everything else around me was changing for reasons I didn't entirely understand. When I was almost nine years old, my parents were on a search for a spiritual awakening and began going to an ashram in Brooklyn Heights. Then they informed the entire extended family at Thanksgiving dinner that we were converting to Sikhism. *Say what?* We had been going to the ashram quite frequently, but this was unexpected.

There I was, in fourth grade, and I had to wear a turban every day. We were only supposed to wear blue, white, or yellow clothes. This really squashed my normal dress-up routine, but on special occasions, I wore the traditional Sikh clothing, which was a tunic and leggings, and I had a knife that was worn across my body on a strap. Imagine a little blue-eyed blonde girl in a turban walking through Flatbush, Brooklyn, in 1979 with a knife slung across her. I spent the whole year getting bullied and harassed. I'd get my turban knocked off daily during recess via basket-balls or footballs. Grown men would shout at me, "Hey, genie, tell my fortune!"

Exactly one year later, at Thanksgiving dinner, my parents announced we were no longer going to be Sikhs. I was just getting used to waking up at 4:30 for yoga and meditation practices, and now I had to change again?! *Oh, you'll get used to it.* What?! Now I felt self-conscious *without* the turban. People were going to think we were completely nuts.

As a child, I wore "No Nukes" and "Pro Choice" buttons on my shirt—thanks, Mom!—and was yelled at by adults who didn't share my budding political views, but I always stood my ground. The thing is, all those experiences trained me to be different. They inadvertently helped me adapt to change and the way people would treat me later in life. My parents unwittingly brought me up to be an outsider.

When I started to dress myself as a teenager—making my own clothes, dying my hair every possible color, and all that shit—my parents were not happy. (I still have a skirt I made out of a ginormous black-and-white giraffe-patterned seersucker bell-bottom pant leg—yes, one pant leg—and some sick bondage pants I made with homemade stencils and hand-drawn band logos.) I would think, "You made me this way." Obviously, I was claiming my identity and lashing out at them and societal norms. My parents and I had huge fights about my clothes and makeup to the point where my dad and I had a major blowout. I ran away from home for a night but still did my homework, which I retrieved from my sister on the subway, and I even went to school the next day. I was still a good student even throughout my most rebellious times. It was just part of my nature. I truly can't imagine what a tough time this was for my parents. I know they must have been losing their minds and didn't know what to do for me or with me. I once told my dad, "I am art." I made my room into an art environment by dragging home various garbage sculptures from the street.

It's amazing I am alive with the shit I did, and it predominantly centered around music. I snuck out to shows and clubs and took the subway home at 4 a.m. I would often almost ritualistically fall asleep to *Ziggy Stardust* or T. Rex's *The Slider* album that Gina gave me for my fifteenth birthday. I loved the Misfits, X-Ray Spex, the Vibrators, Buzzcocks, the Ramones, Sham 69, Blitz, and Channel 3. The first two punk albums I bought myself were the Misfits' *Walk Among Us* and X-Ray Spex's *Germfree Adolescents*.

When I was fifteen, I saw the band that changed my life: Frightwig, an all-female three-piece from San Francisco. I had never seen an all-female band, or any band for that matter, like this before. Frightwig changed my whole perception of bands and women playing in bands in a big way. The bass and guitar players were wearing giant veils over their heads. They looked like larger-than-life gothic witchy beekeepers—and one of them was pregnant! And then there was the drummer, a giant blonde in jeans and a T-shirt. I couldn't take my eyes off her. She was like a real-life Amazon Barbie. And she hit those drums fucking hard! And if that wasn't enough, they switched instruments! Holy shit. My brain imploded. The moment from that set that's been tattooed in my mind is when the real-life giant Barbie of a drummer stood behind her kit, pulled up her perfectly worn-in T-shirt, grabbed her belly, and waggled the skin around. She looked at the audience like, "That's right, motherfuckers! I don't give a fuck!" *My new hero!*

When we formed the Lunachicks, we had a lot of friends in bands, both male and female, who really were excited for us and inspiring to us. I didn't question my power as a young woman and didn't see myself as a vulnerable target. I was empowered, I was sexual. I also always felt a bit male with my female self. Many of the most iconic rock stars are androgynous—Bowie, Prince, Grace Jones, Little Richard, Big Mama Thornton—amiright or amiright?

The only times I felt vulnerable were when something happened to make me feel that way, like getting groped or grabbed on the subway or the street, or when some creep jerked off while staring at me. Only then did I feel threatened because of my gender. One time I actually scared a creep off the train glaring at him with my dagger eyes. That was awesome.

Getting onstage was all-empowering. It was where my best friends and I created a safe haven, a feminist fortress. We were like a benevolent army, and if you fucked with one of us, we'd all come after you together. Not only would we not tolerate that shit, we'd emasculate the jerks and kick their asses onstage or jump in the crowd and take care of business.

Those experiences reinforce how very lucky I was to have grown up in New York City in an artistic home with artistic friends. Going to an arts-focused high school saved my life. I drew our first bat-lady logo there. Being a teenager already made me feel invincible, but being a teenager *and* starting a band made me feel like I could test the strengths and limits of the universe without fear of failing, falling, or dying. I did whatever I wanted and didn't question whether I could do something or whether I would be accepted. I sometimes wonder what might have happened if I had grown up elsewhere. I feel for kids who are in the middle of a tiny town and are creative, weird, or gay and have to wait to get out. I pray for them, and I wrote lyrics for them. For real.

When the Lunachicks first performed, we had a huge, loving show in front of our friends and peers. It couldn't have been better; the show was an out-of-body experience in a way, but I also felt natural, like this was my place. Finally, in my black stretch jeans and red lipstick, I was the lead ballerina, I was Pinky and Leather Tuscadero with Iggy Pop icing, I was Lucille Ball with a side of Alice Cooper, I was Olivia Newton-John in *Grease* with KISS makeup on, I was all my influences and heroes born. I was finally me.

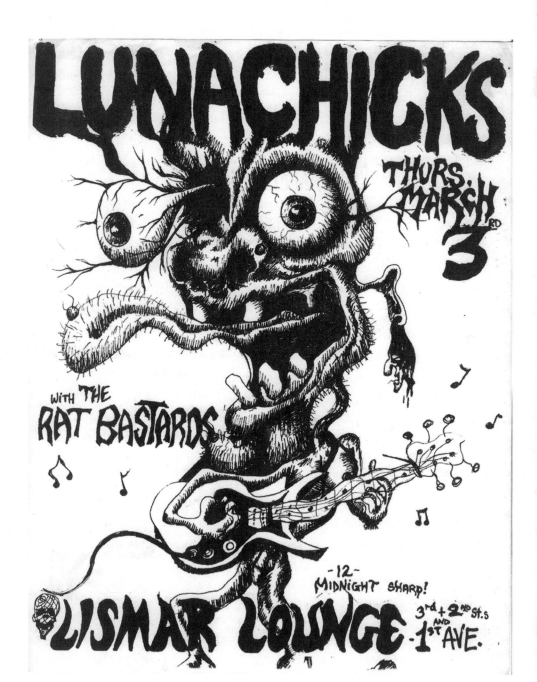

LUNACHICKS

THURS. MARCH 3RD

WITH THE RAT BASTARDS

-12- MIDNIGHT SHARP!

LISMAR LOUNGE

3RD + 2ND ST.S AND 1ST AVE.

CHAPTER 3

GINA VOLPE, ARTEEST EXTRAORDINAIRE

I made my entrance in March 1969, the youngest of three girls. My early childhood was spent in Mount Vernon, a leafy suburb just outside of the Bronx. It was a very Italian American neighborhood; all my neighbors had vowels at the ends of their last names. My dad worked on Wall Street back then, and my mom held various on-and-off part-time jobs. I had an idyllic childhood growing up with my awesome sisters in a house that bordered the woods. I'd spend hours alone among the trees, drawing and sculpting things out of sticks, moss, and crap that I foraged from the woods. I was a strange kid who loved to draw, and ever since I can remember, I was always creating something. I'd sketch insects, cats, skulls, and the beasts that lived in the woods. For some reason, I loved drawing huge '70s platform shoes. Maybe it was a prelude to my fixation with David Bowie and Ziggy Stardust.

I was horribly shy in elementary school. I rarely spoke and did my best to go unnoticed. My friends were the school misfits, of course. Brandi, my best pal, was an unusually large child who looked like an adult by the time we were in fourth grade. Most people mistook her for a teacher. Brandi could draw anything, play any instrument, and sang beautifully. She was brilliant and a total freak because of her size. Naturally, we were attached at the hip.

Brandi and I were put in different classes in fifth grade because a teacher thought there was some kind of budding lesbian romance going on, but we suspected that this was really about race. Brandi was Black, and it seemed the teacher wasn't exactly thrilled about our friendship. Not like that kept us apart.

Brandi turned me on to Stevie Wonder, Michael Jackson, and Earth, Wind & Fire. We loved sitting around listening to her mom's amazing album collection. Our friend Bobby was a weirdo like us. He carried a cassette player to school and blasted Blondie and Devo. We'd roam the school halls singing "Mongoloid," our theme song. Also in our crew was our pal Nellie Kurtzman, whose father was the famous Harvey Kurtzman of *MAD* magazine. We would hang out in his studio in the attic of their house and flip through all of the back issues. It was so incredibly cool.

If I wasn't drawing, I was busy learning about music. My parents were big-time classical and opera fans, which were of no interest to me. My dad would sing aloud around the house—badly and off-key. One of my earliest memories is hearing the song "A Horse with No Name" on the radio. It was the first time I heard a melody and lyrics. I was transfixed. My dad and I would dance to it around the living room. My parents loved music, and there was always a record spinning on the turntable in our house.

My father got really into disco when *Saturday Night Fever* came out. He brought home the record along with the dance book so he could learn how to do the Hustle. I also tried to learn but was too much of a spaz, so I gave up in frustration and just sang along instead. And to this day, I sing the lyric as "strawberry woman" and not "more than a woman."

It kinda all started, musically speaking, when I was six. One of my sisters, Ren—who has always been a huge influence on me—had an idea (one of her many "OMG I HAVE AN IDEA" moments).

"We're gonna start a fan club!" she said.

What's a fan club?

"You know, when you like bands!"

What's a band?

"A band is a group of musicians."

Okay!

"We're gonna start right now. We have one album."

Okay!

"It's a Beatles record!"

Who?

"We're gonna start a Beatles fan club!"

Okay!

Whatever she said, I thought it was a brilliant idea. When Ren first put that Beatles record on, I liked it instantly, but then I became infatuated. We made it our mission to collect every Beatles record we could. I listened to those records nonstop, especially the *White Album*.

Soon after, I acquired a transistor radio, and from then on I was never without it, EVER. That radio went with me everywhere. Each night, I kept it on my pillow and fell asleep listening to the soothing sounds of Captain & Tennille or ELO. I was obsessed with music and songs, and I could not get enough.

My sister Nonda, who is nine years older than me, was a badass teenager during my elementary school years. With her flipped hair, maxi skirts, and Candie's shoes, she would blast all the mega '70s groups that were around at that time—Bad Company, Black Sabbath, Pink Floyd, Led Zeppelin, Elton John—while driving around in my parents' Oldsmobile Delta 88. Those bands became the soundtrack to my early childhood. I spent hours going through her album collection, mesmerized by the artwork on those covers. Emerson, Lake & Palmer's *Brain Salad Surgery* featured H.R. Giger's incredible skeletal airbrush art, which began my fascination with the macabre.

Fortunately, back then public schools still had music electives, and in second grade we got to pick an instrument to study. Ren picked violin, so my mom said to me, "You should pick cello, then you and your sister can have a little duo." So I picked cello and played it for a year or so. Because the thing was bigger than I was, my parents purchased a luggage cart so I could wheel it back and forth to school.

My cello career came to an abrupt end one afternoon while my parents were at work and Nonda was smoking pot in the kitchen downstairs. I was in my bedroom practicing my rockin' version of "Hot Cross Buns"—*screech, screech, screech*—when Ren came bursting through the door yelling, "Fire! Fire!" I didn't believe her because she was always pulling pranks like that on me. She'd lock me out of the house in a snowstorm, tie me to a chair and lock me in a closet, all that torture-your-younger-sibling stuff. So I figured it was another one of her tricks. Then the house suddenly filled up with smoke. Um, don't think this is a prank! I dropped that cello like a hot cross bun and ran out of my burning house. That was the last time I ever saw that thing. We were told the source of the fire was electrical, but years later, my dad got a hold of Nonda's diary and read the entry where she confessed it was she who started the fire by tossing her joint in the garbage can.

Toward the end of the '70s, Ren became a teenager, and she got into punk—the Ramones, the Clash, and Buzzcocks were always blasting from our bedroom. I was in fourth grade when I first heard Blondie's "One Way or Another" while riding in the car with Ren and my mom. *OMG. What is that song?!??* A week later, Ren came home with *Parallel Lines*. I studied the front of the record, then turned it around and looked at the back. Then I'd repeat fifty times over. I examined every inch of those album photos. *She's wearing boots. But on this side she's wearing shoes. Here she's got a thing wrapped on her arm.* I was mesmerized! I loved how strong and powerful Debbie Harry looked fronting a gang of guys with her fists planted on her hips. The epitome of cool.

When Ren came home with a Ramones record, my little mind was blown. The music was so new-sounding. It felt really different from the classic hits that I was listening to on the radio. The novelty of it pulled me right in. *Rocket to Russia* has a drawing on the cover, so I kept repeating that illustration. I'd draw Ren as a punk rocker in ripped-up skinny jeans and a motorcycle jacket. Then I'd draw myself as a punk rocker. Then I drew just about everyone else I knew as a punk rocker. The punk records Ren brought home had such great melodies on top of heavy, driving beats. That's always what grabs me. To this day, I listen to all kinds of music, and if there's a great melody, I'm hooked.

That was the first part of my childhood.

My dad moved out when I was ten. And in 1981, right after I finished sixth grade, my mom packed us up and moved us into the Chelsea neighborhood in Manhattan. Talk about culture shock. This was all so new, so loud, so stinky, and sooo cramped. I didn't know it at the time, but after settling in, man, was I lucky to have moved into the city just as adolescence was about to hit.

When my dad left, my mother all of a sudden found herself solely financially responsible for all of us. With no job after being let go from Macy's and in need of a place for us to live, she scrambled to make it all work. She got a job as a civil servant working for the city and found us an apartment. After the initial trauma of divorce, she was so happy to move back to the city and reinvent herself. By the time I got to high school, as the third child, my mom was like, "I trust you. I'm going to go live my life now. You're old enough to know how to stay out of trouble." Boy, was she wrong about that!

We had a small apartment on Eighth Avenue. Chelsea back then was very different from the posh, gallery-filled neighborhood it is today. The old neighborhood was very Cuban and Dominican, with a burgeoning gay community. It was typical pre-gentrified New York. I knew all the kids on my block and went to middle school around the corner from our apartment. But it was an intense time. Summer of 1981 was when the *New York Times* first reported on a "rare cancer" seen in gay men. One afternoon, my upstairs neighbor collapsed in front of my door, and I helped get him into his apartment. Later that month, he died of AIDS.

New York City felt like it was on edge, and it presented a whole new set of challenges for me. The public schools were kinda rough. When I started middle school in the city, there were fights every day; the kids were violent and out of control, and the teachers couldn't do anything about it. Kids would be openly smoking pot in the classroom. Here I was, this little wallflower from suburbia, getting gum thrown in my hair every day and being threatened by Zoila, the school bully who looked like she was twenty years old. Maybe she was. I was terrified.

Although I was a total nerd, I was fanatical about the Ramones and the Clash. Any song featuring the gritty squeal of a chunky guitar sucked me right in. When I was a few years older, my friends and I crashed a party at Columbia University. The MC5's *Kick Out the Jams* was playing, and I lost my mind. I went around asking everyone, "Who is this?!?" *MC5.* "Who? What? What year is this? Aaaahhhh!!" I was NOT leaving without that record! It was fall, so I had a long trench coat on. I fucking stole that album and played it to death. I'd also steal Ren's Chuck Taylors, ignoring the fact that they were so huge on me. I'd borrow her leather jacket too. Unfortunately, the school bully was not impressed by my ill-fitting punk outfits and still wanted to beat the shit out of me.

I knew I had to get into one of the city's specialized public high schools, otherwise I'd wind up in a general public high school, and rumor was those were even worse than the middle schools. I tried out for the High School of Performing Arts (the *Fame* school) for the acting department, and I took the tests for the smarty-pants schools such as Bronx Science and Brooklyn Tech. But really all I ever really wanted to do was make art, so my main goal was to get into the High School of Music & Art.

I didn't get into Performing Arts (no surprise there) or the other two (also no surprise), but I was put on a waiting list for Music & Art. I was heartbroken when I learned I might or might not be able to get in. There were a lot of kids aiming for that school. At the last minute, thankfully, I was accepted.

In the mid-'80s, punk culture had yet to be assimilated into the mainstream. It was truly still a subculture, and I had found my tribe by befriending the kids in school or on the subway who looked different from everyone else. We cut and dyed our hair, wore fucked-up clothes and makeup, listened to punk, and searched for a place in the world. It wasn't always easy, though, walking from the train to school in Harlem and receiving a lot of commentary (along with the occasional bottle being flung at my head) from the neighborhood kids about the color of my hair. But worth it. It came with the territory. That's how it went.

Because my mom was at her boyfriend's house much of the time, our apartment often housed the gaggle of misfit drug addicts who regularly crashed with me. We did a lot of drugs and tried everything we could get our hands on. Thankfully, I had a level of self-preservation that always stopped me from getting too deep. I could have easily been a junkie. I sat by and watched some of my older punk friends shoot heroin, but I had done enough drugs to know that if I tried it, it would've been the end of me. I didn't want any part of it. By my senior year, I was gravitating out of that scene and spending even more time with Squid and Theo.

The first time I ever saw live music was when some of my new friends took me to a CBGB's hardcore matinee. I was fourteen and had no idea this world even existed! Going to shows became our new thing. Every weekend we'd head downtown to CB's. I liked some of the hardcore bands, but what I really wanted to see were punk shows, but I was too young to get into those. Hardcore matinees were all ages, so that's where my friends and I wound up.

We were a scraggly bunch of teenagers roaming around the city trying to find stuff to do. We spent lots of time at CB's, Danceteria, and Limelight. NYC clubs didn't really check IDs back then, so we were rarely carded at the door. We went wherever we wanted, like the Pyramid and Rock Hotel at the Ritz or the Jane Hotel. I saw Bad Brains, Dead Boys, GBH, the Exploited, the Cramps, and the Damned. My friends and I would always push to the front of the crowd. I wasn't brave enough to go into the pit but I loved being up front, so I'd stick out my elbows— blocking the sweaty bodies flying into me—and push my way up to the stage. I wanted to get as close as I could and observe how all this music that I was so obsessed with was actually made.

When we weren't at a show, our little group of punks staked claim on the West Side, forming a little enclave in Washington Square Park. It was just a few of us at first, then our numbers started to grow. Soon there was a whole clan of us misfit kids dropping acid and hanging out. In a way, it's similar to band culture. We had an entourage and traveled in a group and did everything together. I was used to being in that pack dynamic.

I had always wanted to play guitar, and I fantasized about being in a band some day. Even though I was all punk rock all the time, I was obsessed with Pink Floyd thanks to Nonda and her classic-rock influence on me. David Gilmour's solos on *Dark Side of the Moon* and *Wish You*

Were Here made me want to crawl into the speakers and just live inside of his guitar tone. Back in middle school, my mom's new hippie boyfriend had loaned me his acoustic guitar and showed me some Beatles songs. "Revolution" was the only one that was simple enough for me to learn. I messed around on his acoustic guitar, but it was clunky and the action was like two inches off the neck, plus I could never get it in tune. I got frustrated and put it down. I really wanted to learn, but I had given up on the whole idea.

Then, strangely, when I was seventeen, Ren and her boyfriend came home from college for Christmas and handed me an electric guitar and little practice amp that they'd bought at a pawn shop upstate. It was totally unprompted; I don't even think they knew I wanted to play. I had a blue Mohawk at the time, and Ren said, "Merry Christmas. We think you should have a guitar." And I said, "Yeah, you're right I should!" It was a crappy Kent guitar and a tiny solid-state amp with a short circuit, but I was ecstatic. Ren always had the best ideas.

The first time I ever saw girls playing guitars and drums was at one of the CB's matinees. An all-female hardcore band was onstage, and my jaw immediately dropped. *Holy shit, those girls are badasses! They will kick my ass! I want to be them!* They had big red liberty spikes, black lipstick, and instruments. They looked so fucking cool. A year or so later while flipping through records at Sounds on St. Marks, I picked up Raging Slab's *Assmaster* album. (I mean, that title . . . how could you not?) Elise, the rhythm guitarist, played slide and personified what I aspired to be, a badass muthahfuckin' bitch who knew how to rip! It was finally time for me to get my shit together and make that a reality for myself. I just had to figure out how to play.

I spent lots of time playing—badly, but playing nonetheless. The guitar my sister got me was barely functional, with a cracked neck and broken pickups. Thankfully, my friend Miriam's little metalhead brother Luke, who turned me on to Metallica, loaned me his pink B.C. Rich guitar and gave me the phone number of his guitar teacher, Tim, who I instantly asked to show me how to play "Clampdown" by the Clash. And from there, it was on.

I decided it was finally time to start a band. I was still a terrible guitar player, but I was actively looking for people to play with. I met a girl who played bass. She came over to my house and we jammed on my only song, "Sugar Luv." Coincidently, as if there was something in the air, a day later Theo and Squid came up to me in school: "Hey, we're starting a band and we think you should be in it," which took me by surprise as I had no idea they played any instruments—and what made them decide to form a band anyways? "Tell me more," I said.

Squid came over to my house, and we started jamming in my bedroom on our little practice amps. Other days I'd go to her house with my guitar. I never did see the other girl bass player who I was going to start my band with. I began spending all my time hanging out in Brooklyn with Theo and Squid. We'd cut school and plunk away on our instruments along to our favorite songs. Sindi was older, so she took charge. She'd say, "Okay, so here's what we need to do: we need to book a rehearsal room." It wasn't even in my realm of thinking at seventeen. *And you book a show? Tour? What??*

I had a lot of evolving to do within the Lunachicks. I'd always dreamed of writing songs and recording, but when I got onstage to perform for the first time, I was like, "Oh shit, I didn't think this through. This performing part is a whole different animal. I didn't sign up for this."

Being onstage was terrifying for me. As someone who always tried to fly under the radar, I was not a natural performer and was definitely not loving having all that attention directed toward me. Having to take band photos was also awkward. It took a long time for me to get comfortable with any of it. The first show we ever played, I had my back to the audience the entire time.

By the time of high school graduation, we had a few months of rehearsals under our belt. We were really getting into this band thing, but I faced a dilemma. I was offered a full scholarship to the Maryland Institute College of Art in Baltimore. This was a big deal. But I had a band! I was having fun and didn't want to leave it! I considered going to SUNY New Paltz, which was closer than Baltimore but still about two hours away from the city. The girls weren't having it. "Don't go! We have a band!" I wanted to study art and wasn't yet ready to give up on my plan of being a fine artist. The compromise was that I'd attend SUNY Purchase in nearby Westchester County, and I would come home on the weekends to rehearse.

For my nineteenth birthday, I had a huge party in my dorm. Theo, Squid, and Sindi hopped on the train and showed up on campus to surprise me. The party was a blast, and we even played a song or two. By the time spring semester came to an end, we had played our first show, and after a couple more shows, we had a record deal. *Wow, it's really happening for us.* That's when I decided to take a leave of absence from school. I thought, "I'll go do the band thing, and I'll come back in a year or so." So I left college to go on tour with my punk rock band.

I never went back.

CHAPTER 4

SYDNEY SILVER, DE NIRO UNDERSTUDY

I arrived in November of 1969. I barely made it into the '60s, but I've always thought it was something to be proud of. I was born in Brooklyn Jewish Hospital—say no more—and did all my growing up in a big brownstone in Park Slope which, like most neighborhoods in New York City, has changed quite a bit since the 1970s and '80s.

The Slope was gritty and pretty in those days, sketchy enough to hold your attention but not usually terrifying, and pretty diverse. *Welcome Back, Kotter* meets the *New York Times* Sunday edition—a real mixed bag. The city was practically giving away townhouses in that neighborhood in the '60s, trying to get the "new wave" to move there to save the buildings and surrounding area from falling apart. My parents, along with a small bunch of other very lucky mutherfuckers, scooped one up with $1,000 in their pocket.

Growing up, I never gave my parents credit for much, but I always did reserve ultimate thanks for exactly three things:

1. Naming me Sydney Silver, which I was convinced firmly secured my star on the Walk of Fame or as the recipient of a Pulitzer Prize or something.

2. Giving me the birthday 11/11/1969, which just looks and sounds cool, and I always thought had some cosmic meaning and was inarguable proof of the universe's divine path for me. Later on, it would be revealed quite casually over a dinner visit that my mom had actually been induced into labor on that day around one of my dad's business trips to Cleveland.

3. Always most important of all, raising me in NYC. From the youngest age I can remember, I loved being here. And no matter when and how I felt my parents blew it, I always gave them credit and thanks for having me here, because whatever they didn't have that I needed, it didn't even matter, it was out there, in reach, and mine for the finding. A token in your pocket and a few white lies about whose house you're sleeping at buys a lot of teenage freedom in this town.

My mom was a part-time English professor, and my father worked in an architecture firm. My grandparents were born in Manhattan, Lower East Side Jews, offspring of Russian-Polish-Austrian immigrants, the tailor and shoemaker breed, dodging the draft and looking for something better by way of Ellis Island. They grew up mostly in Brooklyn, found each other in love and matrimony, and then bailed in the 1930s—during the mass exodus of the city—to Long Island (where else?) to raise a nice family in a civilized beachside mecca of bungalows, bagels, and trifold foil tanning reflectors. My aunts, uncles, cousins, etc. all followed suit out into paradise, which sets the stage for family gatherings straight out of *Seinfeld*, but not as funny—a lot of opinions and a lot of yelling and a lot of noshing.

My dad met my mom at school in Virginia and dragged her back to New York, where she studied Chaucer and he art and design at Cooper Union and Pratt, bouncing around town via VW Bug and Vespa. They ditched the home-cooked latkes and Manischewitz for chicken stir-fry and white wine spritzers. I think they may have been the proto-yuppies of their time.

At home, my father always played records, which I'm very grateful for because outside of my grandfather's passion for playing a three-song ukulele set at parties, *no one* in my family was musical. But my dad LOVED to listen (still does) and is a hell of a whistler. I always thought of my parents as classic 1950s squares, Richie Cunningham all the way. I guess there was a little Fonzie hidden under the covers because in truth Dad had a halfway decent record collection, not to mention a stack of *Playboys*—not that he listened to the Stones or anything, but he did love the Beatles and lots of other iconic bands. Also my grandfather had a great 45s collection that included an original copy of Ray Charles's "What'd I Say" and other classics. I would dig through his records and play them on the giant dresser-size flip-open stereo cabinet at my grandparents' house in Long Island. It was the size of a bus. When I was a wee little thing, my babysitter gave me a stack of Monkees records. I was obsessed with their goofy, slapstick TV show and in love with Davy Jones. I used to kiss his picture on the record cover.

My parents wanted me to learn an instrument because it's one of those things you're supposed to do to be a good parent. I took piano lessons for a year, but I didn't dig it. I thought piano was for nerds. I started taking guitar lessons at age twelve. I learned how to play my favorite songs by the Doors, Creedence, Rolling Stones—I probably learned ten songs. I asked my dad to buy me an electric guitar. He said no, so I quit.

As a kid, I must have spent a million hours stoned, in my living room, wearing giant headphones, sitting in the Eames chair and listening to *Dark Side of the Moon, Magical Mystery Tour,* and Crosby, Stills, Nash & Young's *Déjà Vu,* which is still one of my all-time favorites. I was also obsessed with Woodstock and the free-loving dirty hippies and the bad-assed rock gods of that time, Hendrix and Morrison. I couldn't understand how both my parents managed to be alive through the 1960s and still be so painfully unhip.

I have one sister who is three years older and was on the fringe of a social group of high schoolers who frequented punk shows at CBGB and would later form bands like the Beastie Boys and Luscious Jackson. Sister

Sam's record collection was on point, and I was happy to help myself to it. That short stack of classics of '70s English and New York punk contained all the info needed to inform my peewee understanding of music and songwriting. I would spin records in her room for hours, playing air guitar and singing backups to the Undertones' first album and Buzzcocks' *Singles Going Steady* while doing my best Paul Simonon and Dee Dee Ramone impersonations. I studied those songs carefully—the chorus, the riff, the transitions, the endings—not with any real sense of purpose. I just loved the way they made me feel, I wanted to be a part of whatever that was, so I got inside it the best I could. I shut my eyes and pretend-played them a thousand times.

By the time I was ten, eleven years old, I was a total music snob. I had a very narrow scope of listenables. For me, the only music that existed were the twenty-something records that I owned: Ramones, Blondie, Bad Brains, B-52's, the Cramps, Sex Pistols, Buzzcocks, Undertones, X-Ray Spex, Generation X, the Clash, Wire, the Specials, the English Beat, and, ugh, my god, that Stimulators single "Loud Fast Rules!" That changed my life. That was when it hit me. A little kid on drums, on the front cover, same age as me—a little kid in a band!—and the flip side, two chicks fronting with guitars, holy shit, miniskirts, go-go boots, and one with a high pony, black eyeliner, and a snarky "don't fuck with us" face. The first chick I ever saw holding a guitar was not Nancy Wilson, it was Denise Mercedes. Once I saw that, it was over. I knew it could be done. Once you see for yourself what is possible, you never can go back from there. That was the beginning and the end. And that track, "Loud Fast Rules!," is to this day one of my most favorite, an utter classic.

And then there was X-Ray Spex's *Germfree Adolescents*. I would stare at that cover for hours. Poly Styrene was a god, this little-girl singer with a giant voice that seemed like it could slice people's heads off. It's a perfect album and has the coolest cover ever, with the front and back photos of the band stuck in giant test tubes trying to break their way out. I was transfixed. I wanted to be stuck with them inside one of those test tubes. Oh, and the Slits' *Cut*. Whoa, topless tribal-looking women in loincloths and covered in mud, it was so incredible. I was thinking, "These chicks are fucking *naked* and they are afraid of *no one!*"

Those were all my sister's records. She got bored of them at some point and moved on, got a bad perm, and went away to college. By the time I was thirteen, the top two floors of that house and that record collection were all mine.

My next life-altering experience was the first time I ever heard the Stooges. I was smoking enormous joints with my friend Lee Bone in his bedroom, lying on his bed, super-wasted. The needle hit the vinyl on "T.V. Eye" . . . *What . . . is . . . this . . . ???* My first Iggy moment (all punks have one—it's like the punk rock version of losing your virginity). It went to the next level. It changed the game forever.

My long history of starting shit began early. I went to Brooklyn Friends School (BFS), a hippie-ish Quaker school in downtown Brooklyn, and my first "fight" happened on the way back from the park with my class. A boy said something to me that I didn't like, and I hit him in the back of the head. He turned and punched me right in the face, dropped me to the ground. I wasn't expecting that. Live and learn. (Or not.) Somehow this became a recurring theme throughout my life: me standing up and dealing directly with guys talking shit, regardless of the consequences. Sadly, I never learned how to fight, but for better or worse, I definitely have always had a big fat mouth. The stage became by far the safest place for me to be.

When I was a kid, I used to think to myself, why do women get harassed so much more than men? Well, because it's so easy. If a guy harassed a guy like that, he would probably get socked in the jaw. But what if every single woman stood up to that crap every single time they were disrespected, shit-talked, or grabbed and made a big fat stink? Broke some fingers, broke some noses, at the least ruffled some feathers, wrinkled some shirts, made some noise, and just refused to be quiet? My ten-year-old feminist theory was that men would learn to think twice. I bet they would stop. Behavioral reprogramming. Made sense to me! And then women would be treated like normal humans. So I just always felt it was my duty as a female to be part of the solution. For the record, I've never, ever been in a fight with a woman in my entire life (besides Becky Wreck).

Here's the first of many scenarios of me getting in my own way. In 1980, the *Fame* movie came out, and it was a hit. The High School of Performing Arts was actually a real school on West Forty-Sixth Street and the coolest thing anyone had ever seen. I auditioned for the acting department and got in. My shit did *not* stink after that, forget it. But I almost blew it.

The end-of-the-year dance performance at BFS was coming up; it was the dance that I put Theo in. The day before the performance, we did a dress rehearsal, and the stupid teacher actually started to listen to the song I choreographed my routine to, which was Rita Marley's "One Draw," aka "I Wanna Get High." (Of course.) The administration told me I couldn't use that song and they were pulling my dance.

Pssh, fuck YOUUUU...

I jumped on top of the secretary's desk in the school lobby and went crazy up there, screaming my head off, pointing people out one by one, *"Fuck you! And fuck you! And fuck YOU!"* I told off everyone, including the principal. It was like the scene in the movie *Network*, when Howard Beale screams, *"I'm as mad as hell, and I'm not going to take this anymore!"*—but like the *Little Rascals*–on-crack version. This was two weeks before middle school graduation. What an idiot. (To be honest, I wouldn't be entirely sure that this ever really even happened except that Theo was there, apparently, and remembers the entire thing.)

I had my rude awakening the next day when I found out I was expelled, and as a result, I couldn't go to the High School of Performing Arts, even though I had previously been accepted.

Oh shit. Ooops.

So my poor fucking parents had to come to a special meeting and *beg* the administration to let me graduate. I was in that school for nine years—they couldn't wait to get rid of me. So the Quakers took a deep breath and were just like, "Fine! Get out!"

I was allowed to graduate. And once again, I was going to Performing Arts for drama. Al Pacino, Liza Minnelli, and Ellen Barkin went there. This was fucking it. That drama program saved my life. It gave me something to care about. For the first time, I gave a shit. The first year, I was completely absorbed in it. I loved every minute. We had crazy teachers who probably took too much acid in the '60s and would jump up and down and scream at us. It was so beatnik and weird and deep and raw. I was so psyched about it. It was the first big puzzle piece that stuck for me—it was the beginning.

I found my calling, and my life made sense. I had goals, and I was really serious about achieving them. As far as I was concerned, once I hit high school, I had a career. I was on point, on track, and ready to rumble. I had grown up feeling lost and lonely, but now I had something that made me feel important, and I was on a rampage.

The first or second day of high school, I started with some of my usual lip, and a teacher pulled me aside and swiftly put my ass in line. "Nobody gives a shit about you here. You better get your fucking act together or you're out the fucking door tomorrow."

Whoa.

Nobody had ever drawn that line with me. Private Quaker hippie school wasn't like that. I bulldozed over, through, and on top of everyone and everything. Ultimately, I only fucked myself. Looking back, I give them a lot of credit (for not murdering me). They did the best they could, but it was kind of a disaster.

In public school, nobody gave a shit. And in *that* school, there were ten thousand other kids waiting to take my spot. They didn't have time for my bullshit. Get it together or get the fuck out. I heard it loud and clear and I didn't want to blow it. Getting into the drama department at the High School of Performing Arts—fifty kids out of the entire city of New York—was the best thing that ever happened to me, and I wasn't gonna fuck it up.

I did well in my department, but throughout high school, my acting teachers gave me shit for my looks every time I dyed my hair, or shaved a little stripe in my head, or wore too much makeup. "Actors must be nobody so they can play anybody!" screamed Mr. Usim in a thick Russian accent. It was pretty straightforward: I had to conform if I ever wanted to work in the "industry." Play the game of fitting in to get through the door so you can try and stand out? It really bugged the shit out of me.

It got increasingly more annoying. My teachers were hassling me for doing anything out of the ordinary. "You're going to be auditioning for Tampax and toothpaste commercials! You have to look wholesome!" Vomit. Things got difficult around graduation when it was time to start working. The agencies were not loving me. I would try to look the part by digging through my mom's closet to find something that could make me look normal. *Maybe jeans and this blouse (gagging) and this western belt and cowboy boots will make me look regular? I don't even know what that means!* I fucking hated it. I wanted to drink bleach. I wanted to be De Niro in *Raging Bull*; I didn't want to audition for *All My Children* to play the part of the spunky younger daughter named Pamela.

And then . . .

I almost got expelled **again** at the very end of senior year. I got caught selling weed in school (for someone whose name I won't mention, but they know who they are). I tossed a dime bag across the floor and it rolled between the feet of a teacher, total Ferris Bueller moment. *Oooops.* I got in a ton of trouble.

Long story short, I almost didn't graduate *again*. The whole drama sabotaged my part in the end-of-the-year showcase for the casting agencies, and it was a disaster. I bombed it. The response was not good. The long road to nowhere. I was crushed.

And as one door slammed in my face, another opened. Everything that followed with the Lunachicks was in tandem with what I was already doing. It was another crazy scene, but in the movie I actually wanted to be in. Lunachicks happened to get discovered as a band right as we got out of high school. A few months after graduation, we were in a shitty downtown coffee shop meeting with an English record label owner who was telling us, "I love you; I know exactly how to market you. You guys are perfect, *don't change a thing*!" Divine intervention. Suddenly, everything made sense.

Being in a band was just like acting, but the Lunachicks was my dream-come-true stage show and Squid the perfectly cast part. I got to write my own scenes, I got to star in them, and I got to perform in them every night of the week. No more waiting around in auditions for a year to land a single job. I was working and playing and getting paid. It was the role of a lifetime, the one I had been training for all these years. *STELLA!!!*

ZUNACHICKS

WED. JAN. 13th WITH PALE FACE

LISMAR LOUNGE -1st AVE.

CHAPTER 5

SINDI B., MAMA BEAR

I was born in New York City in the summer of 1965. My family lived in a crappy apartment in the slummy section of Park Slope, Brooklyn. It was furnished in the original "shabby chic" style—without the "chic" part. We had a great view, though.

My mother was fantastic. She had lots of albums, and I grew up listening to rock 'n' roll and plenty of hard rock: Rolling Stones, Beatles, Jimi Hendrix, Animals, Cream, Yardbirds. I would listen to them and stare at their albums for hours. My mom was a total hippie, but at the same time she was a tough-as-nails badass who taught me to never back down. And I never did. Studiously, I watched her get in the face of burly truck drivers or whoever else crossed her. Unfortunately, she died before she reached fifty.

My biological father was an addict and a thief. He and my mom split up when I was five. For a while, I spent weekends with him. He lived on St. Marks Place between First Avenue and Avenue A. Boy, have I got some stories. I often found myself in strange apartments hanging out with a monkey or a tarantula. At the supermarket, he would shoplift items and stuff them in MY jacket pockets.

At the age of sixteen, after visiting him in rehab upstate, getting snowed in, having to spend the night there, and consequently missing a Bad Brains show at CBGB, I dumped him. I finally admitted to myself that he was a full-time liar and manipulator, and I'd had enough. The payoff was that I always steered clear of heroin.

My stepdad was around by the time I was six. He brought some stability and normalcy to the situation. We didn't have much, but I had my own room with a loft bed and a hammock. My mom grew tomato plants on the fire escape. The fire escape and the shared roof were our "outdoor spaces."

When I was twelve or thirteen, we bought a brownstone in a slightly better part of Park Slope, still surrounded by abandoned buildings and gangs. Back then, the neighborhood was a dump. Now it's beautiful. I don't think that anyone who wasn't there would believe just how dilapidated it was. I spent years of my life zigzagging my way home from school and shows to avoid being harassed or jumped. On the upside, there were some great candy stores.

The block I grew up on was full of white-trash Irish Catholic families who had no concept of the world beyond Park Slope. We were the oddballs. There were a hundred kids living on the block. We were separated into two groups: the "up-the-block" kids and the "down-the-block" kids. They were okay playmates, but we were worlds apart. They all went to public school or Catholic school. I was in private school, a concept that they could not grasp at all. They could only compare it to a neighbor who had cerebral palsy and went to a special school. They never "got" me, but always accepted me.

If I had my way, I would have spent nearly all of my time reading. I read everything I could get my hands on, although I never enjoyed books about animals or any kind of romance. When I was around eight years old, I somehow came into possession of a small booklet called *Fuck the System*. Not sure how it fell into my hands, but I loved it!!

I also played a lot of sports: stickball, basketball, handball, skellzies (I'm *really* dating myself here), stuff that didn't require much equipment. When I was around ten or eleven, I started doing gymnastics pretty heavily, training several times a week. At home, I would spend long amounts of time standing on my hands. In junior high, I started playing on the basketball team, which I loved.

I was a cerebral kid, pretty shy. But I was also tough and a protector of the small and weak. I kept my mouth shut most of the time, but once I opened it, look out! I never started trouble, but I also never hesitated to jump in with fists flying to defend myself or someone else. No one ever expected it because I was such a tiny, skinny, quiet kid.

I liked school and always did well. I went to Montessori school, a learn-at-your-own-pace kind of thing. It was very relaxed and informal. I have zero bad memories of school in those early years.

From seventh to twelfth grade I went to a small, fancy, private prep school where I found myself, once again, the oddball. Somehow I always managed to have plenty of friends and respect. I was friends with people from every possible group: the popular girls, preppies, nerds. I always had at least one or two really good friends who were completely different from me. I still do. I appreciate other perspectives and different opinions.

Once I was surrounded by all of those smart kids, I realized just what an average student I really was. I had most of them beat on life smarts, though. Even though I wasn't a star student, I was always there, always on time, and never cut class. I had a lot of respect for the financial sacrifices my folks were making to send me there. Also, I was on scholarship and never took that for granted.

When I was in eighth grade, a band I loved called the Speedies played at my school. They were local kids with cool, new-wavey songs. It was the coolest thing that ever happened in my school up to that point. I remember thinking, "What are they doing here? They're so cool, and we are so unhip."

My life changed forever during the summer of 1978. I was about to turn thirteen, and I was visiting family in England. I saw a punk guy busking on the street in London and was completely mesmerized. That same week, I saw a Stiff Little Fingers concert *on television*!! This is something *for me*. Finally! Prior to that, I was listening to the radio, not really caring one way or the other. I was well versed in hard rock and hippie acid-rock stuff, but I wasn't really fitting in with it or thinking about it. Then this weird music presented itself, and I was like, "YES!" Once I got back to New York, I began the search for similar music and people.

By the time I was fifteen, I was living a double life. From Monday through Friday, I kept it straight, going to school, doing homework, and generally behaving myself. I never lost my love of learning. On the weekends, I was going to shows and hanging out with the punks on St. Marks Place, sitting on stoops and drinking. One of the bands I saw was Killer Instinct, which my friend Carolyn was in. She had green hair and was on *Jeopardy* twice. I liked to hang out with her because she was really smart and we could talk about books.

I started going to see shows at the Peppermint Lounge regularly because they never checked ID. At the time, it was located in midtown Manhattan near Times Square. This was the very early '80s, when it was still a super-sketchy area. Leaving there in the middle of the night as a little teenage girl all alone was often an adventure. One of my first real punk shows was the Misfits and the Undead at the Ukrainian National Home on Second Ave in 1981. I dragged my boyfriend along for protection. After that, the floodgates opened, and I started going to shows as often as possible. Most of the punk and hardcore shows were at places like A7, 2+2, or 8BC. They were all very cleverly named after their respective locations to assist the terminally stupid.

It didn't really occur to me to be in a band, but I *did* buy a guitar. I took my meager savings and bought a guitar and little practice amp when I was sixteen. I had a book that taught you how to play punk rock songs, and I learned a few. "Blitzkrieg Bop" was first. I still have the book. Then I was like, "I suck at this," and I put it away. I wasn't all that inspired to really learn how to play nor was I motivated to practice. That never really changed. I'm sure the other Lunachicks would be happy to confirm this.

I can't quite remember the first time I met Theo, Syd, and Gina. I think maybe I met them through some of the neighborhood kids. I barely knew them, but they came to my apartment one night because I was having a party or some friends over. I remember them being (or getting) wasted like pros. I loved them right away. I'm pretty sure they were all around fourteen or fifteen. At that age, four years can be a big difference, but I was never bothered. I can't recall my specific impressions of them, but I was always really impressed by Theo's and Gina's artwork.

They all seem to remember me cooking for them after school, which is funny, because my eating habits were really shit, especially compared to those girls. Certainly I was the master of baking special cookies and ordering Chinese food, but no way was I preparing any vegetarian delights. I mostly ate white foods: potatoes, noodles, bread, and cheese. I'm sure I did take care of them in some ways, just not nutritionally.

Once we formed the Lunachicks, I adopted a fake-it-till-you-make-it mentality in terms of booking shows and helping to get us off the ground. I was very organized; I was like that as a kid. My family was very chaotic, and so I always took on certain roles in my life. I always felt like the protector of everybody, even when I was a little kid. I always tried to hold things together. Shit had to get done. That may be why I left City College in Harlem after a short while spent studying nothing interesting. I really didn't know what I wanted to do and figured it was a waste of time and money to flounder around, so I quit in 1984. (It didn't help that when I tried to sign up for basketball, they straight up wouldn't let me because I was a tiny, white, punk rock girl.)

At my first few crappy jobs, I always got promoted quickly, so I guess it's part of how I am. I think I was managing a chicken-and-ribs joint when we started the Lunachicks, but maybe I was managing a photo lab. I was naturally skilled at being a bossypants.

I had a business head, for some reason. I was really good at math, and I was good with money. I don't know where that came from, certainly wasn't genetic. I figured if we were gonna do this band, we might as well do it somewhat properly. Also, the idea of being ripped off or in any way taken advantage of was unthinkable to me. I wanted to have at least partial control of everything concerning the band.

Sometimes the others resented me for not immediately splitting up all the money that we were paid. I always kept a fund to pay for the rehearsal room, van rental, etc. Everything was documented, and I don't believe there was any distrust, but they still weren't happy about it. Everybody wanted all of their money right then and there. And I knew if I gave it to them, I'd have to ask for it again in three weeks, and nobody's gonna want to give it to me and we're gonna be in trouble. It's how I lived my life anyway: don't spend the rent! To this day I don't get why it was a problem.

I always felt like everybody does what they can do. I never got a driver's license. I took on all those other responsibilities; at least I couldn't drive. Other people in the band had to drive. I didn't love giving interviews, so other people did that. Theo and Gina did all of the artwork. We never had to think about what to put on our flyers or merch. There was a distribution of responsibilities. I took a little bit of flack for having to do the organization and money, and sometimes I got shit on, but it was my role! I didn't mind doing that stuff; nobody else wanted to do that, so I just did it, even though everybody wanted to kill me for it sometimes. Whatever!

What are you gonna do? I loved everybody so much!

It was gratifying to use my brain and my abilities for the gain of myself and my Lunafamily. Rock 'n' roll *was* my life. That sounds so corny, but really, it was glorious. The Lunachicks are sisters. A gang. A team. For years it was no compromise to be together all of the time . . . until it was.

CHAPTER 6

TWISTED SISTERS

THEO: In the eighth grade, I transferred to a private Quaker school, Brooklyn Friends School (BFS). My old school was rough. I was in the smart-kid class, and I was terribly picked on. Kids pulled my hair as hard as they could and stabbed my ass with safety pins and tacks. I had things stolen right out of my hands. The breaking point came when my friend and I were attacked in the girls' locker room by the school bully. The bully got kicked out, and I left for BFS the next year. That's where I met Squid. For a good half year, she wouldn't speak to me. She sort of stomped and bounced down the hall and glared at me.

SQUID: Theo was fuckin' adorable with that blonde hair and those blue eyes, all tall and skinny. I hated her the minute I saw her.

THEO: Squid was a cool girl who had a wild energy exuding from her—it was palpable. I remember watching her drink from a water fountain in awe, stunned with intimidation. Even then, her style was curated and cool. She had a Snow White look, dark hair and pale skin and wore red lipstick (in eighth grade!), long, dark curls bouncing from her head like magic tendrils. I could tell she was a total rebel. When she walked through the halls, I would stop and stare.

SQUID: I first caught sight of Theo standing by the lockers. Hmmm, summing up the new kid ... HIGH WATERS!! Who wears high waters?!? What's going on here?? Grrrrrrr, something different ... points for originality, points for coolness. Possible direct threat. Proceed with caution ...

THEO: I will never forget the day Syd *flllllipped* out when the faculty told her she couldn't perform a dance routine to Rita Marley's "One Draw (I Wanna Get High)." By this time we were friends. With my eyeballs popping and my jaw hanging down, I watched her tell off the principal, the vice principal, the teachers, the dance teacher, whoever was there. She screamed bloody murder. I was enthralled, watching this person be so free with her rage. It was fascinating. I didn't talk back much to elders (yet), definitely not at school. I got spanked as a child and wasn't really allowed to express or stew in my anger. Syd was a different species. When she deemed me cool enough to befriend, I became smitten with her. Little did I know then that she would be my platonic life partner.

SQUID: The boys I hung out with had crushes on Theo. I was seething with jealousy, so I pulled a move and took her into my circle. It was a keep-your-enemies-closer kind of thing. My scheme involved dancing. At BFS, we could take dance if we didn't want to take gym. I fuckin' hated gym, because gym was dodgeball. I was a little chubby, and they were throwing that ball at me very hard. So I went to the dance department. I dragged Theo into one of my performances because I found out she had taken ballet for a long time. So when one of the dancers in my routine dropped out, I said to Theo, "Hey, new girl, heard you can dance. Wanna be in my dance?" It was to J. Geils's "Freeze-Frame." She said yes. Then we fell in love. I had a friend! I sucked her in and I never let her go.

THEO: I hated gym with a passion too, so dance was the only choice for me, and now this alluring creature I had been afraid of all year wanted to be my friend. The first time I went over to Squid's house, it was kinda like she kidnapped me. We were walking to the train from school, and she said, "Come over," and I was like, "Uh, okay." WOW, SHE'S INVITING ME OVER. She showed me photo albums for two hours. I saw pictures of her family and her friends—it was like being welcomed into her world. "Wow, I can't believe I'm at her house!" Hours passed. Finally, I told her, "Uh, I have to go home." From then on, we became super-close.

SQUID: We did everything together—we peed together, took baths together. Not in a sexual way, just because we didn't want to stop talking long enough to use the bathroom.

THEO: The first time I ever got drunk was also the first time I slept over at her house. We watched *The Shining*, drank White Russians, and smoked cigarettes. We wrote to each other from our different summer sleepaway camps, and we stayed friends even though we were in different high schools. She was at High School of Performing Arts (the *Fame* school) for acting, and I was at the High School of Music & Art for art, and that's where I got to know Gina.

GINA: My best friend, Kim, introduced me to Theo briefly a year before high school. It was the first time I ever went to Brooklyn. My friend acted like it was a big deal to go to Brooklyn to meet her friend Theo: "Theo's really cool, so just, you know, be cool. She looks just like Julie from *Fame*." Theo *was* a cool kid. She had a safety pin with beads on it fastened to her sneaker. That was definitely cool. And she really did kinda look like Julie from *Fame*. Now, Theo will tell you that I was wearing a sailor outfit that day, which I wasn't. I had a T-shirt with a sailboat on it and a home haircut that looked like a mullet. But in Theo's memory, I'm in a full sailor outfit and pigtails!

THEO: Gina's hair was in pigtails and she was wearing a matching tank-top-and-shorts set with sailboats on them. I loved a sailor motif, I still do. She was really cute and kind of shy. A year later, we found out we were going to the same high school, and were both art majors. The first day at Music & Art, Gina and I were in our first-period class together. The desks were arranged in a big circle, and we were almost directly across the room from each other. There was a magnetic energy for me with Gina in that first period of ninth grade. I recognized her, as I had met her the year before via our mutual friend Kim Starr. Her giant, beautiful eyes, the Roman nose—it was destiny. Perhaps we were warriors together in another life. I mean, it really was like a magnet. She was someone I knew at first sight that I wanted to be friends with. Maybe her shyness was something I wanted to break through, maybe it was because she looked so damn cool, maybe I connected to the otherness she possesses. In any case, it was for life. To this day, Gina swears I was giving her dirty looks. But I wasn't! I was really sick with a terrible cold! I was stuffy, my sinuses were swollen, I was miserable, and she swears I was glaring at her. I think I was also trying to see if she was the same person I had met—the one with the pigtails and the sailboat shorts outfit—because she had a totally punk orange Mohawk! We've had this discussion so many times, we can sit in a stalemate for hours. Other people in high school thought I gave them dirty looks as well. Usually I was just in my own dazed world and didn't notice them, or I was mad and stewing. Maybe my makeup looked angry.

GINA: On my very first day of high school, there was Theo. She was all new-waved out with an asymmetrical haircut. I had a creeping Mohawk, the kind where you shave an inch or two over your ears, and then the next week you maybe shave an inch higher, and then a little higher and higher. Anyways, Theo was as cool, stylish, and gorgeous as I had remembered her to be from our first meeting in Brooklyn, even if she was giving me dirty looks. She says she wasn't. We sat across from each other that first day of class staring at each other. I was a little intimidated by her but that just made me want to be friends with her even more. Once we started talking, it was obvious to me that we'd be friends for life.

THEO: After the first year, the two schools combined and became LaGuardia High School. Gina, Syd, and I were all together for tenth grade. I wanted Gina and Syd to meet, so I made it my mission to introduce them.

GINA: Theo and I had a drawing assignment to sketch something in the park. Theo said, "Let's go meet my friend Syd, and we'll go hang out." We were in Columbus Circle near Central Park. We picked up Syd and gave her a piece of paper and a pencil so she could sketch with us. I never knew any actors before, so I thought she was a little odd. She had a funny style, a very confident and carefree attitude that I wasn't used to because all my friends were dorky artists. I'd never met anybody like her before—and that holds true to this day.

SQUID: Gina is an absolute creative genius, one of those people that can teach herself to do anything and is annoyingly good at everything, which might have really gotten on my nerves if it weren't for the fact that I always benefited so directly from all of her various skills and talents. But I thought our first hangout was going to see Herbie Hancock at the Roxy. We met in front of a donut shop on Fourteenth Street. I have no idea why we saw Herbie Hancock.

GINA: Nobody did! We probably didn't know what else to do.

THEO: It was my fault. All I remember is that we were the youngest people there, and definitely the strangest. Gina was wearing striped knee socks, combat boots, cut-off shorts, and had her orange Mohawk. My hair was all chopped up. I had one of my first modeling jobs around then and had an asymmetrical haircut swept over one eye, buzzed in the back and all the way around.

SQUID: I was in awe of Gina. She was next-level cool. She had a Mohawk! And the knee socks really blew my mind. I associated knee socks with Sunday school uniforms or church, so when I saw how Gina owned that pair of socks, I was like, "Ohhhh!" I took the whole thing in and started putting it all together. "Hmm ... knee socks, combat boots, orange Mohawk ... knee socks and combat boots and orange Mohawk."

THEO: A year or so later, we met Sindi. We had some mutual friends. I wound up at a party at her house on quaaludes. I passed out, woke up at my house—I have no idea how I got home—and remembered I met this awesome chick. I brought Syd and Gina to her next party. I think.

SQUID: Sindi was the prototype of the tough girl. She was a few years older than us and lived in Park Slope. She'd go stomping around the neighborhood in her combat boots, motorcycle jacket, and jet-black hair. She was the toughest, most badass girl. Nobody fucked with her. The first time I saw her, she walked past my corner. I was with my sister who promptly chimed in, "I know who that girl is. Slut." I couldn't wait to go to Sindi Training Camp. I was her best pupil.

SINDI: Honestly, I don't remember the first interaction I had with the girls. It seemed like suddenly they were just there. I don't know where they came from or how they came into my life, but there they were and I embraced them immediately. They were young, but I often had younger friends. There was something about these girls—they weren't like children. They were crazy-ass teenagers, but so was I. We were all crazy-ass teenagers; I was just an older teenager who was out of school and had moved on. They also had a kind of fearlessness; it was different than mine, which was more of a street-smart fearlessness—a kind of "I know what the fuck I'm doing" fearlessness, whereas theirs was a little bit more "I have no idea what the fuck I'm doing, so I'm not scared of anything because I don't know any better" fearlessness. They were exactly who they were: interesting and creative and up for whatever. I loved them. I brought them into my home. I was living on my own in my first Brooklyn apartment with my boyfriend. It was the party pad! They could sleep there, they could eat there, they could hang out there. I loved them like that kitten you find under a car in the back of the parking lot and you're like, "Ah! You're mine. I'm taking you home. You may have fleas, whatever! Come with me, I'll take care of you." That's what it was. I loved them, and there was no turning back from that. I never stopped loving them.

CHAPTER 7

MAKING A SCENE

The first wave of punk rock that we grew up worshipping was over by the time we were old enough to go out to clubs by ourselves. Some of those bands, like Blondie and the Ramones, were still very active, but by that time they were household names and played big venues. We were looking for our own scene, something we could be part of. That scene was hardcore. Or so we thought.

SINDI: I was a little bit older than the other Lunachicks, so I was in with hardcore early on. At first, the scene was about the love of the music. I was hanging out all night on stoops in the Lower East Side with guys that later became Agnostic Front and Warzone and Murphy's Law. I knew them when it was a much smaller scene, when the punks and skinheads were one group. From '81 to '83, I was very much part of it, and I was accepted just fine. I went to all the old hardcore clubs and CBGB and got to know everybody. And I had my bottle of vodka. Everyone else had their bottles of beer, but I had my vodka, and I could really drink—that was a good party trick to get you recognized. "She's cool, look at her chug that vodka!"

There were so many bands to see during those early years. The Peppermint Lounge on Forty-Fifth Street was my first favorite club before it moved down to Fifteenth Street. I went to the matinees at Gildersleeves, I saw the Damned at a club called the Brooklyn Zoo in Bensonhurst, the Dead Kennedys at the Paramount in Staten Island, and the U.K. Subs at A7. There were women in bands like Killer Instinct, P.M.S., and Wench. The Stimulators had guitarists Denise Mercedes and Anne Gustavsson—they were the cool grown-up girls. And then came Blood Sister and Manon. There were no dressing rooms; the crowd was all mixed in with the band. It was a cool, different experience. I started to drift away a little bit by '83, '84, and then I disappeared. The scene changed in the years that followed, when Theo, Gina, and Squid started going out.

CBGB hosted all-ages hardcore matinee shows every weekend. We wanted to hang out, see shows, and, just like any group of young teens, find our place in this city. This proved a bit stickier than simply showing up to see some bands. The vibe was cliquey and insular, and we were the new kids who seemed to have appeared outta nowhere.

GINA: I went to my first CBGB hardcore matinee when I was fourteen. My friends and I got all dressed up in our best punk rock outfits. The day we went, a photographer was doing a photo shoot on punks for some magazine. There weren't that many girls hanging around, and then here we come, me and my friends with Mohawks, miniskirts, and combat boots, trying so hard to fit in and hang out like we belonged there. I looked like a total poser. Of course, the photographer was like, "You guys! You guys! Let me take your picture!" We were like, "Okay." Then people in the scene saw us and were like, "You guys are

the biggest posers." The skinheads called us "the Mohawks" because we all had Mohawks (clever, as usual).
And that started a whole thing, me and my friends getting hassled by the hardcore kids who were already
hanging out at CB's. It didn't help that one of the
skinheads was flirting with my best friend and that did
not sit well with the skinhead chicks. We were hanging
out in Tompkins Square Park one night and something
happened—it was so stupid, I can't remember what it
was exactly, but it might have involved a bong. A fight
broke out and we got chased out of the park. We didn't
know how to fight; we weren't tough! So we moved over
to Washington Square Park and started our own clique
over there. We may not have been tough bruisers like
the East Side kids, but we were more fun and eventually
some people from the East Side defected and started
hanging out with us.

Sindi was smart to have left the scene when she did. By the time the
three of us were hanging out at CB's, skinhead girls were lining up to
beat our asses. So much for sisterhood. Though there were girls on the
scene and some in bands, the majority of them were girlfriends of the
hardcore guys. Skinhead girls at the matinees would step to us and challenge us, and the boys would tell them to beat us up. It was that kind of
a thing, really fucked up when you think about it—boys on a power trip
pitting girls against each other for their own stupid amusement, and the
girls taking the bait because they wanted to impress the boys. We stood
our ground as best we could, but we were hardly fighters. We were kids
who wanted to see some bands, not get into fistfights with a bunch of
knuckleheads.

THEO: Around this time, I did my first film work as an extra in
Sid and Nancy. I was in a crowd scene outside of a club,
which was cut from the film. A lot of punks and hardcore

kids were there to get paid, but they were not having the fake Sid Vicious played by Gary Oldman. When Gary walked out of the club during the shooting, some skinhead started punching him in the face till he bled, yelling, "Poser!!" Welcome to New York.

SINDI: When I came back in '87, hardcore had bloomed into this bigger thing. There were all these skinhead girls at clubs looking at me going, "Who's THIS poser new girl?" Like, fuck you, you were in diapers when I was doing what you're doing. I was like, "Yuck, I'm out of here." The scene had branched out to the fuckin' jocks and suburban kids trying to be tough, and that's when you get fights. People had something to prove.

The scene became bloated with rage and testosterone; there was always a beef. We'd hear guys talking about how they were going to Christopher Street to beat up "faggots." It was violent, homophobic, and misogynistic—not to mention conformist—everything we were vehemently against.

THEO: One thing I always secretly loved and had an inside giggle about was the amount of shirtless dude-to-dude contact in hardcore. I was always scared to go into the matinees, so I mostly sat outside CB's with one friend and a forty-ounce of Olde English, trying to be cool wearing my black eyeliner and red lipstick, shitting myself on the inside. The guys hanging around were creeps; I felt like a little rabbit among wolves. But in the pit, it was different—like homoerotic wrestling—all these shirtless guys rubbing up and pouncing on each other. HOT! Little did they know my fantasies about them while they were picking fights and pounding on each other. Hee, hee, "pounding."

By '87, we started doing our own thing inspired by local bands like the Kretins, who had become our good friends. Our musical tastes expanded too; we were listening to everything from KISS to the Stooges, a lot of Rolling Stones, Redd Kross, and DMZ. Around this time, there was a psychedelic/garage rock revival in NYC, with bands like the Maneaters, the Secret Service, the Freaks, the Sheiks, and Optic Nerve. All the guys had bobbed haircuts and wore tight jeans and pointy shoes. Everybody was cool and really drunk and just enjoying the music. Nobody bothered us or tried to keep us back. This motley mix of the punk, garage-psychedelic, underground scenes was weirder and a lot more diverse than the hardcore scene. It was really genderbent too. Most important, we were accepted without all of the stupid look-and-act-this-specific-way rule-book bullshit.

Suddenly, the idea of *us* forming our own band seemed really accessible. The gears started turning inside our demented little brains. We didn't have to be KISS or the Rolling Stones in order to get on a stage and make music. Our friends were doing it; there was no reason we couldn't do it too. Plus, they were egging us on.

SQUID: The person who really put the Lunachicks in motion was Andrea Freak, who I met working in this bizarro land of misfit toys called Air Brokers messenger service. I worked there as a foot messenger carrying pieces of paper that needed to be stamped or signed all over Manhattan—before fax machines, baby—randomly alongside Todd Youth, hardcore guitarist extraordinaire (who was somehow even younger than me), as well as with Andrea's then-husband, our weirdo adopted uncle, the legendary Howie Pyro.

GINA: I knew Andrea because she was the drummer for the Maneaters, and I thought that band was so cool because they were one of the few all-female bands out there. I would go see them play all the time. It turned out Squid worked with the drummer.

SQUID: One day I showed up for work and Andrea just said to me, "Hey, you and your friends should form a band, and if you do, we'll let you play with us. And you should write a song called 'Babysitters on Acid.'" Whoa. OK!

Listen, we may have been ding-dongs, but we could also be very pragmatic and pretty damn resourceful too—it's the New Yorker in us. All our favorite, iconic bands had broken up. We missed their music! So we looked to ourselves to fill the void.

Even though it was the exception and not the norm to see women playing in bands, it never crossed our minds NOT to pick up an instrument and start our own damn band. Suzi Quatro and Poly Styrene were godlike, and each of us had the Runaways' *Live in Japan* album. We were enraptured with them. They were kids, we were kids. Their mere existence as young girls creating their own music in the midst of a billion dude bands made us swell with this feeling of *"Fuck yes!!"* We thought we had excellent taste in music, so we figured we knew what it took to write and play great songs. In our minds, it truly was that easy.

GINA: Squid and Theo came up to me in the hallway at school and said, "We're forming a band. Theo's boyfriend Mike is gonna be the drummer. We want you to join!" I was surprised. I said, "What do you mean, you're forming a band? You guys don't even play any instruments."

SQUID: A small detail.

GINA: We were friends, so it was weird that they didn't tell me they played music, which, of course, they didn't! I was already in the process of trying to form a band, and I had been playing guitar for six months at that point.

SQUID: I had talked to Sindi about starting a band. She had a guitar that her boyfriend bought her, but she didn't know how to play. Then I had another conversation with Gina about starting a band, and I had that feeling of

"Uh-oh, I double-dipped. Whoops. Hey, let's have TWO guitar players!"

SINDI: I don't think I was part of the "let's form a band" plan. But they started talking about it. I had a guitar already. It was about hanging out together and, yes, we have such amazing taste in music. We know exactly what's great. Why shouldn't it work? Even if it doesn't work, won't it be fun?? It'll be fun because it's us, and everything we do is fun and great. Sure enough, it was fun and great.

GINA: Squid and Theo said they had started a band with Sindi, and Sindi was playing guitar. I said, "Well, you already have a guitar player." And they said, "Yeah, but you could be a second guitar player. You could be the lead guitar player!"

SQUID: Sindi and Gina both had guitars, but Gina had been playing hers for six months, and Sindi hadn't played hers at all, which put Gina six months ahead, which made Gina the lead guitar player. That was the rationale.

GINA: I thought they were making concessions, trying to be nice. I told them I didn't know how to play lead. But they were like, "C'mon, c'mon, you can do it! You'll learn!"

THEO: I seem to remember Squid telling me that she and Gina had already started writing a song. I semi-panicked because I was afraid of being left out and decided that I was going to be the singer. Squid was deciding what instrument to play, so I made my choice on the fly. I was like, "Uhhhh, I'll be the singer! Right? Yeah?" I imagined having to get a drum set and having to deal with all of that and spoke FAST. I ended up learning to play the drums too and can set up and break down a kit, no prob.

SQUID: Theo grabbed the job of singer, thank god! There wasn't a thought in my mind that there'd be keyboards in this

band, so it was drums or bass. I figured drums were a lot
of shit to carry around. Plus, no one in New York drives
a car at that age, and there's nowhere to practice for
free without some old lady calling the cops. Theo's
boyfriend at the time was the singer in a heavy metal
band from Bensonhurst called Nevermore—they were very
Italian metalheads from deep Brooklyn, so you really
have to pronounce it "Nevamoa" to get the right feel.
This kid in the band, Russell (his mother had plastic
covers on every single piece of furniture in the house,
including the carpet), sold me my first bass, an aqua-
green Aria Diamond for $50. I only had $25. I think I
talked my dad into giving me the other $25.

And that's how the Lunachicks became a band. After we formed, there was no difference from us being friends to us suddenly being friends who were now in a band together. Except that instead of us getting together all the time, smoking pot, and eating snacks, now we would get together all the time, smoke pot, eat snacks, and write songs. Becoming the Lunachicks was the easiest step for us to take. Every single thing that unfolded from this band was a result of the natural impulses, kinda like tides, that drove the way we lived, and we were always following the next thought and idea that blasted into our creative, arty brains.

We formed to satisfy an urge to play great music, fuck with people because we thought it was funny, and blow their minds. But the single most important goal we had was to amuse ourselves. We just wanted to have fun together. It took some time before we realized the deeper implications of our attitude and actions.

Okay, how many songs do we need for a set? Eight? Cool!

We started writing songs in each other's bedrooms. Our influences were varied, everything from Bad Brains to Black Sabbath to Buzzcocks. Theo had certain singers she wanted to emulate, like Glenn Danzig, John

Kay from Steppenwolf, Ozzy Osbourne, and Rob Halford. At first, we were just getting our rocks off. We never felt like we had to sound a certain way. Listen, it's not like we had a lot of choices—we played the only kind of music we were capable of writing at the time, which is whatever came out. That's the beauty of being so young: there were no expectations. We were awful, but we were committed.

We were at such a loss to decide on a band name and failing hard—we thought about calling ourselves the Go Homes (a bad reference to the Runaways)—when Sindi blurted, "Oh well, what are we gonna do, we're just a bunch of raving lunachicks." Our jaws hit the floor. *What did you just say!!!?? That's it! That's our name!* Sindi was the queen of dry, razor-sharp one-liners. One time we were walking past a sidewalk cafe when a guy at a table yelled to us, "Hey, girls, come sit over here," and without missing a beat, Sindi yelled back, "There's not enough room on your face." Zing!

> **GINA:** On my yearbook, I had written "Raving Lunichics," so I guess that was our original name for a hot second. Eventually we dropped the "Raving" (thank god) and learned how to spell.

We rehearsed in a building on Fourteenth Street, which was a popular practice space that nearly every band in the city used. We were in Studio A and made plenty of unflattering noise while working out our songs. One time after leaving the studio, a bunch of boys who rehearsed in the room next to ours followed us down the street yelling, *"Studio A! Pffffft! Bwahahahahaha!"* Ooof. It sucked.

Later on, we relocated to the famous Music Building in Midtown. We had Madonna's old room on the twelfth floor, room 1206 (we think), where she wrote some of her early hits. That's the legend anyway. The elevators were ground zero for a constant graffiti battle. Every band would write their name on the wall of the elevator, and someone would come along and write "sucks" or "eats dick" after the band's name. There was an ongoing war that everybody in the building was participating in.

GINA: Somebody wrote something shitty about us, so I wrote back, "So-and-so is a looser." I misspelled *loser* like a dumb-dumb. THAT started a whole new war. Somebody wrote back, "Nobody is looser than the Lunachicks." It went on and on. The elevator was covered. We were in that building for a good seven years. It was seven years of Sharpie wars.

THEO: That building had a plethora of unwanted odors and was plastered with gobs of graffiti—some of it with priceless grammatical errors. That's where I got the line "We can be worster" for our song "Drop Dead." Somebody wrote that on the walls in the bathroom. I was like, "Wow! I'm using that one!" The building was gross; roaches were everywhere. One practice, I got a quart of Tropicana apple juice to wash down my Little Debbie snack cake, took a swig, put it down, sang, wrote, picked it up, drank, repeat. Suddenly I felt a wiggling inside my mouth and realized it was a live roach. Inside. My. Mouth. I spit it out, watched it crawl across the floor, stomped on it, and proceeded to hop up and down for twenty minutes, screaming with the heebie-jeebies.

As young, not-great musicians, we tried to learn Black Sabbath's "Sweet Leaf," but our attempts turned into different songs every time we sat down and tried to figure it out. We must have written twenty songs while trying and failing to learn "Sweet Leaf." It was a good trick: if you figure it out wrong, it's a whole new song. We also tried the Rolling Stones' "Stray Cat Blues." Bombed on that one too. Sometimes, we'd individually come up with a riff or a part and then mix and match it all together with Theo's lyrics. That was how we wrote our first album, *Babysitters on Acid*.

Television was our surrogate parent. Some of our earliest songs were based on TV shows, horror movies, and after-school specials: "Jan Brady" (the middle sister from *The Brady Bunch*), "Mabel Rock" (about

Mabel King, the mom from the show *What's Happening!!*), "This Is Serious" (inspired by a public service announcement about drugs), "Binge and Purge" (inspired by an after-school special about bulimia). We were huge fans of Russ Meyer and John Waters movies—we can't stress that enough, ever. On our first EP, we covered "Get Off the Road" from the 1968 B movie *She-Devils on Wheels*, directed by Herschell Gordon Lewis, which was about an all-female motorcycle gang. We loved the characters on *Gorgeous Ladies of Wrestling*. We pulled concepts and themes from all that stuff.

Our lives really did change forever the day we discovered John Waters movies, and it was all thanks to our friend Sara. She was a few years older than us, and she always had money—and odd boyfriends. She'd open her thrift store purse and crumpled hundred-dollar bills would go flying. She had some story about how she had a job or was a secretary, but she was always covered in glitter. Turns out she was a dominatrix, but we were clueless. One day, she invited us over after school to hang out and watch a movie she was crazy about, *Desperate Living*. But first we had to convince Gina to blow off her very first lead guitar lesson.

GINA: I really had to start learning how to play leads since I was deemed the lead guitar player, so I started calling around looking for guitar lessons. I called some guy named Robert from an ad in the *Village Voice*. I told him I didn't have much money and couldn't afford his rate, so he goes, "Wait, wait, wait. I can tell you're young, I'll lower my rate for you. Let's have a trial session. First lesson free." I was all excited. The day of my first lesson arrived. After school, Theo, Squid, and I went to Sara's house. She said, "Oh, you have to watch *Desperate Living*! This is the best movie ever, you're gonna love it." But I had my guitar lesson, so I couldn't stay. Everyone was like, "No, no! STAY!" And Sara said, "Here, eat these pot brownies." That was it. I got so fucking high, I was useless. I had to call Robert high out of my mind to cancel. "Um, I ate something and I don't feel good and I can't come." He was all mad because he had reduced his rate for me, but I was so high it didn't matter. We watched *Desperate Living*, and sure enough, our world was transformed.

SQUID: That was the entry point of the John Waters influence. Sara introduced us to the whole B-movie genre. It put a brand-new spin on what we were doing. We felt like he got us. We are one with this man.

Theo really had a gift for taking those underground cult influences and spinning them into gold. Her brain worked in mysterious ways that we were just in awe of. She made ridiculousness an art form and used humor to talk about taboo topics that people rather not think about, whether it was abusive relationships or eating disorders or getting her period. She was not afraid to go there and yank back the curtain. Blew our mind all the time!

Can't have an inch of fat on my bod
Gotta get on the cheerleading squad
Play tryouts are next week
There's a foxy guy I gotta meet
Mom won't let me eat too much
But in my room I go and stuff
Ipecac and Ex-Lax are my best friends
I'll have my head in the toilet till the end
Fingers just not long enough
This time the purge is gonna be tough
People tell me that I'm thin
Then they ask about the bruise on my chin
When I'm home I eat as much as I can
Pretty soon I'll need a bedpan
No guys like me 'cept for Lax
But he's my ex!

Binge and purge the whole day through
I threw up on Mom's good shoes
I made a mess in the school bathroom
Someone's bound to catch me soon
Binge and purge yeah
Mom found me on the floor
Bloodstains on my Christian Dior
Now I'm in the hospital, they feed me
From a bag on the wall
Me and my friends do it all together
Circle purge will make it better
Ruptured my esophagus
But I'm still a hippopotamus
Just can't seem to figure it out
Why my teeth keep falling out!

—"Binge and Purge"

THEO: There was never an agenda to focus on one thing versus another. It's not like I thought, "We're gonna start a band, and I'm gonna write about **this**"—those lyrics were just what came out of me. The reason my lyrics are twisted and funny is because I'm twisted and funny! It's who I've been—and still am—since I can remember. Humor was one of my coping mechanisms (see: Jewish). Being funny is in my bones. You can certainly hear all of that in my lyric-writing. A lot of the bands I loved were funny, even if they didn't mean to be. I thought the Misfits were funny, even though they took themselves seriously. I also related to some of the most fucked-up songs and bands like the Anti-Nowhere League, one of my favorites, because they were hilarious. I never saw how sexist they were because I could see myself writing songs about stupid, annoying dudes. I could be just

as defiant, cold, and mean (and funny) as they were.
The Damned were theatrical and brilliant musicians and
also funny. There was always an element of camp and
The Muppet Show in a lot of the things I liked. My bio
should say, "Raised by TV."

We were so in the moment and doing whatever felt right—and frankly, it *all* felt right. We didn't have any foresight, nor did we think about how people would interpret us. Whatever we felt like doing, we went ahead and did it, including getting naked and putting on Squid's parents' matching orange raincoats and rubber galoshes and going to the deli in between writing songs. No reason, we just did it.

You're really creating art in its purest form when you're not thinking, "Oh, *this* is how it's going to be, and *this* is gonna be the outcome." Although we had an *idea* of what we *thought* we were—awesome and unstoppable rockers primed for world domination—it wasn't necessarily what we sounded like then! All we were capable of doing was letting whatever was inside move through us and come out.

So if we want to write songs about farting in the van or pooping on a cracker because that's what makes us laugh, we're gonna do it. At the same time, if we want to write a song about women being abused because we see it or read about it every single day, we're going to do it. And why wouldn't we also write about our moms and our stupid teacher? Those things were all part of our lives. We were sharing whatever was there without thinking too hard about it. If there was one genuine thought-out intention, it was to crack each other up.

We never grew out of juvenile humor. Ever. Burps are on our live album, burps are on our studio albums. Pooping, farting, burping, and getting our periods feature in a bunch of our songs. Never in a million years did we think a fucking fart could be considered a political statement, but for women especially, shame is associated with body stuff. Those totally normal actions that happen to every single *species* on the planet are deemed foul and improper for women? Fuck you, we're gonna weaponize them and come after you. But the main reason we wrote about bodily functions was because farts are funny and obnoxious, burps are funny and obnoxious, and we were funny and obnoxious.

THEO: A lot of that was because we had parents that were from the '40s and '50s who themselves dealt with very old-fashioned parents. There were different ways we broke free and rebelled against that. For me, whenever I burped at home, my mom would say, "You're never gonna get a boyfriend like that!" And my response was to burp again. It was a rebellion. I'd burp at home at the dinner table, and I'd get yelled at. And I'd do it again. And again. And again.

GINA: My grandmother would let 'em rip, and then she'd giggle. She had a silly streak. She stayed in a mode of adolescence. When she was in first grade, she was taken out of school to work in the fields back in Italy, so she never learned to read and write and she never stopped wanting to play. She loved pranks and was a very funny lady. But for us, burping at the table when my parents were present was absolutely not allowed. And that's what made it so damn funny.

SQUID: My parents would say stuff like, "Someday you're going to have a boyfriend who is gonna invite you to his parents' house and you're going to embarrass yourself," and I was like, "Pfft. WhatEVER." But back to the farting thing, it really all comes from all the stuff we're not supposed to be doing. When I started having serious boyfriends, I would christen them with a juicy one, then be like, "See, I farted on your leg. I own you now, you're mine."

GINA: It's "unladylike." My favorite thing to do would be to belch and follow it up with "Always a lady!" Theo had a T-shirt that said "Always a lady." It was such a funny concept to me: always a lady.

Menstruation is another bodily function that women are taught to feel shameful about and have to hide, and we did not want to hide anything. For one show, we made blood bags and taped them to the inside of our legs. Onstage, we planned it so that we'd slam our legs together at the same time, creating this huge burst of blood. Such a magnificent sight! Many years later, a photo of one of these very moments was part of a big ad campaign for Vans sneakers—except the corporate folks at Vans must not have appreciated our theatrics because the photo was doctored to remove the fake blood from our thighs.

In a lot of ways, we were socially *unconscious*. It's important for us to point this out because a few years into our existence, the press often lumped us in with the riot grrrl movement, which was lazy of them. First and most obvious, we sound nothing like riot grrrl bands. That should've been the end of any attempt at comparisons. Second, riot grrrl specifically began as a way to get more women's voices and viewpoints out into the open. And that's *awesome*, we support it wholeheartedly, but that wasn't our agenda—not intentionally, at least. Unwittingly, perhaps.

Although riot grrrl and the Lunachicks were in the same fight together, we had completely separate paths. It felt like there was a big difference between us and the well-educated, feminist-theory-savvy girls in those bands. They got organized and worked hard building a collective, grassroots movement in punk. Then there was us—we started our trashy band for dumb fun, and we couldn't have quoted feminist theory to save our lives. Our first album was called *Babysitters on Acid*—need we say more?

We were just living, and then one day the band was there, and the microphones were turned on, and suddenly people were listening. We communicated a feminist message from the get-go because feminism was intrinsically part of who we were as individuals, as New York City girls punching our way through a hostile, sexist environment. We can't really say we put any thought into it beyond that. Framework: we are Gen Xers, first-generation daughters of the '70s feminist revolution, born and raised to be equals in every way, and told by our parents and teachers that we could do and be whatever we wanted. We were sent off to fly into a world we were told was fair, equal, and open to everyone, encouraged to be doctors, lawyers, and presidents. *There is nothing standing in your way but you! Go get 'em, tiger!* Every day, we walked out our doors into a world that didn't quite get the same memo. God be with you finding yourself on the same long block with a construction crew posted up for lunch, waiting on their next contestant for the catcall catwalk. Or having to do the side-turn/protruding-elbow maneuver on some guy who nestled his dick in your ass on a sardine-packed D train. Not to mention the endless contradictions coming from inside our households: "Be a leader, but be a lady." Wouldn't YOU want to fart in someone's face??

If we existed as powerful women in the world—which we did—and we were also onstage as powerful women in the world, then hopefully other women were inspired by that.

Together, all that combined energy created an air of "don't fuck with us." Once we were solidified as a band, we became this force of nature that you simply could not fuck with. At the same time, we intuitively knew that every time we walked out on a stage, we were there to represent for our half of the human race. We knew people expected us to suck. We came to battle and to win and prove a point, and it felt important. That is a responsibility we took very seriously. There was a feeling of "Watch this, motherfuckers! Hold on to your face!" We didn't know what that meant, or even what it entailed, but it came with us wherever we went. Our attitude before each show was "We're gonna go into this club, and we're gonna kill it!!!"

LUNACHICKS
DESTROY all BANDS from N.J.
FRIDAY FEB. 16th
PYRAMID CLUB on ave. A btwn 6th & 7th

CHAPTER 8

DESIGNING WOMEN

We always rejected a herd mentality, which included not succumbing to any uniform. And people do have a tendency to wear uniforms, whether that means perfectly manicured eyebrows or a three-piece suit or a spiked leather jacket and combat boots. To us, the stereotypical punk rock look felt so contrived by the time 1988 rolled around.

As a band, we were always about challenging conventions and forcing you to accept us as we are. Society drove us, without us being conscious about it, to really make heads roll and stomachs turn with our appearance. Experimenting with different looks helped us figure out what made us feel the least awkward and most empowered as adolescent freak shows.

GINA: In middle school, it was obvious I was never gonna be part of the popular girls, even though I wanted to be. I was *such* an oddball. I wasn't pretty enough, I couldn't afford nicer clothes, it was never gonna happen. For girls who have been told all their lives that they're pretty, they need to treasure their looks and preserve them as part of who they are. But beauty wasn't part of my identity, so I never felt obligated to concern myself with it.

SQUID: I never felt cute or pretty as a kid. My identity was always about being a smartass/badass. Like Bugs Bunny meets Baretta meets Dennis the Menace. But Sindi was the real tuff-titties model; I couldn't hold a candle to that. I just had a big mouth and a lotta hair. That was the survival personality that helped me navigate the world. The band became an avenue for me to cash in on that, a perfect way for me to channel all the stuff I'd just always be getting in trouble for. People ate it up, like, "More! Spit on us! We love you!"

SINDI: It wasn't until punk that I started dressing in a way that was recognizable as anything in particular. When I was a kid/teenager, there was very little money for new or "better" clothes. I had a lot of hand-me-downs and cheap shit from the department store Alexander's. I had to develop my own style and the attitude to back it up, otherwise I was gonna look like a loooo-ser! Also, I always preferred boys' (and later men's) clothes. In my twenties, I was super-annoyed by my curves. I often wished for a straight, boyish figure that would fit better to the clothes I liked. Whatever, I guess I made it work.

Theo was the pretty girl, but she was also the cool girl—she stood out. She wore daring clothes and had such an awesome style, so original. We were always impressed with her.

SQUID: I never thought of Theo as giving a shit about looking pretty onstage; her more glamorous over-the-top looks came much later, which I think of as more inspired by drag culture. Theo was/is a secret clown, way more interested in cracking people up than being "pretty." She just happens to be drop-dead gorgeous. She couldn't help it!

THEO: I was always into fashion and clothes. I think the persona for the band that I created for myself—confident, strong, glamorous, fearless—was the opposite of how I really felt a lot of the time. I was never satisfied with myself. I knew I was probably pretty because I was told so, and I liked some things about myself, but even as a child I compared myself to other girls. Being told you're pretty—and I know how this is going to sound—is great, but being told you're smart and talented is more important. I was told those things too, but somehow all my real value in my core came from how I looked or was perceived by others (thank you, Barbie and sexism). I know the inside is really the most important thing, but I guess my insides weren't sure about that. I developed cystic acne in my early twenties. With these breakouts, I only felt confident and pretty in my full-coverage pancake makeup—the same kind drag queens use—and my drag queen clothes and hair. The rest of the time, I felt like an ugly, pizza-faced dude. Body issues were deep in my family history. That stuff was in me because it was around me, like a big, juicy boil.

For us together, our identity was about being fierce, and nothing else mattered—especially society's beauty standards. We always dressed differently from our classmates because we were punks. Our early teenage look was old-school NY street punk, kinda like the Ramones on acid. But as we got older, our style morphed into us not wanting to adhere to the traditional punk rock visuals.

We did what we wanted, which really is the essence of punk rock. Gina grew out her Mohawk and dyed her hair blue. Squid had striped jeans that we loved. Theo went through a period of wearing mostly bright orange. We all wore a lot of leopard print. We grew our armpit hair, then we shaved it.

Shedding the traditional punk rock look was also more in line with what we wanted to be as a band and helped us stand out. We ran with it. At our first show, Theo used fake blood, and from there, our look took off. We naturally gravitated toward outrageous clothes, clown makeup, and props such as rubber chickens, giant plastic bones, and oversized fake bloody meat cleavers. Combing thrift stores became our thing. The whole concept of fashion was so different back then. Customizing your look was an art, a hobby, a passion. It was all about coveting bizarre one-of-a-kind finds. We'd score the most hilarious clothes and dare each other to wear them. Theo took most of the dares. And because the stuff cost about fifty cents, we had to buy it! Plus, sometimes you'd get extra-lucky.

GINA: I collected '70s-style brown suede jackets. There was one in a thrift store on sale for $25. It was a little ripped up, but I was like, "I'll take it!" So I put it on, and as I was walking down the street, lookin' good, I put my hands in the pockets. Something was in the lining, not in the pocket. I pulled out a ziplock baggie of two dozen big yellow pills. They had the number 714 on them. I knew what a quaalude was, but I went to one of my druggie friends and asked about these pills. The pharmaceutical companies had stopped making quaaludes and were producing synthetics. But my friend was like, "These are the real deal"—and they were so much fun!

THEO: There was this place called Domsey's, a big warehouse on Kent Avenue in Williamsburg, Brooklyn, that sold old clothes for a dollar a pound. Huge bins of everything you can imagine, from babydoll nighties to crazy polyester pants to go-go boots to stiletto heels. You could dive into one of the bins and come out an hour later with gems for next to nothing. Old clothes, vintage, and maybe some irregulars—which could've been an alternate band name for us, by the way. I miss that place. There were stores like Trash and Vaudeville and Screaming

Mimi's that sold vintage clothes, but I couldn't afford a lot of that stuff, and let's face it, you just couldn't beat a dollar a pound.

SQUID: I used to search the city for sneakers that had been discontinued. Original Pumas, old PRO-Keds, PONYs—those sneakers were out of print for years. You just could not get them ... unless you were me. There were sneaker stores up and down Fourteenth Street. I'd go in and ask, "Hey, you guys got a basement? Mind if I go down there?" And they would let me! I'd find stacks of old boxes covered in dust, like an archaeologist searching for treasure in a hidden tomb, dig through them, and suddenly "OMG! Out-of-print maroon Puma Clydes with a yellow stripe in my size!!!! Yeeee!!!!!!!" I would strut out of the store thinking, "I am theee coolest person on the planet. NO ONE has these but ME."

We all made our own clothes too, not that anyone actually knew how to really sew or anything. We would thrift and alter, peg them plaid golf pants, bay-bee, and add dem bondage straps, hell-o! We used to make regular runs to a place called Diamond Discount Fabrics in Manhattan and buy yards of spandex and make our own leggings and skirts. There was so much silver lamé, ooh là là! We lived in the clothes we made.

THEO: I'd make bracelets out of the plastic from six-packs, and collect flip tabs from cans to turn into charm bracelets. It was true DIY stylings. We wore our trash and somehow it became glamorous. We were literally trashy!

SQUID: I had a pair of homemade FUCK shorts. I had tiny cutoff shorts and sewed red vinyl F-U-C-K letters across the ass.

GINA: I painted band logos and album covers on the backs of jean jackets and trench coats, like the Misfits, the Damned, the Cramps, and of course, our own band. I

even had a little side business getting commissions for
them.

We planned our tours around thrift stores, building time in our sched-
ules to go thrifting. The van smelled like mothballs and old closets after a
few shopping sprees. In the middle of nowhere Mississippi, we rolled out
of our hotel, all rumpled and half-asleep, and as we filed past these two
old ladies on our way into the thrift store, one of them pointed to Squid
and boldly announced to her friend, "Now that's what ya call a heathen."
We'd wake up at a hotel, get coffee, and go thrifting—and then we'd all
have to take a shit. Every. Single. Time. *Great. Now what?* We've taken
shits in disgusting thrift store bathrooms all over the country. But we
never figured it out. Like, *wait* an hour and *then* go shopping!

Our looks got more and more ridiculous. Tutus? Let's do it, why not?!
The tutu look was pioneered by Richie Stotts, the guitarist from the Plasmatics, who were a huuuuge influence on us. Their singer, Wendy O.
Williams, performed looking like a biker/stripper, and she owned the
stage with a fucking chain saw in her hands, blowing up cars and creating
chaos. And Richie would be standing next to her, a six-foot-four man in a
goddamn tutu. Groundbreaking genius, those two.

Makeup was another big part of us. Not properly applied makeup like
pop stars wore, but deliberately over-the-top looks that weren't meant to
make us look even remotely attractive. It'd look like a clown car backfired
in our faces at point-blank range. By the end of a show, all the colors were
streaming down our cheeks, and Theo's enormous fake eyelashes would
be hanging from her lids like loose shingles. It was all about the decon-
struction of beauty and showing the garish, gross reality of it all. We
egged each other on all the time. It was a lot of "I dare you" shit.

THEO: I'd be doing my makeup before a show and I'd turn around
and see Squid had half of her lip one color, the other
half another color, or one eye was the opposite color.
Then Gina would black out one tooth, and then every
other tooth, or all of them. Then one of us would draw

a unibrow. It snowballed. Truthfully, a lot of my intense makeup was self-expression that turned into just me killing time in the dressing room. I can sit and do this for an hour and a half and keep adding and adding like a painting that never feels finished. Kind of like tattoos. I was nineteen when I got my first tattoo, the eyeballs on my arm. There were few women with tattoos back then, and the tattoo community in New York was still very small. If you wanted to get a tattoo, you had to go underground or to Long Island, where it was legal.

SQUID: I was still in acting school when Theo got her first tattoo and I was super-jealous. It was so badass, I couldn't believe it. I was like, "Holy shit, she just got a band of stringy bloody eyeballs tattooed on her arm, she's crazy!! When can I go?!?"

It eventually started to click in our heads: What if we can play better than you, harder than you, faster than you . . . while wearing a fucking housedress and a shower cap? What if we wore tutus or dressed as menstruating cheerleaders and melted your fucking face off from the stage night after night? Women's bodies are scrutinized in a way that men's bodies never are, so of course we knew people were objectifying and sizing us up, and so of course we're going to fuck with that. Women are supposed to wear makeup to be attractive? Let's slap on pounds of it. Lingerie is sexy? Let's wear some matronly toilet-paper-stuffed double-Ds and granny panties on the OUTSIDE of our clothes. You want womanly? We'll show you womanly.

As time went on, this mentality really, really drove us to be as silly as possible. Channeling our hero John Waters, we were aggressively absurd. Some nights Theo would dress like a giant baby with a diaper, bonnet, all but one tooth blacked out, a rattle, and a packet of Nutella in the diaper for fake poop. Visually, we had to be a complete contradiction of who we really were, the epitome of the least-powerful female stereotype you can imagine. And then we were going to rip the fucking stage apart harder and faster than any band you've ever seen.

Absolutely we were repping for girls and women, but also for anyone outside of the norm. We grew up with deep, unsettling feelings of displacement within ourselves, our families, and the world. When you're dealing with any stereotype or a label—female, queer, Jewish, single mom, etc.—that is rooted in sexism, racism, ageism, homophobia, or any other hateful ism, it's all a similar struggle. You want to exist in the world without being harassed or discriminated against for being who you are. This was an ongoing fight for us.

SQUID: Growing up, I really didn't get that people were actually prejudiced against Jews. Of course, I knew about the Holocaust and history, but we grew up in New York City; I thought everybody was Jewish! When we first started touring and headed west, shit got real. I was standing in this gas station in the middle of butt-fuck nowhere when I heard this voice, "Well lookie there, that is a fur real-life Jew," and I realized this freak was looking at me. I was like, "Omg, this is really happening, is this really happening? That is a redneck, I mean that man has an actual red neck (oooh, sunburn, I get it!) and he sounds like Gomer Pyle." Holy shit, I didn't know that was real. I thought it was just something in a TV show. I guess you could say the stares of amazement were going in both directions. We all got a trip to the zoo that day. I started to go onstage with a Jewish star or the word *JEW* drawn on my forehead. I mean, once I knew that would fuck with people and piss them off? Whoopie! Shit, "Yay, I'm Jewish!" How perfect.

GINA: I always thought hair curlers were these strange, archaic items from a bygone era, especially the giant pink ones. I liked to wear them when I played live because I remember my mom sitting at home with curlers begrudgingly stuck in her hair. I even sometimes wore a giant vintage hair-drying cap—hose attached and all—onstage. Also, my grandma, a big Italian woman, inspired me. At sixteen, she came to the United States and worked in a girdle factory in Red Hook, Brooklyn. Being the youngest kid in my family, I wound up spending a lot of time with her. She babysat me, and I tried to keep her out of trouble—she was always chasing after boys, totally uninhibited. We would go out to Fire Island when I was a kid, and my nana loved it out there. Her bathing suit was from the 1950s, and my job was to help her get into it. She had these long-ass slabs for boobs. One time at the fish market on Arthur Ave in the Bronx, I witnessed her stuff a piece of salted cod down into her massive bra. "But Nana, that's stealing," I protested in horror. She shushed me and scooted quickly out of the market. Anyway, I'd have to help her roll up her boobs while she would dump a bunch of baby powder on them to keep them from chafing and stuff them into this vintage bathing suit that was orange and white with a giant petunia print. The whole idea of constricting her big boobs into a suit that was meant to confine her ... maybe that had some kind of subliminal influence on me wearing bras and girdles on the outside of my clothes while onstage. And the word *girdle* cracks me up!

If we could present ourselves that way while playing music that was so fucking ferocious, people would be forced to drop their preconceived notions of what is powerful, tough, strong, and empowering. Annihilating social conventions—especially when it came to how women were told to present themselves—ultimately became a driving force behind our image. *We're gonna wear pink old-lady housedresses, and you guys are gonna love it, and we're gonna blow you all away.*

CHAPTER 9

ALL ROADS LEAD TO CBGB

Our first show was in 1988. It was supposed to be at Gleason's Gym, a famous boxing gym in Brooklyn, but at the last minute, the show got moved to a space on Broadway and Houston Street. The bill included Smoking Gas Truck, Raging Slab, and the Freaks. The room was packed! We got onstage and looked out and saw . . . an audience. For us.

THEO: I was in the bathroom putting on makeup, my Brucci red lipstick in "Tramp" and some cheapo white eyeliner, and thinking, "Wow, I'm actually going onstage, with my own band." I was really nervous, but when I finally got up there, all I could think was "YES! I'm finally free." I found my space, and it saved my life. I felt stifled for so long, I can't imagine what would've happened without this band. There were times when I felt so vulnerable, but then I'd get onstage, and *nobody* could fuck with me. It's such a fucked-up thing because you're putting yourself on display, but the line was drawn. No one could touch me.

GINA: Theo was a natural. She went nuts, rolling on the floor and really going for it. Sindi was hopping around with her guitar, doing all these stage moves, while I looked on, thinking, "Fuuuuuuck—I have to do more than play guitar????? Uh-oh."

SQUID: Gina and I spent the whole set looking down, covered in hair.

But much to our surprise, the crowd went wild and then before we knew it, it was all over. We stepped off the stage with our hearts beating out of our chests. *Holy shit, did that really just happen?! Did we dream this? We just played a show, in front of a room full of people . . . and they fucking loved it! Um . . . when can we do this again?!*

Our second show was in the basement of Lismar Lounge, on First Avenue between Second and Third Streets. The club had to close down a few times because a biker gang lived around the corner and started hanging out there and beating the shit out of people.

SQUID: Sindi and I were at the bar after our show, and here come these giant, scary, no-fucking-joke bikers who sit down at the bar right near us and we can hear them drunk-talking, "Heard there's some pussy band here tonight! Let's find 'em!!" And the two of us were like, "Aaaaiiieeee!" and we quietly, unassumingly slid away from the bar and then ran the fuck outta there.

THEO: We narrowly escaped a beatdown a few times at that club. Like dumbasses, we often thought it was clever to wander around the corner drunk and then drop our pants to pee in any random doorway that suited us. I guess we forgot where we were because all of a sudden one of those bikers was yelling, "You better not be pissing on my street!" and charging straight for us as our pants were around our ankles and our naked butts hovered off the ground.

SQUID: I never pulled my pants up so fast.

Altercations weren't always that avoidable, not when you're us. Wheat-pasting flyers was a big part of band culture back then. People couldn't come to your show if they didn't know there *was* a show, so every band that wanted to have an audience had to hit the streets with a bucket of wheatpaste, some big-ass paintbrushes, and a giant stack of flyers. The number of flyers you were capable of hanging and the amount of ground covered were directly related to the number of people you could draw into the club. Wheatpasting 101: You take your big paintbrush, dunk it in the thick, white, sticky paste, slather a wall with it, put your flyer on it, slather it again. Repeat. It takes a while to do a thorough job. We would draw straws to determine which part of town we had to cover, split into crews, and go for broke until the flyers and paste were all gone. Excellent memories include dead-of-winter shows and freezing our asses off on the streets for hours—tacky, frostbitten, paste-covered fingers and the unmistakable sensation of a giant glob of ice-cold wheatpaste dripping backward off the brush, along your wrist, inside the cuff of your coat, and headed toward your armpit.

THEO: One day, Squid and I were in the Village on Eighth Street, just a few blocks from St. Marks Place, putting up a bunch of flyers. Suddenly, we realized these drunken jock douchebags were following us at a distance and pulling down our posters right as we were pasting them up. As you can imagine, it infuriated us. Would they have done that if we were two big punk guys wheat-pasting? Doubtful. But that's beside the point.

SQUID: Theo and I turned on our heels and went back to confront them. I guess Theo thought I was just going to tell them off, but as we reached these guys and I'm yelling directly in this dude's face like, "Yo, man, what the fuck are you doing?" he grabbed another freshly pasted flyer on the wall and with a giant shit-eating "watcha gonna do about it?" grin on his fat, entitled, white-boy face, slowly ripped that flyer down in front of us. I hit that guy right in the kisser with the bucket. He must have been six-plus feet tall, this big, drunk jock. I remember how tall the guy was because I had to swing the bucket up in the air in order to reach his dumb head. I clobbered the guy. I will never forget the look on Theo's face.

THEO: I froze. Eyes bulged, slack-jawed, once again. It was like watching her tell off all those teachers who told her she couldn't do her dance performance back in middle school, except this time she clocked a guy in the face. I wanted to help her, but I was afraid of a beat-down. I had taken women's self-defense classes and knew how to protect myself, but I just did not see this ending well. And then she dumped all the wheatpaste on him. Greeeeaaaat.

SQUID: Theo was standing there, like, "I love you, but I am not ... What are you doing, are you nuts?!" I would see that look more than once during the years. Like, "I'm a phone call away, but good luck with that." I think he punched me in the head, but I didn't get hurt and, whatever, it was definitely worth seeing the look on that asshole's face after very unexpectedly getting a bucket bounced off his nose by some girl. Funny, he wasn't laughing anymore after that. I don't think that wheatpaste survived the swing, so we were done flyering for that night.

Of course, the one club that we were desperate to play was the most obvious. Lunachicks *had* to play CBGB. While we spent a good amount of time hanging out at CB's, (barely) scratching our way into the scene there, it wasn't enough. Our heroes were made on that stage, and we wanted that for ourselves. Why not? Who could possibly stop us? We quickly learned the answer to that question. Her name was Louise, and she scared the shit out of us.

Louise was a naturally attractive but curiously regular-looking woman who wore plain, nondescript clothes, had brown hair and big boobs. By her image, she could have worked at a stationery store or a bank. She always had the meanest look on her face—a deadpan don't-give-a-fuck-of-a-shit glare—and never once did we see her smile. We sort of had a fear-slash-worship thing going on with her. She was unfuckwithable. We normally wouldn't have any real reason to encounter this lady, but Louise was special. She was the gatekeeper of CBGB; she booked every single band and ran that whole club. She didn't take a drop of shit from anybody—and there were some imposing people hanging around back in those days. But Louise could eat them alive if she wanted to. Her reply to almost everyone and everything was *"Yeah, what?"* said in the sharpest, go-fuck-yourself tone of voice imaginable. It was so weird to see her in action because she wasn't the slightest bit punk rock, but she called all the shots in the most legendary punk club of our lifetime. We were terrified of her.

If you weren't a famous band, the only way you were offered a gig at CB's was if you passed a test: you had to audition. Auditions happened on Sunday nights, and if your band brought enough paying customers to the show, you'd be invited back to play again. Maybe. Otherwise, you were shit outta luck—oh, and have fun restoring your dignity.

So we called and asked for an audition. Then we called again. And again. It took us a long time to finally get on their schedule, and once we did, we transformed ourselves into a publicity machine. We pestered every single one of our friends, friends of friends, acquaintances, and anybody else within earshot and begged them to come to our audition. Beyond just filling the club, our crowd had to be enthusiastic, so we told people, "Act like you're really into it! Please!!" We rallied hard, and it worked! A throng of our friends showed up and pushed their way to the front of the stage.

It was only our third show (or maybe it was our fourth—we can't remember) ever, but we were at the top of our game that night. Deep down, we all believed we belonged there. It wasn't a stretch for us. Maybe it was our youthful naivete, or maybe we were overwhelmed by the support of our pals, but we rocked that sweaty, shitty club to the tits for twenty-five minutes that night like we were KISS playing Madison Square Garden.

CB's took notice of how packed it was, but they were also thrilled with the *type* of crowd we drew: a bunch of colorful, weird, cool kids—a lot of whom were girls. The club decided we passed the test, but that was hardly our greatest triumph of the evening. That night, Louise fell in love with us. The meanest lady in the world *fucking loved us*. From then on, she took our every phone call (that in and of itself was unheard of!) and booked us almost whenever we wanted. When we wanted to see a show, we'd walk to the front of the line and she'd wink, give us a nod, and let us in. We never waited or paid. She even gave us drink tickets to the bar. Louise made us feel special. She always had our backs. Still, we never saw her smile.

One of the bigger shows we ever played at CB's early on was when we opened for Sonic Youth. Sindi was the only one who wasn't clueless about the extent of their popularity; we didn't follow that whole no-wave college rock scene. As we neared the club, we saw a line around the block to get in. And that's how we learned just how big of a deal Sonic Youth were.

We got onstage to do our thing in front of this huge crowd—and they hated us. Positively couldn't stand us. It was the first time, but certainly not the last, that a crowd thought we flat-out sucked. Typical teenagers, we didn't take too kindly to this.

THEO: I was pissed that this college-age artsy-fartsy crowd wasn't into us, so I shouted, "Okay, all you with your coffee klatches!" I was so mad, I had a tantrum. Shit-talked them directly to their faces. I later had to be told that it wasn't such a good idea to berate the audience. "You gotta win them over, not yell at them!" Live and learn.

SQUID: Honestly, they wouldn't have liked us even if we showed up in FUCK shorts. But we were proud of the fact that those stiffs didn't like us.

GINA: It was awkward being onstage staring back at these indie college kids who really did not know what to make of us. Then Theo started lobbing insults at them, and I couldn't stop giggling under my breath. It was such an odd scene.

CB's never lost its magic, regardless of how many thousands of times we walked through its door or on its stage. When we were big enough to headline, we graduated from the smaller, disgusting, flea-infested dressing room that most bands used to the bigger, disgusting, flea-infested dressing room, which, unlike the smaller dressing room, had a door—and that was a big deal.

The club became a backdrop for us through the years. The photos that appear in our first album booklet were taken at CB's. We filmed a movie there called *Blue Vengeance*, which was some of the most hilarious footage filmed of us ever. (It's in the *Naked* video comp we put out.) Gina looked like a cartoon character, our drummer Becky played one giant floor tom with plastic bones, and Theo was singing into a toy shark. It was ridiculous.

Sometime in the '90s, we got photographed with Redman for *Creem* magazine at CB's. Fun fact: originally Debbie Gibson was supposed to do the photo shoot, but she couldn't make it, so the magazine called us. Because when you think of Debbie Gibson's stand-in, you think of Lunachicks, duh. In terms of bizarre career moments, this ranks second only to the fact that one of our songs appears on the soundtrack to the 2002 movie *Getting There*, starring the Olsen twins.

When CB's closed in 2006 and became a John Varvatos boutique, it was a death knell for New York City, but it also took a piece of us with it. Nostalgia gets a bad rap, but fuck it: we miss it there. We really did grow up in that club and loved playing there—getting on the stage and then getting off the stage, covered in sweat, makeup pouring down our faces, going into the little back room, and somebody handing us a joint and some beers, and we'd sit there getting wasted in the afterglow. Thanks, Louise, for giving us kids a break. Love ya. PS: We're still scared of you.

CHAPTER 10

DOMESTICATING FERAL KITTENS

Our third show (or fourth—again, we can't remember) was in the Chapel at the Limelight, an old Episcopal church on Sixth Avenue in Chelsea that was converted into a club owned and operated by nightlife impresario Peter Gatien in 1983. In the '90s, the Limelight became associated with techno culture and designer drugs, but it started as a rock and disco club, and we hung out there a bunch. This particular night, we were sharing a bill with Da Willys, whom we loved so much. Their singer, Lynne Von, had an impressive legacy as the front person of a bunch of our favorite local bands, including the Swamp Goblyns. The show wasn't some big happening or anything like that—it was another night out for misfits like us. But unbeknownst to us, this show would forever change the course of our lives. And it all happened so fast.

We played our set to a sea of familiar faces and friends. Again, nothing earth-shattering, just us kids dressed like goofballs and making an unholy racket. After the show, Sindi told the rest of us, "Kim and Thurston from Sonic Youth are here." With the exception of Sindi, we didn't know who that was (this was before we played with them at CB's). We had to be told that Thurston Moore and Kim Gordon of Sonic Youth were king and queen of the no-wave scene at the time. But we didn't listen to college rock. We were clueless.

Kim and Thurston? Is that good? It is? Okay!

SINDI: For the record, I was not a fan of Sonic Youth. At all.

Apparently, Kim and Thurston were looking for a female band to work with, a so-called foxcore band. For whatever reason, a goddamn mystery to this day, they picked us. They went to their label head, Paul Smith of Blast First Records—an English label that was putting out all the European releases for Sonic Youth, Dinosaur Jr., Big Black, the Butthole Surfers, and lots more great bands—and told him about us. Shortly after, Paul called Squid and expressed his interest in putting out a Lunachicks album, but there was one nonnegotiable condition: Kim and Thurston were to produce it. We were their project. As long as they were involved, Paul would take us on. Of course we said yes. We were fuckin' thrilled! In a weird way, it felt like a self-fulfilling prophecy.

SQUID: Personally, getting signed to Blast First happened at the perfect time in my life. I had graduated from high school, and I was looking to start my acting career. I had a conversation with a casting agent, and they were like, "You're talented and you're really interesting, but we don't know how to sell you." It seemed like the next day we were sitting in a coffee shop with Paul and he was saying the same exact speech, but he was like, "You guys are total freaks, and it's exactly what I need. I'm going to make you famous, and you're perfect."

GINA: I'm laughing because after that, that's the opposite of everything we got told from every music industry lackey. Still, our little teenage minds were blown and we couldn't wait to get into the studio and record.

THEO: Paul Smith talked us up pretty good and filled our heads with grand ideas, like, "And then you'll all have solo albums!" I remember thinking, "Holy shit, we're gonna be like KISS!" I had stars in my eyes and solo album covers and our name in lights.

Done! Show us where to sign! Paul took the entire band to Manny's Music, a big music store in midtown Manhattan on Forty-Eighth Street, known as Music Row. He took out his credit card and said, "Okay, whatever you guys want." There we were, a bunch of wild teenagers—who were not really good musicians yet—running around picking out guitars, amps, drums, the works. We might as well have had a million dollars. We were like, "I'll take that one," pointing at a big Marshall stack. (We would later remove the *ll* so our amps said *Marsha*.) It was amazing, a fairy tale. We thought we were on this incredible career path, and we were just going to keep going up and up and up.

When word eventually got around to the local bands that Blast First scooped us up, the supportive mood we previously enjoyed went sour. Us getting signed wasn't front-page news, and it's not like we got signed by Capitol Records or anything, but when people saw us around town with brand-new equipment, it was obvious that we fell into a pile of shit. This sudden turn of events understandably pissed off some bands who thought the only reason we rose so quickly and landed a record deal was because we were girls.

The truth is that Kim and Thurston definitely wouldn't have taken us to their record label if we weren't girls. It's not like they heard us play some brilliant song at the Limelight that had to be captured on tape. Kim was trying to use her influence to bring more young women into the punk scene—she went on to produce Hole's debut, *Pretty on the Inside*—and happened upon us. We were aware of it, but the significance of her intentions was kinda lost on us at the time. We figured she was looking for a band of rowdy girls and we were it. But as a woman in punk, maybe what she really tried to do was open doors in the spirit of sisterhood, in which case, big belated props to her.

Here's the thing: the greatest successes in the world are combinations of luck and talent. Talent alone doesn't do it. You can be a really brilliant musician writing songs alone in your bedroom, but nobody's gonna know about it. If we were rich kids who got signed, we would've been slagged for that. People will use whatever is convenient to fuel their resentment. And this was just the beginning of the shit-talking. We heard a lot more over the years.

SQUID: The girl thing is really easy to grab on to, and it was prevalent throughout our career. It helped us, and it hurt us. In life, being a woman is the same way. There are advantages and disadvantages.

SINDI: There were some advantages to being female, and we happily accepted them. We were young and good-lookin'! In the very beginning of our career, being an all-female act from New York was a novelty and made people take notice. Certainly people came to see us just because we were female, although we did win them over with the music and the show. Definitely. Once you've got them looking and listening, you have to then keep them engaged, and we were able to do that on our own merit.

THEO: Whether we were girls or boys or whatever, it's true that not every band gets offered a record deal after their third show. But the fact that we got our deal so quickly **and** we were kids **and** we were girls (who went to art school, no less) seemed to be too much for people to deal with. Listen, if Thurston and Kim were in fact searching for their all-girl foxcore band and we happened to be it, then we were simply in the right place at the right time. Hey, that's showbiz. We dealt with the same jealousy years later, in the mid- to late '90s, when we were opening for bands like the Offspring and Rancid. There was a sense of "Who'd the Lunachicks fuck to get that tour?" Well, there was that time one of the other girls spontaneously joined the mile-high club, but we doubt that guy was a record executive . . .

We began recording at Wharton Tiers's studio. Wharton recorded White Zombie and Da Willys, and would go on to record a lot of amazing bands, including Nirvana, Royal Trux, and Helmet, who made their classic *Meantime* with him. Almost as exciting to us was the studio's proximity to Ess-a-Bagel, home of NYC's best bagels. We ate Ess-a-Bagel every single day, this is not an exaggeration. In hindsight, the bagels turned out to be the best part of the whole experience.

Right away, we weren't on the same page with Kim and Thurston. Those two were not warm and fuzzy toward us, to say the least, but we weren't exactly fawning over them either. We couldn't have cared less that they were in some hip New York band. It was as if we were feral cats and they were trying to wrangle us.

Basically, they wanted us to be a noise-type band, kinda like Sonic Youth. When they saw us play, they probably thought we *were* a noise band. But we weren't! We were a rock band; it's just that we were so bad, we sounded like a noise band. Regardless, we wouldn't allow anything of the sort. We knew *exactly* what we wanted to sound like, even though we couldn't possibly make that happen with our then-limited musical abilities. No matter! We were absolutely not a no-wave noise band.

The tension came to a head when Sindi's distortion pedal broke and sounded like a lawn mower. We wanted to fix it, but Kim didn't. She loved the fucked-up sounds the busted pedal was making. Sindi lost it; she wasn't having any of it. We reasoned that if KISS and Van Halen wouldn't record with a broken pedal, we weren't recording with a broken pedal. End of story.

SINDI: It was total discord. Exactly what they wanted was exactly what we didn't want.

SQUID: It was also very businesslike, impersonal. I don't remember one conversation that we ever had with them. About anything.

SINDI: There weren't any.

> **THEO:** It was like they talked about us, around us, but not to us directly. At all. Ever.
>
> **GINA:** I don't remember them laughing or joking or even snacking, which was odd because that's all we did with each other. They both seemed to be stone-faced the whole time.
>
> **SINDI:** Zero common ground. It was the worst fit ever.
>
> **SQUID:** It was almost like we were zoo animals, and they were on the other side of the glass talking about what they were going to do with us.

They didn't even ask us what bands we liked. We were supposed to be molding clay. Can you imagine? We didn't even listen to our parents, and we were supposed to take orders from them? *Fuuuuuuck that.* Did they think we might be grateful, like, "Oh my god, Sonic Youth is going to produce us! Tell us what you want us to do!"

Hahahahahahahahahahahahahahahahahahahahahahahahahahahahaha-hahahahahahahahahahahahahahahahahahahahahahahahahahahahahahahahaha

We were such assholes.

> **SINDI:** Maybe that was the dumbest thing we ever did. Maybe we'd all be millionaires right now if we listened to them.
>
> **THEO:** Doubt it. Nobody would have been able to tell us how to play or sing or what to wear. Ever.

It didn't take long before things got uncomfortable. Kim called Paul Smith and said, "I can't do this anymore. I am *not* a babysitter. These little girls *do not* know what is going on." Trust us, we knew *exactly* what was going on. But you know what? Good for Kim! We *were* bratty assholes.

Halfway through the recording, Kim and Thurston left. Because Paul had already sunk a bunch of money into us at this point, he kept us on his label, figuring he could sell some records. (When the album *Babysitters on Acid* was finally released, we saw that Paul made a twelve-page booklet for it that we had no idea about and never agreed to. The booklet was all about how we looked, that we were pretty, young girls. That's how they sold us. Ugh, great.)

In the meantime, we decided to get semi-serious about this whole new career that was unfolding for us. A local A&R friend got us a meeting with Lyor Cohen over at Def Jam's sister entity Rush Artist Management, who in the late '80s were rumored to be grabbing up a bunch of New York City metal bands. This was our big shot!

SQUID: While Gina and Theo were in college for a hot minute, Sindi and I, thinking it sounded like a good idea, took the bull by the horns and enrolled in a music business course at one of the local universities. My dad was so impressed when he heard that we were going to business school, ha! Well, it just so happened that the volunteer industry professional leading the course was Def Jam's accountant. So at the end of the class, I said to the teacher, "Hey! Small world, we've been talking to Rush and have a meeting next week. Can you give us any advice?" Next day I got a call that Lyor was outraged. Who were WE to be talking to his accountant behind his back! How DARE we! ... Uhh, what? He cancelled our follow-up meeting. We were banished. Oh. My. God. I thought I just single-handedly destroyed our entire future. I was so stressed out, I thought I was having a nervous breakdown. I never wanted to do band business again after that.

We didn't have time to complete *Babysitters on Acid* in full because Blast First was sending us overseas as openers for Dinosaur Jr.'s UK tour. With limited time, the label decided that we'd put out an EP, *Sugar Luv* (named after the first song Gina ever wrote), so the press would have something to cover in advance of the tour. So we finished *Sugar Luv* with Wharton on our own. He was easygoing and indulged our every whim without ever being condescending. But recording came to a halt one day when Paul Smith said we couldn't continue until we found our permanent drummer. We knew exactly who we were looking for. We just had to find her.

CHAPTER 11

BECKY WRECK

We were fortunate in that we could always find a willing friend to generously lend their drumming talents for a show or two, but we really needed a drummer of our own and we were committed to finding a girl for the job because we thought it was so fuckin' cool. We heard of a drummer in Philadelphia named Becky Wreck. Here's what we knew: she was older than us, she rode a motorcycle, and she had lived in Europe. She sounded perfect.

BECKY: I was living in Brussels, Belgium, playing in a goth band called La Muerte. I had been there a little over a year, from 1985 to 1986. It was something to do, get out of America. At some point, I decided to move back to Philadelphia, where I grew up. I had this notorious reputation when I moved back to Philly—I wasn't a rock star, but I managed to get out of town. People were like, *"Oh, you lived in Belgium!"*

Over the summer, my friends from New York came to visit and said, "We saw this band, you would be perfect for them! They can get signed but they need a girl drummer!" I had been in a million bands by the time I joined the Lunachicks. I kinda had never wanted to do the all-girl thing. It's such a fuckin' sellout; I'll play with whoever the fuck I want. It's not a big deal to me that girls can play, you know? I knew that if I wanted to exploit myself, yeah, I could cash in on the all-girl-band thing. But at that time, 1988, there was suddenly all this brouhaha about other girl bands like Babes in Toyland and L7.

At the end of the summer, I got in touch with the Lunachicks. They were like, "Come up and audition." That was funny, because they didn't really know how to play. They were a bunch of friends that were like, "We wanna have a band!" I had been playing since I was eight years old. I'd been playing with dudes, playing in hardcore bands. My friends and I would get in my basement when I was really little and play Yes and Rush. I really knew how to play, so the fact that I had to audition was funny to me. But I understood, they had a label involved. I borrowed a friend's car, drove up to New York, went to the Music Building, and auditioned.

The moment we laid eyes on Becky, our jaws hit the floor. She strode in wearing leather pants and a leather vest, and had long black hair and a dragon tattoo on her arm. Butch dykes were a rarity in our world. They were certainly around, but we were kids and never had cause to overlap with that scene. Becky's look and aesthetic are so assimilated now, but you absolutely didn't see people—women especially—like her back in 1988. We were mesmerized.

BECKY: I knew that I liked girls from a really young age. I was totally comfortable and very much on a mission to be as out as possible, because there wasn't anyone that I could relate to musically that was like me. The images I saw of lesbians were that they dressed badly, had horrible hair, and they had really bad style. I thought, "Well, I might be a lesbian, but I'm not like them."

Early mug shots: Theo, Gina, and Squid yearbook photos, ages 7 to 17.

The end of innocence? Theo and Squid, eighth grade graduation.

Baby chicks: Theo and Gina, ninth grade.
Rachel Maceiras

Squid and Theo, ninth grade, hanging out on the block, definitely not high.

Fast times at LaGuardia High: Squid, Theo, and Gina, tenth grade.

Sindi: Bookworm to Badass, Brooklyn.

Park Slope Rock City: Sindi, Theo, and Squid.

I am a poser and I don't care: Gina, age fourteen, at her first CB's hardcore matinee.

Drew Carolan

If looks could kill, we'd all be dead: Theo, age thirteen,
at her first modelling shoot (for John Dellaria Salon).
Joe Tucci

SYDNEY
SILVER

Roberta De Niro: Squid's acting headshot, age sixteen.

Audition Night at CBGB's, 1988.

Bloody amazing: Theo on stage, our first show, 1988.
Julia Arenson

The infamous "All-Girl Street Gang": Lower East Side, NYC, 1990.
Joe Dilworth

Pleather and lace afterparty: Squid and Sindi.

Rhythm section on the road: Becky and Squid, European tour.

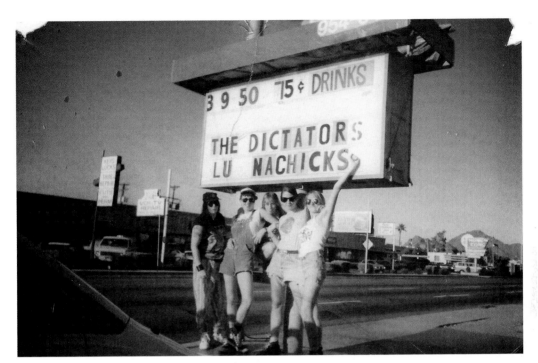

Lu Nachicks on tour with the Dictators, Phoenix, Arizona, 1991.

You're A' Peein' Tour: Gina and Theo backstage.

Backstage during the official Bimbo Sandwich Tur, 1993. Art by Gina.

Binge and Purge outtake, 1992.
Michael Lavine

Boarding the un-private jet to Europe: Gina, Chip, Theo, Squid, and Sindi, 1994.

If you're not on the floor, you're not doing it right: Gina and Theo, Japanese Tour.

Sindi and Squid taking care of business: Offspring Tour, Milwaukee.

Kristin Lee–Ziehler

It's called fashion. Look it up.

Again, it's called fashion.

When I was about sixteen, I met Joan Jett. Kinda. She played at the London Victory Club in Philadelphia, a small club. I was there with my punk rock band the Excuses. You could go up and talk to the bands after they played. I went up to her and I said, "I know you like girls. I *know* you like girls. Tell me you like girls." She wouldn't say anything. She looked at me like, "What the fuck?" At one point, I said, "Can I kiss you?" More than anything she was freaked out.

After the show, we followed Joan and her band back to their hotel because we wanted to party with them. When we reached the hotel, the guys in her band got out of their van—she didn't—and were like, "What the fuck is wrong with you?! You fuckin' followin' us?!" It was so weird because we were used to punk rock bands who were *glad* to hang out and were *glad* people liked them. That really left a bad taste in my mouth. I respect Joan Jett, I know she's a great musician, she can live her life the way she wants, but me, as a homosexual in the society that we live in, I knew I needed to know other people like me.

I never knew what was going to be around the corner as a result of being really open and out. I didn't have to go out of my way to let people know I was gay—it was pretty obvious just looking at me—but I was very vocal and in your face about it. If I thought that someone was intimidated by the fact that I was female and maybe gay or maybe not interested in guys, or their girlfriend was maybe interested in me, I would fight, I would go overboard because I wasn't gonna play small to make others feel better about themselves. I'm not saying I was a good role model, but I certainly was a woman who was not gonna back down for anything. I wasn't worried if people felt comfortable or not. In fact, if people weren't comfortable with me, they were gonna have to deal with me even more.

My first impression of the Lunachicks was that they were young, really pretty, really funny, and they were really healthy—most of them were vegetarian. They were almost innocent, it was refreshing. I wanted it to rub off on me. I had no sense of eating habits or drug intake or anything. I was like, "Wow, these girls are really smart. They already know what's up. They already know how they want to live their life." They were smart and artistic. It was interesting. I thought we could really make a splash. These girls had a lot of things going on, they weren't only one thing.

Becky was a hot commodity. Back then, female drummers were scarce, which is why it took us so long to find one, and when we finally did, we always had to worry about her being poached by another female band. There was a bit of a bidding war between us and the LA band L7 over who would get Becky. She was on the verge of joining our band when she went to see L7 perform. It was then that she had reservations. L7 were awesome, *really* awesome. We started to get nervous. Ultimately, she chose us.

BECKY: There was no bidding war. I met L7 at one of their shows in Philly. They were girls, but girls or not, I was like, "Oh my god, they are fuckin' great!" I had made an impression on them, because I was like, "If you ever need a fuckin' drummer, man, you should call me!!!" all crazy and shit. The song "Fast and Frightening" is about rad girls, but that one line is about me ["Poppin' wheelies on her motorbike / Straight girls wish they were dykes"]. I was in the alley behind the club after their show, and I was like, "Come on! Hang out!" Donita

[Sparks, singer and guitarist] was like, "Whoa. This girl is fuckin' crazy," like she wanted to hang, but she wasn't sure.

Months later, after I committed myself to Lunachicks, L7 reached out to me. It was days after I completely moved myself to Williamsburg, Brooklyn, when I got a phone call from Jennifer Finch, the bass player of L7, saying, "We want you to be our drummer. We'll fly you out here. Can you move to LA?" I was like, "I don't want to live in LA." I told Jennifer, "You guys are fuckin' great, but I just joined this other band, and they're really good, and I want to see where it goes."

And truthfully, I loved the heroin in Williamsburg. I was really into it; I was just starting, didn't have a habit. I started doing it here and there in Belgium. I was liking the heroin in Williamsburg a lot. The Lunachicks might've been like, "Oh, you're not gonna join L7, are you?" But I was never gonna join. I was really high, but I don't recall there being any tug-of-war thing.

Once Becky joined, we had to redo a bunch of our press material, Lunachicks-style. Because we'd already shot the band photos for the cover art, Becky had to be photoshopped—before that technology even existed. It was one hell of a slapdash cut-and-paste job. But we were really pressured to get the *Sugar Luv* EP out as fast as possible in advance of our tour, so there was no time to reshoot the band photos. The cover looks ridiculous—on top of it already looking ridiculous because our faces *were* ridiculous.

GINA: I remember dreading the photo shoot for the EP. Michael Lavine was the photographer. "What? I have to get in front of the camera? Nooooo. I don't wanna look into the lens!" I was so uncomfortable. I didn't know how to be, and it shows: in every picture, I am making stupid faces or trying to hide behind the other girls.

Becky had to record over the drum tracks to our EP that were put in as a placeholder by Theo's boyfriend Mike. She had much more experience than any of us, so she was familiar with the studio environment and knew how the process worked, a pro. Walked right in and did her thing. We were super-impressed.

BECKY: Talk about paying dues in rock 'n' roll. I felt like I paid the dues so they didn't have to. It's kinda hard when you spend years in a million other bands tryin' to get any attention and nobody gives a shit, then you get in a band—and you know they're good—but you know the real reason people care is because they're girls. The Lunachicks, that was their first-ever attempt at playing music, and they got so much attention. It wasn't because they were so great—it was because they were girls. It's kinda fucked up because I was selling myself out, but I did it because I knew they would be great. They came into their own, and I knew that would happen. But I was like, "You guys don't know how fuckin' lucky you are." All the years I spent sleeping in vans, all that shit, it made sense that I could bring it to something. I love what we did. I love the music that I made with the Lunachicks.

Shortly after joining the band, Becky became an unlikely celebrity. It was all because she was on the "Lesbian Dating Game" on Howard Stern's cable show.

BECKY: One night, I was drinking wine and watching Howard Stern on TV. Different booze did different things to me: Jack Daniels always made me get into a fight; gin, I was havin' a good time; wine, I was laughing, funny, and very egotistic. So I was watching this show, drinking wine, and I was pretty fucked up. They said, "Anyone who wants to be on the 'Lesbian Dating Game' who lives in this area, call this number!" So I called the number and left a message: "My name's Becky Wreck. I'm the coolest dyke in New York City! I play in a band called the Lunachicks! You want me to be on your show!"

You couldn't be more over-the-top and full of yourself than I was. By the next day, I don't even think I remembered that I made that call. I didn't think anything of it. But Howard Stern's people called me and were like, "Wow! You really left quite a message! We want you to come on the show."

I thought, "This is great. I'm gonna give him a T-shirt, I'm gonna give him a record. If he fuckin' wears a Lunachicks T-shirt on his show, or if he plays the record ... " Everybody was listening to him! He was numero uno. He didn't really respond to the Lunachicks the way I hoped he would, but he mentioned the name of the band on his show, but like a joke: "She's in a band called the Lunachicks!" But still, he said the name!

A lot of the other "lesbians" who were on the show weren't really lesbians, or they were bi. They said they were lesbians so they could get on the show, be on TV, and meet Howard Stern. There were only a few that were real lesbians, but they weren't like me. Fact is, back then, nobody really wanted to be branded "gay." Howard Stern was making fun of us—he didn't think we were cool. He knew he would get good ratings if he put lesbians on TV, and he knew that I was the real deal. They all did.

The producers kept asking me to come back on the show. A few girls wrote in saying they wanted to meet me. So the producers would have me come back, but they wouldn't tell me what their plans were. I'd be like, "What are you gonna do, fix me up with a farm animal?" Whatever. I'd be on the show, but Howard Stern didn't talk about Lunachicks. It wasn't about the band, it was about the gay thing.

As a result, Becky became the most famous of us all, hands down. We showed up at the airport to go on tour, and all these jocks went nuts, "YO, BECKY! YO! YO, BECKY! CAN I GET YO AUTOGRAPH?!" We were stunned. When we think about it, Becky's appearance on that show was one of the first out lesbian/gay moments in the media, and it caused such a giant reaction from jocks and suits. To see them at the airport, surrounding Becky, like, "Yeaaaaah! Dykes!"—that had *never* happened before (to our knowledge) on such a large scale. And it was *our drummer* in the middle of it! A bunch of straight guys thought she was fuckin' cool at a time when nothing about being gay was cool to straight America. It really blew our minds.

BECKY: One time I parked my motorcycle near a construction site. I thought, "Oh god, here it comes, I might get my ass kicked." So they were like, "Hey, hey, hey!" and I was like, "Oh fuck ... " but they go, "We saw you on *Howard Stern*! We know who you are! Maaaan, you were great! You really told Howard! That was great!" I was like, "Holy shit, they weren't like, 'Hey, you're a fuckin' queer!'" They thought I was funny! And that's what I was hoping to achieve by being out: I wanted to let people know that lesbians weren't what they thought. We're whatever! Someone else called me and was like, "Becky! Sebastian Bach was on *Howard Stern* this morning and he said you were fuckin' cool!" I guess Robin Quivers was making fun of my leather overalls, and Sebastian Bach was like, "No, Becky Wreck's cool!" I was like, "Really?" That was a really cool thing.

I had no idea how the Lunachicks perceived anything, so it's really funny for me to hear that they thought it was cool. If anything, they seemed annoyed at it! One time, I told the show I couldn't go in because I had soundcheck, and the show sent a white stretch limo to pick me up from the club. Well, the Lunachicks did not like that, lemme tell you. It interrupted soundcheck. I also think they didn't like that I was getting all the attention.

But I never felt like I was in competition with any of them. I always felt like, "This is fuckin' great! We're the shit!!" I would come out and sing one song, and Theo would play the drums. Not only can I play the drums, even our fuckin' singer plays the drums! Sometimes people would come up to me in the dressing room afterward and say to me, right in front of Theo, "Wow, you're a fuckin' great singer, you should sing more!" Theo would turn around and be like, "I'M a fuckin' great singer!" I'd be like, "Whoaaa!!" And then Theo would be mad at me! Stupid shit. "They're not saying you're not a good singer! What the fuck!" When I'm in a band, I love that people love the other players in my band! But I'd been in tons of bands. Guys aren't like that—none of the ones that I worked with anyway.

None of us ever took issue with her fame. We were grateful for it, and we were proud of her! Sometimes it was annoying because the attention she was attracting was from a lot of hetero meatheads, who were the last kind of people we wanted for fans—but it was better than no fans. Really, it was kinda awesome. She added to our kick-assness, another element of "just you try and fuck with us."

BECKY: I think I brought a certain amount of street credibility and authenticity to the music. I had already been

livin' my life and doing what the Lunachicks wanted to
do. Because I really could play, when I joined the band,
it was like people had to take us seriously. Whatever
was cute and interesting about the Lunachicks before
was all of a sudden like, "Holy shit!" I was like glue
that took all those pieces that were not yet quite together and brought 'em together. We became a wall of
fuckin' sound.

Having Becky made us stronger, another piece of explosive to add to
our pile. She was really impressive and people were kind of blown away
by her. She's such a character. She added to our mystique and our power.
Henry Rollins was one of her biggest fans; he loved her. She was a great
drummer and the most experienced musician out of all of us put together.
She gave us credibility, and we knew it. Fired up, we practiced four times
a week and got to know each other on an even deeper level than we
thought possible, one that merged our individual artistic impulses into
one thrilling current. We were hell-bent on becoming unstoppable musicians ready to BRING IT!

Right around the time Becky joined the band, an unlikely romance blos-
somed between her and Squid.

SQUID: We all hung out with gay men, but we didn't really know
any gay women. I mean, I didn't. I thought all lesbians were crunchy, hippie, frumpy, sandal-wearing
lesbians. Girls like Becky—really beautiful, badass,
leather-wearing girls—were uncharted territory. I was
definitely in awe of her at first sight. Do you remember
the first time you ever saw the Meat Loaf album *Bat Out
of Hell* cover? That's what I'm talking about—that kind
of "Whoa." But that was it at first. I don't get any more
credit than that. I was nineteen and way too clueless

to even have come up with the idea of having a crush on Becky. I had never been with a girl before. I remember the day I finally started putting the pieces together, genius that I am. We were hanging out at Howie Pyro and Andrea Freak's apartment in Williamsburg, which was the middle of absolutely fucking nowhere in the late '80s. I was having these hot flashes, like menopause, seriously, and these little tingles. I was like, "Is it hot in here? What the fuck is wrong with me? Am I sick? Do I have a fever?" Of course, then I started realizing that every time Becky came into the room, I was having the flashes and the tingles. Then, like the junior detective that I am, total dumbo, I started putting all those subtle clues together and then suddenly—*ding!* "Oh shit, I think I have the hots for BECKY!" Oh god, I knew it was gonna be so bad and everyone was gonna wanna kill me for fucking shit up with the band, but I seriously could not help myself. I was freaking out. I had to kiss her.

BECKY: Syd's amazing. Drums and bass, there's the rhythm section right there. If you're a drummer, you have to love your bass player. You have a bond in the band that's not like anybody else's—you're the heavy end. Syd and I had chemistry. I wanted her good stuff to rub off on me, but it went the other way. My bad stuff rubbed off on her. She was beautiful, super-smart, really funny—she's gorgeous. Who wouldn't want to be with Syd? I bought a van and we would go visit my brother in Philly. We spent time together. It just kinda happened.

SQUID: Initially, the rest of the band didn't know the two of us were hooking up, but eventually everybody figured it out. I wondered if they thought, "Oh, what, you're fucking gay now?"

BECKY: The other girls weren't happy about it at all. They weren't like, "Good for you!" Gina probably was the most indifferent, but in general they were like, "This could be bad." Even we knew that.

GINA: I figured, "Oh, Syd's just trying to piss off her parents even more." We'd laugh, but I remember thinking, "Is this a good idea?"

THEO: It was like, "Oh boy, here we go. Didn't we learn this was a bad idea from Fleetwood Mac?!"

SQUID: I moved Becky into my house. My parents said she could stay in the spare room, but I said, "Nah, she's gonna stay in my room." My parents were like, "Oh-kay."

Having two people in your band be in a relationship with each other is generally not the smartest move, but it wasn't unheard of. Our heroes had done it: Debbie Harry and Chris Stein from Blondie, Lux Interior and Poison Ivy from the Cramps, Joan Jett and Cherie Currie from the Runaways—it can work. Or not.

SINDI: Syd was my best friend. We did everything together. We saw eye to eye and then along came Becky, and Syd did a complete turnaround and became somebody else. She changed. As soon as Becky moved in to Syd's house, it was like . . . We used to hang out so much! We were always together!

SQUID: You're breaking my heart.

SINDI: Becky and I had a power struggle from the get-go. I did all the organizing shit for the band. It's not like I wanted to be in control in any way, it was just my personality type and I fell into that role, making a lot of decisions that nobody wanted to make. And then Becky wanted to come in and tell me what for. And I wasn't having it. We were butting heads. She and I were never buddies.

BECKY: I think Sindi felt like she was the toughest girl in the band, but I never felt like I was competing with anybody, so that was weird to me that I had to deal with that. I wasn't used to playing with girls. I wasn't used to the cattiness that girls can have between themselves. I never really thought of myself as a girlie girl. I embrace the masculine side. If you were tough and you were female, great. Whoever you are, great. It didn't matter to me. I didn't feel like I had to one-up anybody. I was being me; I can't help who I am. I thought Sindi was cool! But I also noticed that she had this animosity toward me.

SINDI: There were qualities that I appreciated about Becky. We needed her, and she could be a kick-ass drummer when she had her capacities together. She had experience being in a band and was older than me, but I felt like she was working someplace totally different than me. I was more reasonable. We were a little bit at odds. Not a little bit ... we had some issues, definitely.

GINA: Sindi and Becky were four and five years older than we three were, so in a sense they were the adults in the band, at least early on. When they would have an argument, it was almost like parents fighting.

SINDI: Becky and Syd didn't mind sharing a bed on tour, so that made some things easier, I guess. Luckily, it didn't last forever anyway. I wasn't so upset by them dating except for the change that it made in Syd. And I felt that Becky had a little more power because she now had Syd, so Becky had two votes because Syd was gonna be Team Becky no matter what the situation was, even if it was a bad vote. If that makes sense.

The main problem had nothing to do with who was dating whom.

THEO: One time, Becky called me on the phone while snorting heroin. Loudly. "You probably don't want to know what

I'm doing," she said. I was like, "Uh, I think I can figure it out." I was not as dumb as I looked.

So many of our punk rock heroes from the '70s were casualties of heroin. It was really well known that you didn't want to be on dope. It was
not popular or in fashion with anyone we hung out with. There was an
"everything but" drug policy among our friends—everything but heroin
was okay. We all got fucked up together using all sorts of combinations of
drugs, and there was never any judgment between us and our friends. But
heroin was always a no-no.

BECKY: I didn't have skills to handle a lot of attention, and
I think that's why I really liked drugs. I knew all of
a sudden I was gonna get a lot of attention and people
were gonna know who I was because I was in an all-girl
band, not because of my drumming. I had to be ready for
the fact that the only reason we'd get more attention
than any other band I'd ever been in was because we were
girls. I had spent so many years in bands that got NO
attention, and that's fine, because if you're a true punk
rocker, it isn't about attention anyway. It's almost
insulting that people were so impressed by us. I was
like, "What the fuck's wrong with you? You're part of
the problem." When I was high, I thought I at least had
something to say to everybody. Otherwise I'd feel like,
"I'm just a fuckin' drug addict. I really just wanna
go smoke some crack, and you're fuckin' in my way and
takin' up my time."

Becky was in pretty good shape when she first came to New York; she
wasn't strung out and never came to rehearsal high or shitfaced. But addiction can destroy a person, doesn't matter how tough she is.

SQUID: When I started using heroin, it was definitely in secret because I knew everyone would be pissed at me if they knew.

THEO: When Squid first started using and I would catch her, she'd say, "No, no, don't worry, I'll stop, this is the last time." Her eyes were like Muppet eyes to me, blue and wide and kaleidoscope-like and her pupils were big too, but when she (or anyone for that matter) was on heroin, her pupils would shrink to pin size, a telltale sign. I wanted to believe her, but I'd worry, and I'd say, "I'm watching you!" as if I had any control over anything. I was really scared, but I still held on to hope at that point, though I also felt my friend slowly slipping away. I saw her less, we hung out less, I knew less about her day to day. Much less.

CHAPTER 12

SQUID + DRUGS, PART 1

SQUID: People knew there was something very wrong with me by the time I was in fourth grade. I was a problem in school and got sent to the principal's office every day—literally every day. I fought with kids, I spit on teachers, I was a nightmare. Self-prescribed anger therapy included regular trips to the girls' bathroom, where I would try my best to rip the sinks off the walls by wrapping my body around the bowl and bracing my feet on the wall. Other helpful coping mechanisms included getting stoned. That started when I was ten. I recall declaring to my mom, "I'm smokin' pot and there's nothin' you can do about it." She seemed silently to be weighing her options on this conversation and went with *ignore*. She probably knew well enough there really was nothing she could do about it.

One day I was losing it. I was probably eleven or twelve. I was spiraling. The weight of emotion was over my head and I knew I was in trouble. I walked into the living room, crying, hyperventilating a little, and squeaking out the words as best I could to my parents, who were sitting on the couch watching TV. I thought I was going to hurt myself, or maybe someone else. My dad got that stink look on his face, the one I

129

knew so well, like someone just took a hot, steaming crap on the carpet. He responded, "People who do that sort of thing get locked up," turned his head away, and resumed his episode of *M*A*S*H*. Scenes from *One Flew Over the Cuckoo's Nest* and *Endless Love* flashed through my head. "I'll never make it out of there," I thought. I went upstairs, ate a bottle of pills, said my goodbyes to this cruel world, and passed out. Just my luck, it was a bottle of Tylenol. I woke up the next morning puking my guts out, told my mom I got food poisoning, and that was the end of it.

Honestly, I hated being a kid. I couldn't stand the way people talked down to me, talked over me, ignored me, and disrespected me. I couldn't wait to take over the reins of fucking up my own life before a bunch of misguided grown-ups could beat me to it.

One of the first times I got drunk was at a party. I was almost twelve, it was 1982, and Grandmaster Flash & the Furious Five's "The Message" had just been released and was playing in the background of this groovy carpeted '70s basement. *"It's like a jungle sometimes / It makes me wonder how I keep from goin' under, huh huh huh huh huh . . ."* I heard somebody say, "If you drink this giant glass of beer in really fast gulps, you'll get drunk." I jumped on it. "I'll do it!" It worked great. There was a rumor floating around that if you crushed aspirin into powder and sprinkled it into your eyeballs, you'd get high. "Me first!" Yes, it burns. No, it didn't get me high (no need to try this one at home, kids). I was always game for anything, first on the list, fearless, and idiotic.

At an early age, I had broken the world down into two kinds of people: those who can deal and those who can't. I was perfectly aware I belonged to the latter category. It never occurred to me that I wouldn't be able to use drugs to feel okay, or that being reliant on them might be a bigger problem. With high school came regular trips to Washington Square Park to score acid, and the usual shenanigans. There was an incident of freebasing coke with a babysitter (she was seventeen, I think her boyfriend was fifty), but that was a one-off. For the most part, it seemed like pretty normal teenage stuff to us. My friends and I—some of whom *might* be mentioned in this book—had a regular habit of partying at my house when my parents were away. Best practices included chopping coke and sniffing lines off this awesome old framed picture of my mom, probably her yearbook photo, late 1950s portrait-studio style. We were being bad, and it was fun to be bad. We had great times.

But there came a point where the road appeared to split. One night, probably around age fifteen, we were on the Lower East Side waiting to get into a club. This down-and-out homeless guy approached us saying gross things and slurring, trying to get with us girls. My friends were like, "Eewww, beat it!" Then he tapped out some powder on his filthy, bloated hand and growled, "Anybody wanna get high?" I stepped up and sniffed it right off his hand, which sent my friends flipping out on me, like, "What the fuck is wrong with you?" and then the guy started yelling and threatening them; a whole scene ensued. I was like, "What?" Everyone was mad at me. I got belligerent. "It's free drugs! Who doesn't take free drugs? Who cares?" That's where I was at.

After high school I got a job waiting tables downtown, but I only wanted to work on the graveyard shift when there were no managers and I could get away with being a bad employee and hijack the playlist with Black Sabbath and AC/DC. Overnight clientele were forgiving—they were mostly strippers and bouncers, musicians, and other club workers. Cheetah Chrome would come in, and sometimes Johnny Thunders. By the late '80s, these guys were not looking well. Poor Johnny was the worst. He was so fragile, maybe ninety pounds soaking wet, wore five inches of pancake makeup over his rotting skin, and looked and moved like a walking corpse; it was so sad. Everybody knew that our heroes had fallen because of dope. That drug just wasn't acceptable. We knew some people on the fringes who were doing it, and when they died of overdoses, people were like, "See?!" And yet, no amount of finger-wagging or dead rock stars was gonna make a difference to me.

There's this episode of *Charlie's Angels* where Kelly gets kidnapped by drug dealers and they tie her to a bed in a dark room and shoot her up for weeks until she's strung out and begging for more. When the other Angels finally rescue her, she's a hot MESS. *See what can happen, kids? Drugs are bad! Don't let this be you!* I thought, "Wow, that looks so dramatic! I love the part where they rescue her and half drag/half carry her out of the drug den!" I wanted it all, and I wasn't afraid. I didn't know I could get stuck down there forever without the other Angels. Fuck you, ABC, and you too, Aaron Spelling.

I met Becky Wreck when I was eighteen. She was into heroin but wasn't strung out. She joined the band, we got tight, and started dating. I did heroin for the first time with her. I didn't like it—I sniffed it and puked. But if at first you don't succeed . . . We dated for two years, but I never got deep into drugs with Becky. I was too busy as her girlfriend trying to contain her crazy, unmanageable ass. Becky was a handful from hell. But once I was out of that, I was free to get back to center stage in my own soap opera.

CHAPTER 13

TOUR TIME

THEO: In 1989, I was going to California to see some friends and hopefully hang out with our pals Redd Kross—we went to all their shows in New York and New Jersey; as groovy guys who dressed in bright, kooky '70s clothes like we did, they were a huge influence on us. We loved that they embraced their freakiness so brazenly. It was my first-ever trip west, and I was planning to celebrate my nineteenth birthday out there. Then the band informed me that they were coming, like, "Let's make it a little tour! What a great idea!" Grrrr. I was so mad; I just wanted to go on a vacation. And it would have been my first vacation on my own. Not so fast, Kogan.

L7 were from Los Angeles, so Becky called the bassist, Jennifer Finch, and asked for help booking some shows. Jennifer was really cool, and it was super-generous of her to set the whole thing up. She even let us stay at her house. The little we knew about California mostly came from the Penelope Spheeris movie *Suburbia* about punk kids in LA. We would go see it repeatedly at the Waverly Theater on Sixth Avenue. *Suburbia* was what we assumed California was like. Well, that and *The Brady Bunch*. A lot of punk bands that we loved came out of LA too: Circle Jerks, Black Flag, Angry Samoans, Germs, Fear, Blitz, Agent Orange. The soundtrack of this particular trip was Jane's Addiction's *Nothing's Shocking*. We listened to it nonstop.

Upon arrival, LA blew our little minds. It was like paradise compared to New York City. We walked around gawking at the foliage, completely bugging out at all the plant life. We felt like we were tripping on acid, screaming, "It's like Dr. Seuss! But it's real!"

GINA: The first time we ever saw the desert, we pulled over to the side of the highway so we could see those giant cartoon-looking cacti up close. A photo shoot was of course in order, so I posed like the ham that I am by sticking my butt out and pretended to be pricked in the ass by an enormous cactus. Except I misjudged the safe amount of distance from it and OW! Dozens of spines in my ass cheek. The band had to pluck them out one at a time. Not one of my prouder moments. It's all fun and games until someone gets thirty cactus spines in their ass.

SQUID: I stood in front of Jennifer's house and stared at the shrubs for ten full minutes. I saw one of those bird-of-paradise plants, the ones that look like cranes. I was like, "Is that real?" I was poking at it with my finger, like, "Where are we? It's fucking weird here."

THEO: Gina and I busted into a laughing fit over foliage. FOLI-AGE. Bahahahaha! It was like we were in *The Flintstones*. I walked over to the La Brea Tar Pits and tripped out on the bubbling tar and fake dinosaurs. So. Not. NYC. All the newness had an effect on me. I got to LA and I was like a lunatic that was let out of the asylum to go mad. I stayed with friends in the band Celebrity Skin for a night in an industrial office building that wasn't supposed to be for residential living. All night, I went on a rampage—basically, I left Brooklyn and I went bananas. I ran down Hollywood Boulevard laughing

hysterically while smashing long fluorescent lights. After our show at the Gaslight, I was drunk and started
throwing and smashing any and all beer bottles I could
find in the stairwell of the club while laughing my ass
off. I was having the time of my life!

The other thing about LA that cracked us up was the vernacular. We
didn't believe people said stuff like "dude," "rad," and "babe" until we got
there and heard those words firsthand. It was hilarious. Years later, when
we were headed to Paris, we joked that every other person would probably
be carrying a baguette and a poodle, and then we got to Paris and every
other person actually had a baguette in their purse, a bottle of wine, a be-
ret, and was riding a bike with—you guessed it—a poodle. It was like the
episode of Bugs Bunny when he goes to Paris! Turns out, clichés come
from somewhere. We have to thank LA for another perfect cliché that
happened a few years later.

SQUID: One of my favorite memories is when Gina and I met Gene
Simmons at a party in LA. He was a caricature of himself, a total lothario type. He had a giant comb-over
helmet of frizzy black hair. His shirt was unbuttoned
and his chest hair was on display, and he slid up next
to me, all sleazy and hitting on me. I said, "You have
to meet my guitar player!"

GINA: Squid brought me over to Gene Simmons, who reached
his hand out and started stroking my hair and saying, "Ohhhh, so nice to meet youuuu." So in return, I
said, "Ohhh, so nice to meet YOUUU" and reached out my
hand and touched his hair. And his entire head of hair
moved. In one piece. It tilted forward and back like a
Brillo helmet. I screamed and pulled my hand back immediately. I was horrified.

SQUID: It was like watching a car accident in slow motion. "No,
Gina! NO! No touch!"

> **THEO:** At that same party he told me, "Ya can't make money in punk rock, ya gotta do somethin' else." It felt like one of my Jewish relatives doling out unwarranted advice.

We weren't entirely sure how the West Coast crowd would take to us New York City bozos. In fact, LA was really awesome to us. We played the Gaslight, Coconut Teaszer, and Raji's, where we met Wino from Saint Vitus. Our big gig was opening for Redd Kross at the Roxy on Theo's nineteenth birthday. That didn't go as planned. We played our set, but then one of the members of Redd Kross was sick, so they wound up canceling. They came out onstage and announced, "Sorry, we're not playing tonight." We're lucky we didn't get killed. But at least we got to play the show we had come all the way out there for. Although it was Jennifer who mentioned, after seeing our set for the first time, that we might want to work on our overall onstage energy, a relatively new concept for some of us in the band. And she was right. Punk rock is adrenaline, it's mania, it's unabashed, and that needs to come off in not only your music but also in your physical performance. But we were still punk rock rookies, too busy wrangling our guitar cables and trying to remember which notes to play to think about going crazy and jumping around. Okay, well, guess it's time to step up our game.

> **THEO:** I was a classically trained dancer, and from the early to mid-'90s, I took African dance classes with teacher and drummer Djoniba Mouflet at Lezly Dance and Skate School. African dance is so incredible and such a release; it taught me to move my body in a different way than all my ballet studies did. It's extremely expressive and a lot of the movements are fairly acrobatic. These classes are where I learned how to jump really high. Thanks to this training, I could even jump while wearing high heels. During our shows, the stage became a combination of launchpad, trampoline, and three-ring circus.

GINA: I started to challenge myself to stop looking at the floor, stop looking at my guitar, stop worrying about what the audience was thinking, and just have fun. And I began to notice that the more fun we were having on-stage, the more fun the audience was having watching us. It was infectious and we fed off of each other. On the other end of the stage, Sindi was becoming more and more animated during our sets, bustin' out all these stage moves, hopping up and down, and going nuts. She was having a blast.

SQUID: Don't look down! Learn to tie your fucking shoes with your eyes closed if you have to. Perfect that snotty punk-ass look on your face like you do not give a shit, stick your nose in the air, and pray to god you hit the right note. If you didn't practice, you'll be sow-weee. Step to the mic, hit your cue, nail that backup sharp and loud, leave some glitter on it. Watch for the crowd—fans smash into mic stands, and microphones break teeth.

We came home from LA right before the *Sugar Luv* EP was released, which was right before we left for the Dinosaur Jr. tour. Stop us if you've heard this one before: three of us (Theo, Syd, and Gina) didn't know who Dinosaur Jr. was, but it didn't matter. We couldn't believe it! We'd played our first show the year before, had a great couple of shows in LA, and there we were one year later headed on a sold-out tour overseas. The crowds were huge to us—fifteen hundred to two thousand people. It was surreal.

Merry old England was really cold and bleak-looking. We flew in and they took us right to eat. *"Yor gonnah 'av a real English brekfist."* Ooooh! Dainty teacups with roses on them! Scones the size of our heads! Endless jars of clotted cream! Wrong! Turned out that "brekfist" was served in a little diner and consisted of beans, fried mushrooms, fried tomatoes, and fried toast. *This ain't no bagels and cream cheese.* But the candy and chips (called crisps over there) were off the hook! Of course, we immediately went out and spent all of our per diem money on snacks.

Paul Smith's friend Susan, of Band of Susans, loaned us her one-bedroom flat for the tour. We explored everything and ate lots of strange English food. It was fascinating having a funny-looking bathroom with a weird English toilet and limescale on everything. There was even a plug-in teapot, which we didn't even know existed. Plants in LA and electric kettles in London—now we'd seen everything! There was all this interesting shit for us Yankee city girls to get into. And you better believe we got into all of it.

This tour was where we got introduced to the wonders of hash, courtesy of our friend Mat Fraser, who gave us blocks of the stuff. This wasn't a drug we had much access to back home. We had so much of it and had to figure out how to get rid of the leftover chunks by the end of the tour. We couldn't smoke it fast enough, and we'd be damned if we were gonna throw it away. Solution: fry a bunch of margarine, add the hash, add sugar to it, and then drink it.

THEO: That night, I was lying on a kid-size foam mattress, and the lights were out, and the air was swirling around me, like an illustrated movie from *Sesame Street* or *Fantasia* or something. I was tripping my brains out. I woke up the next day sick as a dog, and I had my period. I couldn't get off the toilet. I was like, "You guys have to go without me"—as in go home, on the plane, back to New York. "Have a nice time." Somehow I got myself together, but for a while I was positive I couldn't leave. I thought I was going to die on that fucking toilet, shitting hash and bleeding. So disgusting. Not that I learned from this experience ... There was always a hunk of hash at the end of a European tour, and somehow

```
I'd always wind up sick. Waste not, want not! There are
starving children that want to eat this! Fast-forward
to me crying on a toilet. I somehow made it onto the
plane and most definitely vomited on the flight home.
```

Not everything we got into was illegal, just really fuckin' obnoxious. At one of the universities we played, a records room doubled as our dressing room. Snoopy little bastards that we were, you know we had to start digging around into all these massive file cabinets. Bingo! In there, we found hundreds of student ID cards, each with an attached passport-sized photo. After our set, we killed time by going through these pictures and laughing our heads off. ID pictures are usually unflattering, and these were some extra-dorky college kids, so you could imagine how hilarious some of them were. HOLY SHIT, were they funny-looking. American idiots in Europe, day one observations: mmmm, no fluoride in the tap water. Everyone's teeth were EVERYWHERE. We were dying laughing for hours picking through them.

We must have swiped a hundred photos, took them back to the flat, and proceeded to hide them all over the place in this poor woman's apartment: in drawers, under mats, in boxes of tea, inside pillowcases, under floorboards, in medicine cabinets, inside bags of frozen foods, in boxes of tampons, in light fixtures, in the cat litter. We put those tiny pictures in places that probably weren't discovered until two years later—little faces with notes on the back of them, like, "Hi!"

Till the day that woman dies or relocates, she will never be free from this. She didn't know us at all and was nice enough to let us stay at her apartment, and we showed our gratitude by bombarding every room with a zillion pictures of goofy English kids. That was one of those hoot 'n' hollerin' times. We were such assholes.

We doled out the shenanigans, but England made sure we got it right back, one way or another, and it began at the first show, which, if memory serves correctly, was at a place called the Mean Fiddler. There we were, onstage in England in all our glory. Such fun! Here's what nobody told us but what we learned really quickly: the British have a very strange way of showing their enthusiasm. The crowd liked us, but boy, were they wild! If we took a break between songs, they bellowed at us, *"Git on wivvit!!"*

SQUID: Something went whizzing by my face. I was like, "What the fuck is that?" It kept happening. I couldn't figure it out. Then I realized people were chucking fuckin' pint glasses at our heads. I was convinced one of us, if not all of us, was going to end up in the hospital. That was a cultural learning experience for us. We thought we came from the hardest place on earth, New York fuckin' City. NOT SO. The Lower East Side can't hold a tea bag to London. Nothing like that had ever happened to us before. We ain't home, holy shit.

GINA: I was amazed at the rowdiness of the crowds; they just did not give a fuck! They were loud, drunk, sloppy, and out to have fun, and I loved it. Of course I was terrified at first, dodging flying pint glasses and loogies, but aside from that, the audience actually really liked us and were having a great time. It was a thrill to get such an animated reaction to our music from a crowd that had no idea who we were. I was psyched.

THEO: I lost my voice at the end of the very first set we played there, and I just started to cry. I was really, really upset. The crowd was throwing things at us and I couldn't talk. What was I going to do? Then I found out it was a bunch of girls throwing the pints at us. Even more lame! After I got over it, I walked around the bar area and found a bunch of money. One of the genius things about England was that they still had the pound coin. People were drunk, and they'd drop shit out of their pockets. So I walked around the bar and cleaned up. That became my new post-show activity. I bought a lot of Ribena (a popular English black currant drink) and sweets with that extra cash.

At first we just sort of rolled with the antics. But it didn't take long before we fired back, as was our nature.

BECKY: One of the best times I ever had was on that tour. The Lunachicks were very pretty and young—even though they did a lot to make themselves not look pretty—and I have always kinda had a belly. At one of our shows, I came out to sing my song, "Superstrong," while Theo played drums, and I thought I heard someone yell out, "You fat fuckin' bastard!" And so I went, "What? FAT? You callin' me fuckin' fat!? That's right, I'm fuckin' FAT!! Fuck you, you skinny fuckin' piece of shit! Come up here and fuckin' say it to my face, I'll fuckin' kill you!!" When I went back to my drums, there were all these fat people on the right side of the stage lookin' at me with their arms up, like, "YEAH, FUCKIN' A!!" It was one of the best moments of my fuckin' life.

SQUID: We played at a club that had a setup similar to CBGB, with a long bar area and then the stage. We were on-stage, and I was rocking out with my eyes closed, la la la la, and suddenly I heard this weird, loud feedback. I opened my eyes and saw Sindi's guitar on the floor. It didn't register right away with me that Sindi was gone, but I looked up and out into the crowd, and that's when I saw it. Sindi made her way from the stage all the way to the back of the club, and she was fuckin' pounding some dude square in the face. *Bam-bam-bam!* I don't know how she got there so fast. Somebody did something, and she saw who did it, and she went after him. And he was trying to escape! It was one of those moments where you think, "Who does stuff like that, bolting offstage like the Road Runner to hunt down some guy and crush him in the face mid-verse? Who can even move that fast?" Answer: Sindi. That is the kind of girl she is.

SINDI: We were getting pelted with pint glasses. Not cups or plastic bottles—pint glasses. Those things don't break when you drop them. We were getting hammered. At one point I got hit with one, and I managed to put the pint and the pint-thrower together. I saw him from the back, saw the thing coming, couldn't move fast enough to get out of the way, but I identified him. I blinked and I was at the back of the club, punching him. Luckily, security was right on my tail and the person was removed. I was furious. I don't like to be hit, and I did something about it. I turned around and the band was like, "Where is she?" Well, I got hit in the face with a pint glass, saw where it came from, and I took care of it.

THEO: A few nights later, I got nailed right in the forehead with a full can of beer. I had a bright red *C* in the middle of my forehead from the can for the rest of the night. I was so fuckin' angry. It must've come from the back of the room, but I looked down from the stage and saw some kid giving me a look, so I jumped down and clocked him in the face.

BECKY: Theo picked up a bottle and threw it right back at them. Nobody told her. She knew exactly what to do. The girls, they were just being themselves! They all showed they had balls.

At another show, the crowd spit all over us. We had heard that that was how the English expressed their love for a band, by hocking loogies. Talk about culture shock. So disgusting. *Really? This is how you show your love?* Squid was *covered* in loogies. Her arms, her bass, it was so fuckin' gross. The rest of us were jumping around the stage trying to avoid the spit, a great way to work on our latest stage moves.

Honestly, none of the aforementioned antics bothered us to the point where it threw us off our game. Being targets of thrown pints and cans and spitting was an occupational hazard and also nasty, sure, but mostly it was fucking annoying. That all changed in a flash.

SINDI: Toward the end of the tour, we were playing a huge show, and during our last song, a couple people were stage diving, so I did too. I was expecting what happens when you did that in New York—the crowd passed you around on their hands, and you eventually made it back to the stage. Not this time. The crowd ripped my clothes off. Suddenly, I was in the crowd and topless. A bouncer took his shirt off and covered me with it and got me out of there, which was really awesome. I was pissed and also thought it was a bit ridiculous. I wasn't traumatized or anything, but it was really fucked up. I had jumped in with joy in my heart and good feelings, and then it was like, "Fuck, man, you people suck so hard!" What the fuck?! Why!? The answer clearly was, "It's a chick and here she is and I can touch her boobs!" That was horrible. It was the first and last time I ever jumped into a crowd. I don't know what possessed me to do it in the first place, it wasn't my style. I did it, and it sucked.

We were immediately thrown into the backstage area. The show was over. Becky was flipping out.

BECKY: That was one of the worst things I ever saw in my whole life. Ever. And I'm the only one who saw, because the other girls were rolling around on the ground. Sindi jumped in the audience, and the first thing that happened was someone ripped her shirt off and grabbed her tits. And the look on her face wasn't "This is cool"—it was horrible, but she had to play it off. It was like watching someone being molested in front of you. Your fuckin' bandmate. Your sister. I stopped playing and went to help get her back onstage. Where's the fuckin' security? When security knows you're going to jump in the crowd, they can be prepared for any situation. So I was mad at Sindi that she had done that without telling anybody. I understand why she did what she did, but that's not safe! The girls told me, "Oh, you're mad that you didn't do it." That's what they thought! You know how many times I jumped off a stage? I don't give a shit. I was mad because she got fuckin' molested. I was mad because if a dude jumped in the audience, the crowd wouldn't do that. The other girls completely misunderstood why I was so upset. It was really horrible for me. Sindi was really mad at me, and I was mad at her, and it definitely put a tear in my relationship with the band. They were never gonna see it from my perspective, and I can only have my perspective in a situation like that. It was terrifying. It was unjust. And it was wrong.

SINDI: Becky got furious. I think she was mad at me for doing it, and that got me mad. Like, do you think I'm feeling good about this? I was already upset and then to have her attack me for being attacked was really sad. Instead of comforting me and being a team and like, "We're gonna get 'em!" or something like that, it was suddenly my fault. I understand that she was upset and angry about it and maybe felt violated herself somehow through me, but it was really not cool that she attacked me for getting assaulted. Whatever. I got over it.

The only reason the rest of us weren't freaking out was because Sindi was safe and assured us that she was okay. In that moment, that was the only thing that mattered. There was a lot of yelling and confusion backstage. Becky was toe to toe with someone, maybe our tour manager, yelling and freaking out, then, for some unknown reason, she pivoted left and socked our soundman square in the face. He didn't do anything. He unfortunately happened to be standing there. Members of Dinosaur Jr. were watching all of this unfold, like, "Whaaaat theee fuck is wrong with these chicks?" And the hits just kept on comin'.

SQUID: Later on in the tour, Becky and I broke up and were seriously getting on each other's nerves. We were soundchecking and both ended up in the bathroom. We got into it. I have no idea what started it, but we went from zero to one hundred. We had each other by the hair and were beating the shit out of each other, spitting point-blank into each other's faces, wrestling each other to the ground. The rest of the band was waiting onstage, finishing soundcheck. We could hear someone say, "Hello?! Kick drum!" as we were trying to drown each other in the toilet. Finally, we were exhausted, and the show must go on! So we called a one-two-three truce, dropped piles of hair on the floor, and headed for the stage. For the record, Becky is the only woman I've ever been in a fight with.

BECKY: At that point, we had broken up. Everybody wanted to be with Squid—everybody. I think the fight had something to do with that. Mind you, if I was in Europe, I was on hash. If I was in the States, I was on heroin. I still love Syd to this day. I will always love her.

THEO: I went into the bathroom looking for them because soundcheck was happening and was like, "What the fuck happened in here??" There was spit and clumps of hair

```
everywhere. It was disgusting. It looked like somebody
had been torn in half.
```

Apart from all that, we had such a great time during those two weeks, and the audiences were really amazing. By the time the tour made its way through England and returned to London for a show at the University of London, we had our own fans waiting outside. They'd never seen anything like us and couldn't *not* like us. It helped that the press was like, "Wow, these New York City girls are *not* backing down."

At our hotel, members of the press lined up for us one after the other. Every magazine gave us full-page features! It was shocking. Goes to show you, when there's money behind you, that's what you get. Blast First had big clout and big bands, and the amount of coverage they set up for us was huge. We were kids, so fuckin' sassy and full of ourselves. We didn't know how to play the publicity game—that was part of our charm. We even signed our first autographs on that tour.

```
GINA: In a short amount of time we gained a huge following
      over there, bigger than the one we had at home. In En-
      gland we had a record (which wasn't released in the
      States), we had press, and we had awesome fans. It was a
      little strange to feel more known in a foreign country
      than we did in our own city.
```

Paul was also promoting us as American teenage chicks from Brooklyn who were in a street gang. He had this whole sensational pitch that was so stupid and kinda embarrassing for us because if some real street gang from back home got wind of that, we would've had our asses destroyed. But it worked. We even recorded Peel Sessions for the legendary DJ John Peel's BBC Radio 1 show. We went to a fancy studio in a giant orchestral room, plugged in, and everything sounded perfect. How insane that our band joined the likes of David Bowie and X-Ray Spex on the list of artists who did Peel Sessions? Whose life were we living?

We never had a grand plan, but the fact was, after our third show, we got signed to a record label *and* were flown to the UK *and* woke up in a nice hotel *and* had back-to-back interviews *and* multipage spreads in *NME* and *Melody Maker and* recorded Peel Sessions. After that experience, we were like, "Maybe we're rock stars."

CHAPTER 14

CLOSE ENCOUNTERS OF THE TURD KIND

As teenagers, whenever we'd go see shows with our gang of punk rock girlfriends, we always had to protect each other from boneheads in the pit who saw us as moving targets. So when we started playing live and got increasingly comfortable in that role, we wanted to make sure nobody messed with the girls who pushed their way to the front of the stage just like we would do. We wanted people of all colors, creeds, and sizes, and anyone who felt like an outcast, to exist front and center so they could express themselves and dance and know that we had their backs.

SINDI: When I was at punk rock shows as a teenager, safety was so far from anyone's concern. Whatever, that didn't stop me, but I had to throw punches a lot in my life. But how nice that we could offer a sort of protection to our crowds. We were watching out for them.

GINA: In high school, I saw a show at the Ritz. I looked down from the balcony and saw a girl crowd-surf and get her ass and tits grabbed. It made me so goddamn mad. The more we started to understand that there were women in our audiences who were getting pushed around or stomped on, the more it made us aware of the platform we had. There were a lot of young gay kids at our shows too. It made us realize that, yeah, we want everyone to feel welcome. This is a place for us outsiders, and it's a safe space for us to rock out together, no matter what you look like or who you love.

Absolutely nobody was better at watching out for fans than Theo. Nothing got by her. She would always make sure the crowd was respectful and that women were up front. She'd be like, "There's too many dudes up here, let the women through. Move! Move!" and she'd direct the crowd. She could act very much like a schoolteacher when she was up there, like, "I saw that. Stop that shit." She didn't mess around, and it really made a difference. It made people stop and think, "Oh yeah, maybe I am tall and big and blocking everybody's view or not allowing people to dance and have fun because I'm too busy being up front 'cause I'm a dude."

SINDI: But men didn't feel like second-class citizens either, and that was very important to me. I didn't want to be in a band that was like, "Fuck the dudes. Dudes, get outta here!" We were able to keep that balance. But absolutely Theo would stop the show if she saw something out of line. She would stop mid-song and take care of it. Even if it was sometimes like, "Ohh, that song was going great!" but safety was more important. Those were our girls, and we were there for them. Nothing was gonna happen. If we had to jump in there and take care of it ourselves, it was gonna get taken care of. And I think the audience felt that, and felt good and safe, and that's a big deal to be at a punk rock show and feel that. That's something about the Lunachicks that we did awesomely.

THEO: Because I knew all too well what it was like to be in a crowd and get pushed around and thrown on the ground,

I couldn't let it happen at our shows. It was my safe superhero power space onstage, and I wanted our fans to feel they were in a safe space too. When we were opening for bigger bands that had jock-ish or, in some places (*aherereherm*, Florida), racist skinhead types in the crowd, I would stop mid-song to end the stupidity.

There were a fair amount of oddball fans who, for whatever reason, went bananas for us. This small portion of very hopped-up people would do outrageous things to get our attention or to satisfy whatever bizarre Lunachicks fetish they had. Some of them were harmless, even flattering, in their fanaticism. You tattooed our band name on your body? That's cool! You tattooed a portrait of Theo's or Squid's face on your body? A little much, but yeah, sure, go for it.

But some people were outright dicks. Who the fuck knows why people do the things they do. Wasn't Selena murdered by her biggest fan? If somebody in the crowd was yelling something at us that we didn't like, Theo would have them come to the front of the stage to say it in the microphone, and as they opened their mouth, she'd whack them on the head with the microphone. Funny as shit.

THEO: Immediately, the crowd would love us because they could hear the *thwump* of the mic landing on someone's head. Unfortunately/fortunately, this violence made the crowd love us when they had decided to hate us on sight. Someone once wanted to press charges because I whacked them hard enough and drew blood. But that got kiboshed. Phew.

SQUID: One way people tried to show their love for me when we were playing was by smiling right at me while unplugging my guitar. Why?? All the fucking time—on purpose. I have a tattoo on my right knee, *F.T.W.* in hot pink. That's the knee you get in the face when you mess with my stuff. We're tryin' ta do a job here! Another one of

my signature moves was gum in the hair. I always had
a mouthful of gum. Ammo. I'd be standing at a perfect
height where I could grab guys by the hair and grind
gum into their head if they did something to deserve
it. I did that so many times. The girls loved it. A real
crowd-pleaser. Plus, I loved to think of some dude waking up the next day with a hangover, trying to cut a
giant clump of Bubble Yum out of his hair.

We get it: we're women in a band *and* we're kooks, so we're gonna
attract some special kinds. But we drew the fuckin' line at sickos. One
time, Gina's friend Howard had recently bought a small yellow school bus
for his band the Pineapples to tour with. We borrowed this mini school
bus, the kind that takes developmentally disabled kids to and from school
(aka a short bus) to drive to a show in Boston. Some guy pulled alongside
us on the road with his dick in his hand. We shrieked. And then it happened *again*. Mind blown.

SINDI: It was terrifying because we would see drivers with
their penises out, and that was *before* they even knew
we were grown women sitting in the bus. What could be
more terrifying than that? Okay, you see us and then
whip it out—bad, but normal-bad. But your dick is already out at the sight of a school bus? Horrifying!
Traumatic!

GINA: It seems that a bunch of young punk-rock chicks driving a short bus was just way too much for any bona fide
perv to handle. They lost their minds at the sight of
it. It was really unsettling just how many disgusting
reactions we got from gross men driving alongside us on
I-95. Each one of them had something to say about it,
all of which involved some kind of gesture with their
crotch. We never borrowed that creep magnet of a bus
again.

We wound up as guests on *Midnight Blue*, a cable show hosted by Al Goldstein, from *Screw* magazine. To absolutely nobody's surprise, every question he asked was grosser than the last. He had no intentions of asking us about our music and tried to get us to talk about really lewd, deviant stuff. We are *not* squeamish girls, but we were repulsed.

GINA: I babysat for his kid once, and I told him that, and he immediately asked if I slept with his son. His *child*. Yulch! I remember eating the whole time during the interview. I was so, so uncomfortable. There was a plate of food next to me. I just sat there and stress ate. I really did not know how to deal.

SINDI: Al was hitting on me. All the old, fat Jews always hit on me. He kept saying to us, "Show us your tits, show us your tits, show us your tits!" Finally, Becky lifted her shirt up. Stills were printed in *Screw* with Becky's blurry tits.

Another guy showed up with cassette tapes of him playing along to Led Zeppelin, and handed us folded love notes that were sort of stuck together. We discovered the reason the paper was stuck together was because there was dried cum all over these notes. Eeeeeeewwwwww! The fuckin' hammer came down whenever he'd come to our shows wearing nothing but nude pantyhose. Because our shows were so packed, if you got yourself to the front of the crowd, nobody could see you except the band. You were basically pressed against the stage, which was usually only waist high. He would get up front and start masturbating. He was particularly fixated with Squid.

SQUID: He started telling people that we were married. I fuckin' lost it at one particular show. I had had enough and went after him with the butt end of my bass. I remember the neck of my bass slipping out of my hands. I didn't mean to throw it, I just meant to hit him with it, but

```
        it flew out of my hands in the direction of his face. I
        was like, "Shit, my fucking bass" as I saw it sailing
        away into the crowd. I don't remember if I hit him.
 THEO: You hit him.
```

We weren't scared of him because we never really felt like he was a physical threat; he was just fuckin' creepy and annoying. There was always that sense of being violated and us being like, "You're gonna pay, you motherfucker." It wasn't only about us. He'd be violating anyone who had the bad luck of standing near him or bumping into him at our shows. We really prided ourselves on our shows being an empowering experience, especially for our female fans, and that immediately goes to shit when some dude is being a gross creep in the middle of it all. That's an act of sabotage that we would not stand for. We told every club in New York, "If you see this guy, do not let him in." The ban remains in effect.

Once, we were on tour and staying in a shitty motel outside of Salt Lake City. While we were screwing around by the pool, we suddenly saw a woman hurrying by and her face was smashed up. She was a prostitute; a john had been hitting her in the face with a bottle. We tried to call the cops, but she threatened to run if we did. Because she was a sex worker, she was afraid she would get arrested and thrown in jail instead of getting help—great system we have.

The whole ordeal was devastating and reminded us of when we used to practice near Times Square and would see pimps beat the shit out of hookers in the street. Seeing that poor woman with her face all fucked up and knowing we couldn't help her gave us nightmares for literal years.

We weren't afraid to get physical or teach someone a lesson, especially when defending each other.

```
 SQUID: One time, we were offstage and I was carrying a bunch of
        shit through the crowd when I felt someone touch my ass.
        Well. The next thing I knew, the whole band surrounded
        two dudes and started yelling. It was really crowded,
        so we were pressed against each other; it was a sea of
```

arms. Out of nowhere, Theo's fists started moving at lightning speed. She was getting in these shots like a fucking kangaroo boxing. Ducking and weaving and, *BAM*, catching this guy in the fuckin' face and picking him apart. The dude was reeling. It's not like she practiced boxing; I mean, I've known Theo my whole life and I'd never seen her do anything like that. She was landing perfect punches. We were all like, "Daaaaaaaaamn!" For the record, I have a tremendous mouth but no actual fighting skills. I was so impressed.

THEO: Oh, I had to punch that guy. It was an animal reflex. DON'T FUCKING TOUCH MY FRIEND!

While in Sweden, we played at a club that had dorms next door. So after the show, we went back to the dorms, got in our pajamas, and started brushing our teeth, but people were still hanging out and milling around. The promoter was a super clean-cut, square dude. We paid him no mind until he had a bit too much to drink and got a little too touchy-feely with one of us. He passed out. Bad move. You just signed your death warrant, dude.

Out came the Sharpies. We went to fuckin' town. We wrote "I heart Lunachicks" across his whole fuckin' head and neck, drew a penis on his cheek—he was covered front to back. We gave him the royal treatment. *Don't. You. Fuck. With. Us.*

What we didn't know was that he would be driving us the next day— six hours in the van with this guy. He was bright red from trying to scrub everything off. So now his face was bright red with "I heart Lunachicks" and a giant penis on it. It was SO awkward. No regrets, though. We'd do it again in a heartbeat.

There were times when we probably drifted toward incurring bodily harm in exacting revenge or standing our ground or reclaiming our time or whatever you want to call it. One tour stop was in a big skinhead town in Florida. Social Distortion had played the night before, and the resident skinheads had tried to set their hotel on fire. Tensions were REAL high by the time we rolled in. The promoters warned us ahead of time. Of course, us being us—and the fact that collectively we're at least half Jewess—the warning translated to a dare.

SQUID: I couldn't help myself. I came out onstage with *JEW* written across my forehead. The skinheads were mad-dogging me from the audience. I thought, "Okay, this might be one of those moments where I'm pushing it too far." That only made me more "FUCK YOU, there is NO WAY I'm passing up this moment." But, yeah, this could get nasty. There was a question mark in my mind, and that was rare. I paused, you know? It wasn't like, "Well, the bunch of us are gonna kick their asses!"

THEO: It was more like, "Well, we might die." These guys had swastika tattoos on their chests and backs. It was full-on white-supremacist scary.

SQUID: I thought, "Okay, they might do something to us," but it egged me on. I couldn't keep my mouth shut. We were being told by the club that we should keep quiet, but that was like when producers told Jim Morrison to not sing the word *higher* on *The Ed Sullivan Show* and he went for it and shouted the word straight into the camera when it came time for that lyric. SURE, tell me not to. Good luck with that.

THEO: But that's your personality, and it's been like that since I've known you. After a similar neo-Nazi-ish crowd experience at a venue in Seattle, a bouncer came up to us after the show, shook our hands, and said, "Thanks for that, I'm a Jew from Queens."

SQUID: It's a job, a calling really. It's what we're living for, right? Where better to fuck with a bunch of roided-out poser Nazis if not in front of twenty-five hundred fans and a crew of beefcake bouncers versus, you know, anywhere else at any other time where you know for 100

percent sure you're gonna get killed. SOMEBODY'S GOTTA
DO IT!

Among the various types of characters that would show up in our audience was a phenomenon we came to learn of called the "creepy girl-band guy" aka Mom's Basement Guy—their moms probably still made them lunch. Every female band we know has had this same experience: there's always at least one weird, old guy who is at every show, just sort of hanging around, leering. Every city on our tours had its version of creepy girl-band guy. They were odd, but harmless. Mostly, Mom's Basement Guy would have a stack of stuff for us to sign when we got offstage.

Men and women tended to show affection differently. Most straight men from the audience never lined up to be our hot sex toys in the same way that we saw girls do for dude bands. Granted, we were a bit off-putting, so we can understand why anyone would be hesitant to talk to us. Compared to the guy bands that we traveled with, we ladies didn't remotely have the same kinds of groupie conquests on tour, coined "road sausage" by L7. It's something we've openly joked about with other female bands—that kind of hook-up culture didn't really seem to translate the same for women in bands. When we got down with dudes on tour, it was usually with someone from the other band or their crew, except for that hot guy in Florida who had a pet goat named Jessica.

Sure, we had our rock-star moments—the double makeout on the sidewalk, or the guy we called Amtrak after we had our fun with him for a week and then plopped him on a train back to his hometown—but by and large, only the strangest of bizzaro dudes ever had the guts to offer themselves up to us, instead of the hot, good-looking guys that we would have hoped for. On the other hand, some girls at our shows were not at all shy about expressing themselves to us.

GINA: If I was gay, I bet I would've gotten laid every single
night. A girl came up to me after a show, ripped off her
bra, and was like, "You guys rock so hard, you rocked
my bra off!!" Becky always had a slew of fans. One of

them was an enormous butch dyke in Germany who never stopped staring at Becky and followed her around all night going, "Whoa . . . whoa." Becky got a lot of attention, whoa.

BECKY: I definitely would go home with chicks on the road. I think in Malmö, Sweden, I went home with two girls and a guy. The guy might have been one of their boyfriends, but I was like, "I'm not doin' nothin with him." Yeah, I had my share of fun with women, for sure.

SQUID: One cute girl got on the stage and asked, "If I kiss you, will you punch me in the face or kiss me back?" I was like, "I am not gonna punch you in the face." And we started making out. She was adorable! It was a great line!

We understood groupie culture, even if we didn't participate in the traditional sense. As music fans and young women, we'd have died to be close to bands, but not because we wanted to have sex with them, but because we wanted to BE THEM.

THEO: Squid and I were going to see Frehley's Comet at the Cat Club with a group of our girlfriends. We were maybe sixteen. We were all dressed to the nines: miniskirts, platforms, fishnets, varieties of Manic Panic hair colors, and lots of glitter. But the club wouldn't let us in because we were underage. Security was like, "Nope!" We sat on a car outside, crushed. Near to tears. Suddenly a small guy came up to us and in a thick English accent said, "Hello, girls! What's the matta, can't get into the show?" We were like, "NO, we came to see Ace but we can't get in!" The guy said, "Well, I'm Peter Frampton, and I'm gonna get you in! Come with me." No way, shut up. We followed him as he said something to the guy at the door. The seas parted, he walked us in and was like, "Bye-bye!" and left. Didn't ask us for a thing and then disappeared. We saw the show, I met Ace, and I got my jacket signed. Thank you, Mr. Frampton, wherever you are! Fast-forward to when we were making *Terror Firmer*, a movie for Troma Entertainment, in 1998 or 1999, and the production people called me and were like, "Lemmy's coming from the airport. Can you go pick him up? He wants to ... hang out with a chick." Lemmy was rock 'n' roll royalty. He was the singer and bass player of the iconic Motörhead and was also in the trailblazing psychedelic band Hawkwind. I was a fan of both bands and him big-time. Lemmy was a fucking legend but not a legend I ever wanted to get with—know what I'm saying? Plus, I was not an escort. I was so insulted by this request. And unabashedly I was like, "NO! Are you fucking kidding me? Are you trying to pimp me out right now? HOW RUDE!"

Sometimes, it's what our fans *didn't* do that best demonstrated their devotion. An LA band called Goldfinger opened for us at Tramps in NYC right when their hit single was all over the radio. Our label head, Greg Ross of Go-Kart Records, overheard the band and crew concoct a plan to impress the music press in attendance: even though their camp knew it wasn't the norm for an opening band to play an encore, they didn't care. (Think they'd have attempted this little stunt if we had fuckin' dongs? Doubt it.) When their set was done, they left the stage and their roadie ran up and tried to get the crowd cheering for an encore. Lunachicks fans stood there, silent and annoyed at having to wait any longer for us to come on, and effectively killed this master plan. The band got onstage to play a last song, only to face a room full of pissed-off crickets.

Reminds us of the time some local opener (dudes) was getting annoyed at our audience's obvious impatience as their set dragged on. "Don't worry," the singer sneered, "the GIRL band will be on soon." A riot almost ensued. The crowd launched an onslaught of boos and hisses while we were backstage waiting to smash bottles over the band members' idiot heads.

Perhaps the most ridiculous display of bonkers Lunachicks fandom (if you can call it that) occurred during a show in New Jersey. Nearing the end of our set, some people began stage diving, nothing unusual. It's important to note that we were soaking wet with sweat, to the point that we looked like we had stepped right out of the shower.

> **SQUID:** So there we were, in the middle of a song, when a guy jumped onstage, grabbed my arm, hoisted it high in the air, and slurped my sweaty, hairy armpit—I'm talking a field of armpit hair. He locked on. I didn't even push him off.

He then immediately jumped down, ran to the bar, and broke a wooden barstool over his head. We all saw it happen. It was one of those moments where, in the middle of the madness, we had a sudden moment of clarity: everyone is insane. That insight was quickly followed by another one: sometimes we bring out the best in people.

CHAPTER 15

BINGE AND PURGATORY

The experience of making our second album, *Binge and Purge*, can be metaphorically summed up in one story. It was during the early summer months of 1992. We borrowed a friend's car to pick up Squid's amp and drive it to the studio where we were recording. Squid opened the door into oncoming traffic, and a car whizzed by and tore the door clean off. Turned out to be pretty symbolic.

For a while, we were being managed by Jane Friedman, Patti Smith's and John Cale's former manager. We loved her. We called her "the Ruth Gordon of Rock 'n' Roll." We would go over to her house, and she would make us salad and give us seltzer. She was like a cool auntie. Our contract with her included securing a record deal, but when the A-list labels took a pass, followed by the B-list, she got us a quick last-minute deal with Safe House.

We recorded the album at SST in Weehawken, New Jersey. We drove the engineer nuts. One of the employees got drunk and a little too cavalier with his affections. *No touch.* After one too many drinks, the offender passed out. Theo drew a flower on his head, we put his hair in pigtails, and we topped it off with a pair of panties (you know who you are, and yes, we have pictures). He learned quickly to keep his hands off.

SST was a huge space that was almost like a venue and doubled as a van rental company. The recording process wasn't as intimidating now that we had been through it once. Our confidence was up, and we really wanted to become a better, stronger band.

We had spent the year rehearsing, touring, and writing in between various shitty day jobs, which we had to work because the band was never a reliable source of income.

SQUID: I was a super-stoned waitress who got fired from every job and finally ran away on my motorcycle during the middle of a shift to beg for a job as a tattoo artist.

THEO: I was a babysitter, failed waitress, longtime go-go dancer, and later a model, actress, and professional ham.

GINA: Among a thousand odd jobs, I scooped ice cream at Häagen-Dazs and worked my way up to painting Day-Glo parrots on bejeweled acid-washed denim jackets for a cheesy Long Island clothing company.

At some point or another, we all cleaned toilets.

Meanwhile, we had moved a few more rungs forward from being the struggling teenage musicians who were writing songs in our bedrooms. We still had a ways to go yet, but for sure we were making progress. We were a bit more (semi) conscious about song structure, tempos, and overall tone.

SQUID: Getting through a Lunachicks set was half skill and half stamina. Preparing for tour was like training for a mini marathon. One of my "workouts" entailed playing along with all four sides of the Ramones *Alive* album. They're playing twice as fast because it's all recorded live, and then I'm playing double time to that. If your wrist doesn't snap off and go flying through a window like a rogue helicopter blade, then you're damn sure building chops from that. Downstroke, baby! You gotta play through the hand cramps and no pee breaks! And make it through all twenty-eight songs without stopping. And learn how to recover your pick without missing a beat because those things go flinging out of your grip like little torpedoes (gotta keep 'em tucked in your pick-guard). The downstroke rhythm is an unspoken tradition and weird source of punk rock pride (if you hit the string on the way up, you're cheating). I have no idea why, but I will tell you this is something Sindi and I took VERY seriously. It's like a ridiculous test you put yourself through just to prove you can; same thing goes for holding your guitar as close to your knees as humanly possible without breaking your arm. I am willing to swear this all makes it sound better.

Not sure most people understand how physical an adventure playing bass guitar is—those strings are FAT and that neck is long. And I liked to hit it HARD, so it sounds like a poke-poke-poke in the chest or a smack in the head. My profile includes "firm handshaker." And for the record (no pun intended), I never, ever, ever—not sick, not stoned, not tired, not hungover—ever practiced sitting down. You could play like Eddie Van Halen sitting in a chair, and no one's gonna give a shit. If you can't stand and deliver, it doesn't count. To this day, one of my shoulders is three inches higher than the other from spending so many hours in that contorted position. I never knew exactly how, but I left blood smears on that guitar most nights, and you know I was proud of that.

GINA: I had to work on getting the wrist on my right hand loose enough to chunk and strike to the speed of the kick drum, while also strengthening the fingers on my left hand to be ready to rip when it was time to stomp my foot on my RAT pedal and kick into a screaming lead. I built up tough, leathery calluses on my fingertips so that I could bend, pull, and draaag the strings across the fretboard. Nothing better than the warped sound of the low E string pulled way out of tune and smashed up against the other strings. Add some ear-bleeding, high-pitched feedback, and I swear your facial expression will automatically twist and pucker into an ugly grimace—Guitar Face—it ain't pretty but you just can't fucking help it! Live AC/DC records were a great workout. I'd play along to my hero Angus Young to whip my lead-playing fingers into shape. Envisioning him shredding away in a constant state of frenzied motion taught me what was possible. Can I jump up and down and still grab that note? Nope, not yet, but I now had a goal (much to my downstairs neighbor's dismay), and I knew that as long as I stuck with it, it was only a matter of time.

THEO: I started taking voice lessons with Don Lawrence. Everybody went to him: Dee Snider, Jon Bon Jovi, and a lot of the metal and hardcore singers. But his method didn't work for me. Methods aside, maybe the real reason I couldn't learn from him was because I couldn't stop staring at his hair plugs. It was the early days of hair plugs, so they were incredibly obvious, especially when you've got a bird's-eye view like I had. Don would sit at the piano, I would stand over him, and he would tell me what to do, and I would be like, "Wow, how many hairs are going into that one plug??!" I couldn't stop staring. When I loop my days with Don into all my fascinations with wigs and makeup, it makes sense that I got distracted. I had to get another teacher. I found more of a Broadway guy named Bill Reed. I couldn't get away with not knowing how to sing or not being trained—not anymore. The screamy and growly stuff I did on the first album was hurting my voice. I was forced into learning how to sing properly, otherwise I would have developed nodes and wouldn't be singing anymore. Plus, I wanted to do it right! When I think about bands I really love—Judas Priest, Blondie, Black Sabbath—there was so much good singing influencing me. I wanted to be able to sing well. That was a point of contention because some of the girls wanted me to growl, and I was like, "Well, you're not getting that now because I'm going to hurt myself." It wasn't like, "Oh, okay, sure, let's figure this out." I was like, "I need to learn how to do this without killing my voice or I'm not gonna be able to sing at all, let alone talk." There were differences of opinion, but we made it work.

Our songwriting was collaborative, a constant back-and-forth. It's messy, it's dirty, it's hilarious, it's frustrating, it's thrilling and maddening at the same time. We want to choke each other, hug each other, question why we are even trying to attempt this feat. It's a wrestling match and we are in the ring working it all out and someone is going to get slammed to the mat. Egos bruised, feelings hurt, creative visions crushed, but such is the war that is art. We wanted to explore, take risks, and create something new. Some were wins and some were fails, but at least we can say we weren't afraid to try. And in the end, that quirky, all-over-the-map, sometimes-fast-sometimes-slow-sometimes-slow-then-fast metal-then-punk-then-pop worked (most of the time), and we'd wind up with a song that we were so proud of and that we knew kicked ass. It's sometimes hard to even imagine how we ever got anything done. Maybe it's because ultimately there was a deep level of trust in each other's creative input—we believed in each other's talent.

GINA: I knew that if Theo, Squid, and I could stick it out through all of the back-and-forths and ongoing opinions, our three brains together would ultimately pump out a higher level of geniusness than each of us independently.

As a collective, we were making something bigger than our individual selves, and we were fearless when it came to the creative process. We dove in headfirst, determined to discover what possibilities lay ahead. The end results melded our multifaceted sensibilities—high-energy punk, dirgy-riff metal, classic rock and blues riffs. As we grew into our artistry, we were eager to show off. Theo's versatility as a vocalist put her in a league of her own. She could go from tough, husky barks to stunning operatic roars. Gina pulled from every genre you can think of (seriously, from blues to bossa nova and everything in between) to create different textures and tones that were lit with a billion watts. Squid didn't just play the root note of the chords; she got underneath, inside, and all around the melodies. As varied as our songs' musical styles were, they shared a common pursuit: liberally smack the listener on the ass and in the face with NYC attitude. Yes, we wanted to write excellent music. We also wanted you to see colors, hear feelings, and smell power. These songs were the purest means of our collective self-expression, one-way tickets to the nerve center of this entire operation.

We made the cover for the album with photographer Michael Lavine again. On the front, it's us eating a bunch of food, and on the back, we're throwing it all up. The whole concept for the title song and art came from an after-school special about bulimia. Now, bulimia is a really serious, awful condition that affects mostly young girls and women. We decided, in our deranged way, "Let's fuck this up." It was also kind of a feminist fuck-you thing. People tend to binge and purge in secrecy; there's a lot of shame associated with it—literally, a lethal amount. Naturally, we decided to do the exact opposite. Food and diets and body image and self-loathing aren't topics befitting conversation among young women? Load the cannon. Light the fuse.

Also, as friends, we'd bonded over food before we'd bonded over music. Think about what teenagers need: food and sleep. Snacking was very important to us (we were potheads then, after all), and we ate whatever the fuck we wanted. We'd get together and get high and eat.

THEO: Though we did not have the inter-webs then, we had magazines and television and billboard ads blaring that we should look like Farrah Fawcett and Barbie, and clearly that didn't involve enjoyment of food. *Binge and Purge* is also a metaphor of us as a band, how we ingested everything from the world and pop culture and then vomited it back out. That aside, we sure loved to eat. My paternal grandparents were not religious, so when we did Passover seders, it was a lot of skipping pages to where we could eat or drink. I loved the rituals of all the snacking and drinking. Grandma would feed us till we were bursting and then send us home with chocolates and snacks in the car. Food = love. Squid and I have what we call the (Jewish) food memory. We can recall a meal we had from eons ago, down to every little detail: what we ate, where we were, who was there, if it was good. Like how one can't remember pain, I have a tough time remembering a bad meal.

SQUID: I'm pretty sure there are people I've slept with that I can't remember. That being said, the Dutch word for garlic mayo is *knoflooksaus*.

GINA: I grew up with a loving Italian grandmother who was constantly trying to feed me. She was an amazing cook. Need I say more about the role food played in my life?

We can still recite the contents of each other's childhood refrigerators. Theo's mom always had giant chocolate bars in the freezer; Squid's dad had Jujubes, seltzer in old-fashioned glass bottles, and Jarlsberg; Sindi ate strictly starchy white foods and Pop-Tarts for dinner; Gina only had Steak-umms in the freezer (her mom left her money for food but Gina never went grocery shopping). We'd go to each other's houses after school, raid the refrigerator, and we'd make food for each other. Sindi used to make us pierogies like she was our mom.

> **THEO:** Squid and I spent countless hours snacking, and at a peak of creative condiment combining, we had the brilliant idea of making each other lunch for school. We did this for a period of time until it went over the top.
>
> **SQUID:** It was a dare. We'd show up for lunch period and swap our brown paper bags with disgusting sandwiches in them. Banana with peanut butter and pickles and kiwi.
>
> **THEO:** The kiwi one did me in. It got the bread all wet and mushy. The line was drawn. That was the end of the lunch-making challenge. There was a lot of hot-pickled-pepper-eating at her house as well. We stuffed pepperoncinis and cherry peppers into cheese sandwiches and chomped down.
>
> **GINA:** I would just go on a snacking tour when visiting Syd's kitchen. Especially when stoned. I was awed by her family's giant fridge filled to the brim with food.
>
> **SINDI:** Squid and I would play a game called "condiments on a cracker." We'd take out the stone-ground wheat thins that her family always had in the cupboard. And then we'd take out every single condiment, everything that you could possibly put on a cracker, and it became a vessel to get the condiments from the jar into the belly. That was our sport.

New York City is one big global buffet, and we were exposed to all kinds of cuisines from different cultures. Snacks-R-Us, from all-nighters at Kiev full of blintzes and borscht, to Mamoun's for the best falafel-hummus-and-tabbouleh sammies, to the mirrored ceilings of Spumoni Gardens in pursuit of that sacred square slice, to dinners at Rose of India under canopies of Christmas lights where we'd pretend it was our birthday so the staff would go nuts flashing sirens and making a fuss. In an interview Sindi and Gina did with *Guitar* magazine, the writer notes that Sindi answered a question "in between stuffing her face with popcorn and cherry pie simultaneously."

Absolutely nothing delighted us more than candy. We were *really* into it. Candy is similar to who we are—bright colors, very visual packaging. It was sensory overload, between looking at it and smelling it and tasting it. With the exception of Sindi, we grew up in households where sugar was restricted. Not surprisingly, candy was the very first thing we bought with our own money. It was associated with freedom.

Touring further exposed us to all different kinds of candy. We were hell-bent on trying everything, like it was a challenge. Every tour, we would buy shitloads of candy and snacks, dump them out into a pile, and proceed to stuff our faces—salt, sugar, salt, sugar. We'd all gorge on sweets until we wanted to throw up, no joke.

So for *Binge and Purge*, we had a whole plan of doing a garish John Waters–inspired, very done-up, rococo front cover—chiffon, ruffles, elaborate wigs—and then, because we're us, we'd be a disgusting, puke-covered catastrophe on the back cover. We were surrounded by a bunch of junk food, soda, cake, bags of chips, the works. The labels on the food had to be hidden, otherwise it would have been considered copyright infringement. So we took a bunch of tape and covered the brand names, or we got creative. "Diet Coke" became "Die ok." For the back cover, we're splayed out and covered in grayish-brown fake vomit, which was a mix of canned soup and other disgusting slop. Just the smell of it had us gagging for real. Again, we were not exactly the cerebral type, but we were so amused at ourselves. Second only to those photos was our cover of "Feel Like Makin' Love" by Bad Company.

GINA: Because of my sister Nonda's classic rock influence on me growing up, I really wanted to cover a Bad Company song and have fun with it, which Theo did in hilarious fashion as usual. We recorded it for the album, but it never made the cut.

Because we had changed some of the lyrics, we needed to get permission from the band. Paul Rodgers from Bad Company heard it and supposedly was so appalled that he remarked, "This is an abomination." He was so insulted by our version of his song, he wouldn't give us permission to release it. We doubled over laughing at his rejection letter. Talk about a badge of honor. That's pretty much where the good times ended.

Recording *Binge and Purge* kind of mirrored the album cover—it seemed great at first, but then was a vomitous horror show. Becky's heroin addiction was off the rails. She was always so high.

> **BECKY:** I don't remember, but I was a junkie for over eight years, strung out every fuckin' day. This was probably the beginning of that time. So this might have been the first or second year of what ended up being eight years. I think I trusted the process and the people around us— not everybody, but, like, our manager Jane. I was very happy to have them make the decisions. I don't think I wanted to know anything about being in the studio because I knew our first album didn't sound the way I wanted it to.

We struggled to get through the recording. Every take was like, "Cut!" "Cut!" "Cut!" Becky was being a pain in the ass and was really moody. Such a drag. Look, the four of us can be massive jackass goofballs—until it's time to put on our instruments and get to work. Then there is zero fucking around. Laser focus. But Becky was out of it, and it was impossible to record.

> **BECKY:** You know, you shut yourself completely off when you're a fuckin' junkie, especially when you're the only one doing that drug. Nobody wants to be around you. But I will say this: I don't think I ever fucked up a show or a song. When I listen to the recording, I'm playing it

the way that I play it. I'm not saying, "I wish I wasn't high there, I'd have played it differently." No. I just wish the drums were recorded better.

Squid was also sneaking off and getting high in the bathroom, but she had yet to come apart. She might have caused us greater concern at the time had Becky not been such an overwhelming distraction.

Our partnership with Jane was also deteriorating. It started out great—we always loved her—and she certainly bumped up our profile, but our career was stalling, and we were impatient and didn't entirely trust Jane to get us where we wanted to go. But Becky loved her, so that was another point of contention.

BECKY: Jane and I are great friends. I call her my aunt. I love her to death. But anytime Jane tried to get us a show or do anything, she had to call every single one of the girls to get their approval. Do you know how insulting that is to someone like Jane Friedman? It was shit like that, business-wise, that would drive me crazy. I was like, "Why is it you think you know anything about business? Why would you even question her? Let her do her job!"

Safe to say, we had a 'TUDE. We had A LOT of opinions about stuff. We were young, headstrong, and for whatever reason we thought we knew better than the adults in the room. It was just in our nature to question authority, or rather, anyone older than the age of twenty, bahahahahaaaaaa. That same year, we went into the studio with Lenny Kaye—legendary musician, Patti Smith's right-hand man—to record a seven-inch single, "C.I.L.L."/"Plugg," and rejected 99 percent of his ideas. Lenny suggested that we start "Plugg" with a guitar solo. We were totally against it, but we did it. That was maybe the one time we listened to him. To *Lenny Kaye*. (You were right all along, Lenny.)

We also went into the studio with Richie Stotts, the tutu-wearing guitar player of the Plasmatics, one of our heroes, and rejected his ideas too. We told him, "You can put your name on the record, but we're doing it our way." You can't herd cats. People really did try to produce us, but we did not listen. We were such assholes.

CHAPTER 16

ON THE ROAD AND ON THE RAG

Our first headlining European tour was booked by Pyramid Entertainment, the same company used by top R&B acts like Kool & the Gang. We'd show up to dressing rooms and there'd be shopping carts full of snacks waiting for us, like seven kinds of fruit juice and nine different cheeses, five kinds of crackers, chips, dips, spreads, breads, fresh fruit, dried fruit, candied fruit... At Easter time, one venue presented us with a full-on feast complete with a bunny-shaped cake. *This is how it is?!!? Europe is AMAZING! The people here are so niiiiice!* Promoters started complaining.

> **GINA:** At the end of our first European headlining tour, a promoter pulled me aside and was like, "Your rider is meant for an arena rock band. We're spending hundreds of dollars running around the city trying to find this shit and you're losing money because we could be putting this money toward your guarantee instead." Ummmm... what's a rider?

It turned out Pyramid was using Janet Jackson's rider as our own. Thankfully, one of our North American bookers, Scott Weiss (whom we called Squat Twice), taught Gina how to coordinate a tour and budget for important things like gas and hotels. No more bunny cakes.

We excelled at other parts of touring, namely inventing ways to amuse ourselves during the countless hours between showtimes. We fucked off everywhere—dressing rooms, the van, hotel rooms, friends' houses—being stupid idiots until we got onstage. Honestly, it was for the sake of our own mental health.

> **GINA:** Our life was spent crammed in a van. I remember coming to the realization of what touring really was about on our first tour in England. After the sixth day in a row of stuffing ourselves and our gear into a van, then sitting there for hours on end while the world whizzed by, it suddenly dawned on me, "Is this what it boils down to? All for just that forty-five minutes onstage? I dunno 'bout this." I slumped back into a mild state of panic envisioning a lifetime dictated by highway blur and being contained in a vehicle. I wanted to jump out of the window. And yet somehow I toured consistently for fifteen years after that. I guess you just have to eat some shit in order to get to the gravy/cream/light at the end of the tunnel or whatever the fuck the saying is. There's always a price for something is what I'm trying to say.

Because we toured before any sort of portable TV was invented, we had to come up with distractions. One way was by playing a game we called Let's Watch a Movie, where we'd recite an entire movie to each other, line for line. Crying laughing. Collectively, we're still capable of reciting *Pee-wee's Big Adventure* from beginning to end. Drawing was another way to kill time. Theo and Gina would spend hours making elaborate, grotesque drawings on every wall of every dressing room we ever walked into. Farting women covered in stubble and warts, lactating she-beasts, enormous spiders in high heels—everything that congealed in the recesses of their zonked brains after devouring hours of B and C horror movies mixed with *MAD* magazine, Wacky Packs, and Garbage Pail Kids came rushing to the surface.

THEO: Gina was and is still the only person I can art-jam with with complete abandon. We have been drawing and painting things for and with each other since we were fourteen years old, and I can't say I ever see it ending. I have had some of my life's biggest laughing fits drawing on walls of dressing rooms with her. She is a much better visual artist than I am in both talent and technique, and I am constantly in awe of her work. I have always trusted her implicitly as an artist. I realize that it's really in every way that I feel this.

GINA: I remember going into hysterical fits of laughter with Theo, my forever partner in art crime. Since high school, Theo and I were always making art together, passing drawings off to each other in class, creating ridiculous comic strips, and making cartoons of our teachers. When we'd go on tour, Theo and I always packed boxes of Sharpies and we would create these elaborate drawings on the walls of our dressing rooms featuring our grotesque and ridiculous characters—lactating three-titted hairy-chested beauty queens framed by our signifying touch: hearts and flies. I always loved that we had that connection and that we would inspire each other to reach into the depths of our imaginations to pull out the most outrageous visuals. Many of Theo's brilliant characters have become iconic mascots for us and some of my favorite Lunachicks artwork.

If we had a dressing room that was covered in posters with photos of bands, no one was safe with the two of us armed with markers. Theo and I would go to town. Everybody got a dick, unibrows, boobs, hairy warts. We would

be crying laughing. We at some point put out a poster
where we did that to ourselves. We defaced ourselves by
drawing dicks in our mouths and adding Bozo hair and
unibrows to our faces. We knew somebody else was going
to do it, so we did it to ourselves first. That's what I
would do if I had a Sharpie.

Traveling internationally was always full of surprises. One cold, wet winter morning, we were bleary-eyed from the show the night before and super-cranky at having woken up extra early because of the especially long-ass drive we had that day to get to some other German city. (For a country that's not that big, it seemed endless. It was one of the biggest markets in Europe, so no matter how small the city, there was always an offer to book a show. We joked that Germany was the Ohio of Europe because that leg of the tour and drive was never-ending.) As we sped down the Autobahn that morning, we noticed a van in the next lane keeping pace with us. Like our van, it too was stuffed with humans, gear, and luggage. *That's gotta be another band!* It was always kind of exciting to cross paths with fellow freaks on the road. It made us feel less alone in foreign territories. This van was purposely driving close to us.

> **GINA:** I could see a bunch of really big, hairy dudes smoking
> blunts, downing beers, and doing shots, lifting their
> bottles up to us, smiling, going, "Cheers, mate!" WTF,
> it was 7 a.m.! We hadn't even had coffee yet! They began
> to shuffle in their seats and then boom! Pressed hams
> against each one of their windows—an entire vehicle of
> ass cracks and naked hairy butts mooning us at 90 mph
> on the Autobahn.

Velcome to Chermany! What a sight to behold! We were awed. Who were these people?! We all pulled over at the next rest area to formally meet. The band was Portland's legendary Poison Idea. Our European tours were overlapping, so from then on, we spent the next few weeks running into each other, attending their shows on nights off, etc. We became fast friends. After all, we are the *Luna*chicks and they did offer up some impressive moons.

Not all interactions were as cheerful. Sometimes we had to stop at two or three machine-gun-guarded borders in a single day, and there was no being waved through. No border cop *ever* took a look at us and figured, "You guys are all right, keep driving." Wasn't happening. We were searched regularly. It was nerve-racking seeing guards walking around with all those automatic weapons. There was never anything bad in the van, but it certainly was an interesting search for those guards.

SINDI: All the stage props! We were driving around with rubber
    chickens, giant flies, Theo's big plastic bones—I can't
    even imagine what the border police thought. But we got
    some fans out of it—some of the guards made it onto our
    guest list.

The only band that had it rougher at customs was Gwar. When we toured with them, we met their entourage at the border and watched as guards pulled out their enormous latex demon costumes with three-foot-long dicks. We thought we had it bad, but those guys, whew. They made us look like a bunch of grannies traveling to go have tea on the other side of the border. We loved that band *so much*. Talk about family. They were good people, and there were like twenty-five of them! We really felt they were a kindred spirit. Some of our most cherished memories in the whole world are from when we'd be in Richmond, Virginia, where Gwar is from, tripping on acid, driving around in pickup trucks, and skinny-dipping in the quarry in the middle of the night.

When Gwar were on *The Joan Rivers Show*, which taped in New York, we met up with them, got wasted, slept in their hotel, stayed up all night, and made sure we were in the front row of the audience in the same clothes we wore the night before. Ah, memories.

Gwar wasn't the only band crossing international borders with large genital prosthetics. We had plenty of experience with that too. We got a lot of laughs out of Becky's big double-dong dildo. She'd pretend it was a microphone and she was a talk show host. She'd be like, "So, Squid, what do you have to say about cheese doodles?"

```
SQUID: Becky's dildo needs its own chapter. Border guards were
       always pulling it out of her bag and talking about it
       like it was a conversation piece. Happened all the time.
 THEO: One time a really cranky female border guard started
       going through our bags. She got to Becky's bag and
       pulled out the giant dildo. Then she dropped her keys
       into Becky's bag—I'm not sure it wasn't intentional—and
       started really going through Becky's stuff and found her
       leather chaps and whatever else she had. My eyes were
       popping out of my face watching this all go down while
       trying desperately not to guffaw out loud.
```

Touring was often a test of our health and will. There was a period of many, many years where it was unheard of for us to get a hotel, and whenever we did have enough and sprung for a hotel, we all piled into one room. But the majority of our tours were spent sleeping on floors in the homes of strangers, some of whom would be tripping on acid and threatening to murder people in the middle of the night.

Here's how it usually went: We'd be at the club getting ready for our set, and we'd meet some speed freak with three teeth in his head and who looked about as stable as a three-legged stool . . . and we'd learn we were staying at his house that night because a friend of a friend set it up for us. Great. Can't wait to see the accommodations.

One such guy who hosted us in upstate New York was this older Johnny Thunders type who looked like the crypt keeper from *Tales from the Crypt*. His son had a friend who was over who had recently gotten out of jail and was staying there. His friend's name was PCPete. This guy was craaaaacked out or on angel dust, had tattooed eyelids, and looked like he'd probably killed somebody(s). It was the middle of winter, the ground was frozen. Mattresses were spread out on the floor in the living room.

We put our sleeping bags on top of the mattresses and huddled together, except for Becky who was in an adjoining room. We were trying to sleep while PCPete was talking about grinding up glass and putting it in someone's eyeballs. We were quietly freaking the fuck out. Becky had found a pan or a pot and was standing behind a door in the kitchen, waiting for someone to start screaming so she could run out and hit the guy over the head. We were terrified and started thinking about the logistics of how we could all get out of the house without drawing attention to ourselves, and then debating if we could all fit in the van to sleep without freezing to death—which we did. Barely.

> **THEO:** I went to sleep in the van sitting up and crying, and I woke up in the van sitting up and crying.
>
> **SQUID:** And the whole time I'm thinking, "This is just great. I love being in a band!!" Believe me, we weren't in any way prudish, but this was WAY over the top. Terrifying. Okay, you got me, I choose not to be sleeping in a room with a hallucinating, jail-breaked psychopath murderer. Call me a party pooper. Not a safe situation.

Furthermore, out of any band we knew, we had the worst experiences with vans and transportation. It was like a curse. Nearly every tour involved some fiasco with a deathtrap on four wheels, and Europe was the site of some of our more ridiculous breakdowns. We'd fly overnight, get zero sleep on the plane, and arrive tripping with exhaustion. Most of the time, we'd be greeted by a stranger who was about to take all five of our lives in their hands. Within an hour, without fail, we'd be stranded and/or have barely avoided death.

> **GINA:** A new tour manager picked us up at Heathrow. We piled into his van at 6 a.m., sleep-deprived. We headed north on the highway toward the next show. We fell asleep only to be woken by the van bumping into the side rails as it drove off the highway. The new guy fell asleep at

> the wheel, and we were headed straight into a ditch
> at 70 mph. Luckily, he woke up and swerved back onto
> the highway before we all crashed and burned, but holy
> shit, that was fucking close, dude! Reminds me of an-
> other one of our drivers. After being on tour with her
> for a while, we found out she only had one working eye.

This cycle has repeated itself so many times, the events blend together. One time, we were driving through the Scottish countryside, passing beautiful fields and mountains and tons of sheep on the side of the road. As we gazed out the window, admiring how green the landscape was, all of a sudden, the van made the loudest, most horrifying sound. We were hurled forward and then came to a startling stop.

The engine dropped out of the van and sat smoking in the middle of the road.

What the FUCK.

There we were, stranded, with sheep running around in the grass. There's something about those situations where you're just so fucked, it's actually freeing and you have fleeting moments of clarity and peace. *At least we didn't explode! There's a lot worse things that could've happened! NOW WHAT?*

We were lying in the grass on the side of the road and chased our sheep friends around for hours. Our driver went and found a pay phone, and someone picked us up and took us to an inn above a pub in a tiny one-street town. You can only imagine the stir we caused: a bunch of freaks from the States come to this quaint little Scottish village. It was like the movie *To Wong Foo, Thanks for Everything! Julie Newmar*, when the drag queens broke down in a conservative Podunk town. We were the drag queens.

Somehow, the whole village found out we had unexpectedly arrived. Throngs of people filled the pub, and everyone was asking us, "What team do you play?" And we were like, "What? What team? Uh, I don't know? What kind of sports are you into?" They were asking "What *time* do you play?" Ha! We gained a bunch of new fans that day in true Lunachicks style.

The closest we ever came to luxury accommodations was touring Europe in a minibus. All that space—and bunk beds! One problem: there was no air-conditioning, and it just so happened that we were driving through Germany during a massive heat wave. The locals were saying, "Zis iss zee hottest summah in Chermany zince 1872" or whatever. We lay in our bunks, night after night, sweating ourselves into altered states of consciousness. It didn't have a bathroom, and we were stuck in it for such long stretches. That's another reason we wished for a bus—the convenience of an actual toilet.

THEO: That minibus made me feral. The world basically became my toilet. I dropped trou whenever and wherever I had to go. We'd be on a long drive, and we'd stop to get something to eat, and I wouldn't feel like walking to the bathroom, so I'd piss in the parking lot next to our vehicle. Right in the middle of it, with people and families all around me. I remember walking through a city, and I was like, "Oh, there's a bush, I'm going to go pee behind it." I turned into a cavewoman. Not a proud moment in my life but just plain truthful. Also, I think I still have a scar on my back from the repeated times during that tour when I scraped my spine while trying to get into one of the 900-degree bunks. I would wake up in a sopping soggy pool of sweat every damn *MORGEN*.

SINDI: Theo was inarguably the master of peeing in a cup. She could do it anywhere, anytime—in full makeup. I have photo documentation of some of the cup pees. The peeing happened in the woods, on the side of the road, everywhere. We'd be stopped at a gas station or truck stop, but instead of lining up for the bathroom, Theo would decide to drop trou and let it happen.

Occasionally, human error was to blame for our travel fails. Back in ye olden times, we toured without cell phones, GPS, or the internet (how was that even possible!?). To get to the clubs, we had to pull over at a pay phone, call the club, and handwrite the directions on a piece of paper. One such time, we were speeding down the highway through the middle of the desert with all of the windows down, taking in the summer breeze.

GINA: I was co-piloting, directions in hand, and went to rest my elbow on the windowsill, which, to my surprise, was hot as hell from the beating sun. I yelped when my skin hit the metal, causing the directions to fly out of my hand, directly out of the window, and swiftly vanish into the distance. FUCK!

The next pay phone wasn't for another seventy-five miles. Looks like we're gonna be late to the gig tonight.

Another time, at 2 a.m. in the middle of Buttfuck, USA, we were lost, tired, and had to pee. We saw a sign for a Days Inn, but they were more expensive than the motels we usually stayed at. *Ugh, just do it! We have to stop already!* We pulled off the highway out of the pitch-blackness. The Inn's fluorescent-lit entrance was an oasis in the desert and had us salivating with visions of clean sheets and beds. The carport signaled luxury. Was there a valet too? Wonder if they have vending—

SCREEEEEEEEEEEEEEECH!!!! THUMP, CRAAAANK!

Holy shit, what the fuck was that??

OMG, OMG, what just happened!

We hit something!

We're stuck!

Back up! Back up!

I can't!

Something's on top of us!

Squid gunned the engine.

SCRAAAAAAAPE!

We looked out of the rear window to see the carport leaning over to one side in a crumpled mass of aluminum. *Oh shit, that's right, we have the high-top van on this tour. OOPS. Anyone see us? No? Let's get the fuck out of here, like now! Guess we're not stopping tonight. Back to the highway we go.*

CHAPTER 17

BOTTOMS UP

In the summer of 1992, we headed back to England to promote *Binge and Purge*, which was already out over there. Our first tour of the UK with Dinosaur Jr. definitely laid a foundation for us, because when we returned this time, we discovered we had some pretty die-hard fans, especially in London. We'd play shows and get three encores. Three. We were stunned. Not every member of the band was thrilled about this.

THEO: There was a brawl backstage after our first show of the tour. The audience was screaming and stomping their feet for an encore. Becky didn't want to go back out, so we were fighting backstage. It was so intense and crazy—cinematic, even. Becky tried to attack Gina, a table almost flipped over, and I was holding Becky back from trying to hit Gina. It was full-on mayhem.

GINA: Becky was dopesick, as was usually the case after any international flight. Not wanting to try and smuggle drugs across borders during international tours became a de facto opportunity for Becky, then later Squid, to get clean. This meant that the first week of shows were usually hell on earth. Our first show was in Birmingham and Becky was really dopesick. Despite that, the audience loved us and when we walked offstage, they pounded their fists on the waist-high stage demanding an encore. Our dressing room was behind a door just off of the stage. While back there discussing which song to play, Becky threw a full-on tantrum saying she was done for the night and that she refused to do another song. When I protested, she underscored her point by kicking my guitar over onto the floor. WTF!? DON'T TOUCH THE AXE, MAN! I pushed her, so she went to slap me and then somehow we all ended up in a dogpile on the floor yelling, kicking, screaming, and spitting. In all of the commotion, the backstage door flung open and we all tumbled out onto the stage. I remember lying on the floor with the band on top of me looking out onto the audience, who were right there just ten feet away witnessing this odd brawling mass of tangled, glittered, tattooed, spandex-ed rage. They just looked so perplexed. You want an encore? How's that for a fucking encore!

And that's how the tour *started*.

Paul Smith and Blast First were no longer in the picture, and neither was Paul's expense account. In order to save money on hotels, we had a home base—a houseboat on the Thames River. The owner of our booking agency in London knew somebody who had this houseboat, and they were willing to let us take it over for a month or so for free. Every night, we would drive to a different city, play a show, and return to the boat.

Our tour manager in England was a guy named Dean Kennedy, an old-school punk who had toured with a ton of English punk bands. He was the father of three little girls and also became our tour dad. Along with Dean was Oggins, aka Ogs, who was the drummer in Peter and the Test Tube Babies. He sold the merch at our shows. Ogs would get so drunk and pass out with his clothes and shoes still on. There were times we had to pull him out of the gutter because he was so wasted. He was filthy. When we were in Scotland, his girlfriend was with him and he finally bathed. Swear to God, he turned a different color. He was so dirty because he hadn't touched water in so long, and afterward, he was pink like a baby gerbil. We were like, "Oh my god, is that you!?" He was such a sweet guy even if he was a bit woeful. His catchphrase was "It's a shit life. See you at the bott-um."

The boat wasn't fancy, but it wasn't disgusting. It was just sort of fine. (Did we mention it was free?) For some reason, a few door handles were replaced with spoons. If you wanted to open or close a certain door, you had to futz with a spoon. Oh, the glamour.

Something to know about sleeping on a houseboat on the Thames: in the middle of the night, the river's tide goes out and the whole boat tips. We slid from one end of the boat to the other in our sleeping bags. In the afternoon when we woke up, we were all pressed up against the wall in a pile like little hamsters.

In addition to naturally occurring hazards, Becky had acquired an independently wealthy girlfriend who was taking care of her. Bad move. We told our manager Jane that Becky was forbidden to bring anything (i.e., drugs) or have anything (i.e., drugs) sent. Becky was furious, but Jane eventually calmed her down. Then Jane left after a few days. Becky started drinking, which made her violent and unpredictable. One night on the ride back to the houseboat, she got drunk in the van. Sindi was playing a tape of some SoCal punk band, and Becky was yelling at Sindi, "Turn that shit off!"

BECKY: We had different taste in music.

THEO: Becky would show up for a photo shoot in a Grateful Dead shirt, and we'd be like, "Uh, no."

BECKY: I had spent a really long time when I got into hardcore only wanting to listen to hardcore and being a punk and saying, like, "Fuck this and fuck that" to shit that I grew up listening to. At some point as I got older, I was like, "You know what? Fuck that shit. I like everything. I don't fuckin' care."

Finally, Becky snapped, flew into a rabid fit, and madly attacked the speaker in the back of the van, punching it over and over in a rage until it smashed into bits. There we were, driving on the highway, like, "You're gonna hafta pay for that. Hope you enjoyed it."

When we arrived back at the boat, it was around four in the morning. We stood on the dock with our mounds of luggage and instruments, looking at the boat. Everyone was cranky and exhausted, and we just wanted to get on board and go to sleep.

That didn't happen.

In order to get onto the boat, we had to haul all our shit along the dock, go down some stairs, walk along a boardwalk and then along a narrow plank that led onto the boat. Theo was among the first people to successfully navigate the maze and make it on board. Becky had other plans. She didn't feel like lugging her huge duffel bag all the way around the dock, so she yelled to Theo that she was going to throw her bag across the dock for Theo to catch. That meant Becky's big, heavy duffel bag would have to clear a good ten- or fifteen-foot gap between the dock and the boat.

THEO: Even though I was half-asleep, I knew it was the worst idea I ever heard. I shook my head no. Becky decided she was going to do it anyway. So she took her bag and chucked it in my direction. And what do you think happened? It hit the side of the boat and splashed into the river. Nice one.

The second the bag hit the water, we all doubled over. We were laughing so hard, we were crying—stomach-cramp-peeing-our-pants hilariousness—while Becky's screaming, "No! No! Help!" The funniest part was watching Theo's eyes get wider and wider as the huge bag sailed through the air, thudded against the boat, and flopped into the Thames. Ogs had to get a rake and fish this soaking-wet duffel bag out of the river before the tide carried it away. We were still laughing when we were trying to fall asleep.

A couple of days later, Becky had started sleeping with some gorgeous blonde British chick who worked at our booking agency. One night, Becky brought her back to the houseboat. A few of us heard a noise, so we popped our heads up to see what it was. Turned out to be the girl sleepwalking butt-naked onto the deck outside. Our eyes nearly fell out of our heads. She walked off our boat and onto the neighbors' boat. (The neighbors were an old couple, and they fucking hated us, of course.) She proceeded to steal a coat from them and then make her way back onto our boat.

BECKY: She worked for whatever promoter was helping us at the time. She was the girlfriend of the singer of a really famous band from that time and was so, so, so fuckin' hot. I guess her job was to take care of the band, so she took us out to a club. We hit it off. Big-time. So after, I was like, "Fuck it, just come back to the boat. I think everybody's asleep." We had killer sex, and I guess in the middle of the night, I think it was Gina who saw this girl walking around naked on the other boat.

That was part one.

Part two: Back on the boat, the girl reached between her legs, yanked out her tampon, and threw it onto the neighbor's boat. It landed on a little ledge by their window where they would never see it, but we sure did. It stayed on that ledge the entire time we were living on the houseboat. It turned black as the weeks went on, so fucking gross. This chick then fell asleep in the stolen coat, so we had to sneak back onto the neighbors' boat in the morning to return it.

BECKY: I only heard about it the next day. I was like, "Hey, where'd you get that coat?" I didn't hear about the tampon thing at all.

The biggest show of that tour was the Reading Festival, the first big festival we ever did. *Oh my gawd, it's so legendary, we can't believe it!* We drove out to god-knows-where and had to go through all this security. It was 1992, and the main stage lineup that year was wild: Nirvana, Public Enemy, Nick Cave, Public Image Ltd, PJ Harvey. We played the Session Tent in front of probably five thousand people. We weren't as well known as the big names, but it was still great.

> **THEO:** We were in a tent getting ready, and I was wearing a pink curly wig. I was like, "This is it, we are clowns. We are fucking clowns in a tent, and this is the circus." I'd always dreamed of this. The day had finally come.

It was incredible to poke around behind the scenes and see all those bands. It was like in *Wayne's World* when Wayne and Garth are backstage at the Alice Cooper concert and they kept showing their all-access passes to everyone. We were like, "See?! We really do belong here!"

We went back on the final day of Reading to see more bands, including L7. God forbid the organizers let them and us play on the same day. Nirvana also played. It was right when they were first gigantic. We climbed a fence next to the stage and watched the crowd during "Smells Like Teen Spirit." Fifty thousand bodies, as far as the eye could see, pogoing on the same downbeat under the floodlights—that was really something to behold. The whole day was loads of fun, so much so that when it came time to return to the houseboat, we had a tough time trying to pull Becky off of L7's tour bus. She was so pissed after being on their bus and then having to stuff back into our shitty van. As we drove away, she seethed, "L7 has a fucking tour bus, but I have to sit here with you assholes in a van; why didn't I choose them?!" Haahaha.

CHAPTER 18

GIRL BANNED

While we loved all the hijinks on the Thames, we were battling a different kind of tide change. See, our first trip to the UK was full of nice hotels and back-to-back press meetings where we juggled high-profile interviews and photo shoots for what seemed like days. We expected the same royal treatment the second time around, but it became very apparent that that wasn't happening. Our eyes were yanked wide open and we experienced the music industry very differently.

From the beginning, our tour itinerary didn't look right. The route had us skipping prominent cities, driving out of our way, and generally sent us all over the place. We'd say, "Why can't we play X city? It makes more sense geographically for the tour." We heard plenty of vague excuses and brush-offs, but never any clear answers. We were being given the runaround and couldn't figure out why. Finally, it all came out one night while we were sitting downstairs on the houseboat. Our booking agent laid it out for us.

Hole and Babes in Toyland were touring Europe at the same time as us. Apparently, some clubs weren't willing to have bands with women in them play within a month of each other. We'd never before heard of anything like this happening. Growing up in New York City, we saw plenty of great bands that had women in them. It wasn't unusual to see a girl onstage. So what the fuck were these clubs even talking about? They wouldn't book multiple bands with women in them? Why? What's the issue? Look at the Runaways! They were the coolest band ever! Who wouldn't want *more* of THAT?? There were four hundred guy bands playing that month. Do we need to point out how many Nirvana and Pearl Jam clones were all over the radio during those years? But the clubs filled their "girl-band quota," so they wouldn't book any more? What the actual *fuck?*

We were so naive. Bands that featured women were often seen as a novelty act—not real musicians—and weren't given the same access as dudes who did the exact same thing. It was as if these clubs viewed bands that had women in them as this one particular thing. Like, "Sorry, we already booked a Bon Jovi cover band this month, so you'll have to wait until next month if you want to play here."

We didn't believe shit like this actually happened until it actually happened. That was the first time we heard "Sorry, no thanks, we don't want you because we already had a girl band, so we can't book you." It wouldn't be the last time. And yes, those were the actual words we were told. They didn't see this as sexist. To them, it was business as usual. Why beat around the bush? Pun intended.

There were venues that flat-out rejected us. Promoters wouldn't let us play a club because Babes in Toyland had played there a week earlier, or shall we be so blunt as to say because we had vaginas and they had vaginas. Only a certain vagina limit per month in these venues was acceptable to these promoters. Doors were slamming in our face. Full-blown unapologetic sexism at its finest.

SINDI: People were turning us away from clubs and magazines because they had filled their quota. That was not a hunch; that was a fact that was plainly stated as if it were reasonable: "What do you want us to do? Repeat the same shit over and over?" And then clubs would put up promo posters that said "all-girl-band music," as if that were a musical genre. What does that even mean? We'd be put on bills with other female acts simply due to gender, regardless of whether the music made sense as an

```
event. That was very, very frustrating. Those were the
facts. And it wasn't just that UK tour; we encountered
that throughout our career. It was always there.
```

Then there was the press. One magazine was supposed to feature us in a big spread, but because it had already done a piece on another band with women in the previous issue, we got relegated to a little blurb. And when certain media outlets *did* write about us, they had an agenda. Interviewers would ask us what we thought of other women in bands, as if they wanted us to be at odds with each other. Like, "Oh, girls! They must hate each other!" But it wasn't like that at all. We were psyched to be around other badass rockers like ourselves. We couldn't help but wonder if every woman in a band got asked these same questions. And did the press ever ask Nirvana what they thought about the guys in Soundgarden and Mudhoney? What the fuck's wrong with you? Fuck off.

Back home in the States, we started experiencing the same kind of sexist bullshit that greeted us on tour, and it lasted for years. More than one record label, radio station, and club said, "We already have a girl band signed to the label." "We already have one girl band on our playlist." "We already had a girl band here this month."

In 1996 the huge radio station K-Rock (WXRK) in NYC switched to an alt-rock format. The day it was announced, Go-Kart Records (the label we were on from '95 onward) owner Greg Ross raced up to the station with a package for Howard Stern and Kevin Weatherly, who was the station director of KROQ in LA, which was arguably the most influential rock station maybe ever. Greg followed up with loads of calls. He told us that when he finally got Kevin on the phone, Kevin said he was a Lunachicks fan but there was no way he could play us, and if the station played more than one girl band at a time, the ratings went down. At that moment, KROQ had Hole in rotation and couldn't even play No Doubt (or maybe that was reversed). When Greg tried to persuade him, Kevin again pointed to the data: more than one girl band equals a drop in ratings. We encountered that shit time and time again and responded appropriately.

GINA: Sometime in the mid-'90s, Theo held up a KROQ banner onstage and said, "Pure KROQ, pure cock rock!" because they wouldn't play us and then rrrrrrriiiippppp went that banner right in half. Welp, guess they're definitely not gonna play us now!

It was really extreme in certain areas of the country. Some radio stations wouldn't even play bands with female vocalists. Not "We already have one," but more like "We don't want any." A few years later, Fat Mike from NOFX told us that "girl bands" just didn't sell records.

The whole mindset was bizarre to us. The women we knew in punk and rock bands were take-no-shit types. We were all carving our way forward more aggressively than people were used to seeing. We wanted nothing more than for women to form bands to help bulldoze people's belief that rock 'n' roll's just for boys. But when we actually got out there and started touring and the clubs turned us away because another "girl band" beat us to the punch and nabbed the one slot that was up for grabs, it became clear that not everyone felt the way we did. Instead, we were presented with a kind of *Hunger Games*–type scenario, a deprivation exercise, one in which guy bands never had to participate. Our mission as a band and a sisterhood became even more solidified: take up a fuck-ton of space in order to make room for every woman who wants in.

SINDI: Friendship was the most important thing. Women are and were pitted against each other, but we didn't let that happen. Like, these are our girls! We want success for all of us and the best for all of us. What one of us achieves, we all achieve. Neither we nor any of the other women on our level had a feeling of competition because that would've sucked. In reality, it really was sisterhood. L7 brought us out to play shows with them. They helped us out. And when we were booked to play with other females where it made sense and the music was similar, it was great! When people on the outside tried to pile that kind of competitive shit up, we weren't buying it. We didn't give it any sort of time at all. We shot that shit down because that was not what we're about.

――――――――――――

As much as we believe in the power of sisterhood, we were helpless when it came to Becky's addiction. Nothing could have saved that relationship. Drugs put her on a severe decline. Not only was her using getting completely out of hand, she just didn't seem to enjoy being in the band anymore. Looking back, that could've also been attributed to her worsening addiction.

BECKY: When Squid and I broke up, at one point, it was like, "Well, okay, I'm gonna quit the band." In my mind, I went through that. But I didn't move to Brooklyn to be with Squid, I moved to Brooklyn to play with the Lunachicks. So I needed to separate that. But it was really hard, seeing her with other guys. If I hadn't already been a really bad drug addict, I would've become worse, and I think that's part of why I did maybe become more into drugs. The band would tell me, "We're going on tour, you better stop, you better get it under control." Yeah, yeah, yeah. I'd get on the plane and I'd have a ten-bag-a-day habit. Whatever I had to do to get through. I still love Squid, and I know she truly loved me. And I fucked it up. I fucked it up for a lot of reasons.

SQUID: Becky had a new girlfriend in about three hours.

GINA: At the time, I didn't see Becky's addiction as getting any better. The idea of doing an intervention ... we were so young, and I don't think I even knew what an intervention was. And I was so angry at her. On top of the drugs, her moodiness was really intense and made her hard to be around. She was resentful of us, and condescending. I get it, in hindsight. She was older and we were young, and we were fucking brats. But she was just constantly putting us down. I loved Becky, she was funny and great, but I also wanted to strangle her half the time. I was so worried she was gonna overdose. Thank god she came through in the end.

THEO: The last show we played with Becky made it very clear that things had run their course. When we parted ways with her, I was relieved that we didn't have to deal with her addiction, resentment, and out-of-control emotions anymore. She came to see us play in San Francisco a year or so later and she was still a mess. I remember hugging her goodbye after the show and thinking she was definitely going to die so I better hug her a little extra. But she made it, and I am so glad she did.

We reached our absolute breaking point on Halloween night, when we were playing a show with Murphy's Law. We dressed up as old men and had bald caps on. The house was packed, and during our set Becky was so high that she played everything half-time. We knew we had to move on without her.

SQUID: I thought I might murder her between songs. Nothing in life sucks worse than being sabotaged by your drummer in front of a packed house, except maybe add being in a bald cap and giant mustache.

BECKY: First of all, I hated Murphy's Law because Syd had had a thing with the singer. Once some guy has fucked the girl you're in love with, you don't want to be in the same room as them. But a lot of the things I did back then were because I was confused about my own gender dysphoria or whatever. I knew the way women were treated and I refused to be treated like that, therefore I was

completely embracing my masculine side—but never re-
jecting that I was a woman or denying it—and was the
most masculine woman I could possibly be. I was an addict in almost a competitive sense; I was gonna drink
every guy under the table. I was so proud that I drank
Gibby Haynes from Butthole Surfers under the table when
they came to play in Brussels and I was in La Muerte.
I would black out and start fights with men. I must've
thought of myself as a big, tough guy, so when I got with
a girl, I had to be that guy, because that's who they
must have seen. I didn't get that people just liked me
because of me. Because Lunachicks were my band and were
like family, they got the worst of it. Yeah, I remember them dressing like old men, and I think I thought
it was stupid. I had enough of the shenanigans and felt
that our music was good enough on its own. I stopped
seeing it through their eyes. I don't really remember
the show, but by then I was just like, "This is so not
fucking funny or cool. Just fucking play." I think that
was probably my mean, fucked-up-junkie attitude.

It wasn't until I got sober that I realized I had
taken all those bad masculine traits and magnified
them as a defense mechanism when I would drink. I was
horrified. I can't tell you why I had that mean streak.
Thank god I got in recovery and realized I had gotten it all wrong. People that I knew in other bands
in New York that I totally respected would try to give
me a hand and take me to a meeting and show me what
was up. I was always stoned, but I'd go and listen to
them. Eventually, around '96, I ended up in a homeless
shelter in San Francisco. Some opportunity presented
itself to come to LA because a band wanted to play
with me, and they said they would only play with me if
I got clean. So I came to LA and began to get clean. I

started to see people in the [recovery] rooms in LA, like people in bands that I had met who were my idols. I was among my angels. When I saw these people at meetings, I was like, "Holy shit, *he's* here?! Well he's fuckin' cool as shit. If he can do this, I can do this!" And I did it! I guess everybody's life happens the way it's supposed to happen.

CHAPTER 19

SQUID + DRUGS, PART 2

SQUID: When I was around twenty-one, I got into an accident on my motorcycle and hurt my knee pretty bad. My ba-dass girlfriend bike mechanic showed up to the house with a big plastic ziplock bag full of Tylenol 4s. That's a shit-ton of pharmaceutical dope. Jeez, they were great. I started eating those things like candy. I was perfectly happy, finally, for once. Right around the same time, I got dumped, hard. This guy I thought was in love with me decided he was more in love with his *wife*. (Uhhhh, your what?) I got the dumping by way of a long-distance call, no less—heyyy, wait a minute, which one of us is paying for this? I was out. Thanks for all the blow jobs, see ya around. I hung up the phone with one hand and picked up that giant ziplock bag with the other. It was like, "Okay. I'm just gonna do this now." The rest is herstory.

Crawling to walking to running, truthfully I couldn't wait to stick a needle in my arm. All my dreams would soon come true. By twenty-two, people were already calling me "junkie." That little motorcycle accident had landed me a settlement: $50K minus lawyer fees, that's 33,000 dollaroonies. I was young, broken, and loaded. Now I can stay high for-EVER, in style. I bought myself this incredible 1964 Chevy Nova, four-door, off a little old lady in Bay Ridge named Veronica Stalupi who needed a cataract operation. Nineteen hundred ORIGI-NAL miles, garage-kept, mint, aqua-blue with a match-ing interior. This car even had the original tires on it. I loved that car, it became my own private shooting gallery on wheels. Me, wasted, 3 a.m., lost in Queens (again), driving clueless *up* the *off* ramp on the BQE, headlights coming *at* me, whoooops, *reverse! Reverse!* Oh shit, and I forgot to turn my lights on! I have memories of trying to find a vein while maneuvering that big ol' steering wheel. I'd be tied up with a needle hanging outta my arm just out of sight while I'm cruising past cop cars on Ave C. Extreme sports of the lost and idi-otic. The more insane, the better.

I started dating this sweetheart of a guy I re-ally liked. Let's call him X. He was a soft-spoken, weed-smoking, good-natured little thug from the Wu-Tang-infamous Stapleton projects on Staten Island. He refused to identify as white due to being seriously Sicilian, mostly mistaken for Puerto Rican, and was uncharacteristically obsessed with the Clash as much as Brand Nubian. He also loved the Lunachicks, and he really loved the absolute shit outta me. No stranger to excitement—he and his buddies used to run and rob drug spots back on Staten Island as teenagers—but he never did heroin and he looked down on junkies. Love, you know, is a powerful thing. Within six months we were both strung out and made the prudent decision to join our junkie powers in matrimony.

GINA: I was not impressed by X.

THEO: I was like, "What? You're dating **him**?" And then Squid said she was going to get married. And I was like,

"WHAAAT?" She was like, "I want to have a baby." I re-member telling her, "I WILL PERSONALLY ABORT YOUR BABY." No fucking way. At their pin-eyed wedding, there's a photo of me that was taken when the officiant was like, "Does anyone have any reason why these two should not get married?" I looked directly at the camera, and the photographer snapped the picture.

SQUID: The plan was to skip down to city hall and ruin my life in privacy, but my dad caught wind of it and decided we needed to have a proper wedding, in the backyard. Oyyyy, the drammmma. I cracked very early on as the de facto wedding planner and started getting high more than ever. My parents thought it would be a great idea to send me and X down to Jamaica on a proper honeymoon, and then I had this amazing idea. We could go down there to this gorgeous little beachfront paradise and kick dope! Then come back all squeaky clean and live happily ever after. "No, listen, honey, this is going to be SO GREAT!" Cut to day three—fucking dying, kill me, kill me faster. Puking, shitting, shaking, sweating, freezing, stabbing pain, crushing fever, my skin hurt, my hair hurt. "Bungalow" translation: grass hut, open air, 90 degrees, 100 percent humidity, swarms of mos-quitoes, sand in the bed everywhere like sharp little rocks on top of sandpaper sheets. No sleep for seventy-two hours, just turning, twisting, flipping, flopping, burning in everlasting relentless eternal hell.

Then came even more amazing ideas; light bulbs were flashing one after the other for me and X. Cut to the chase, we were in the back of a car driving for some time on a dirt road through dense jungle, and this was where it finally hit me: they are never going to find my body. This was like all the collective stupidity of one hundred thousand lifetimes jam-packed into one really seriously bad decision. At some point, we arrived at a scary abandoned building. I followed suit inside a decrepit bathroom stall, waiting to be executed. Much to my surprise, we didn't get murdered and the next thing I knew, we were back in our shitty bungalow with a bag of drugs. Let's get this party started! I had never seen a syringe the size of a football; maybe that's what they use on horses? But that's what we got, and whatever the hell we just spent all our money on, it didn't look anything like heroin, but hey, strangers in a strange land. I was SO sick at this point, I insisted on going first. I somehow managed to manhandle that giant foot-long needle into my arm and SWOOOOOOOSHHHHHHHBUZZZZZZZZZ- BWAHHHWAHHWAHHHH ... vomit ... "Oh crap. I think that's crystal meth." Shooting crystal is a feeling so wrong it can never be right. But in the absence of immediate agony from withdrawals, we diligently banged it all.

In the brief sweet spot, we had the wherewithal to formulate a new and improved plan. We quickly changed our plane tickets, packed our bags, and headed for the airport. Top on the list of new concerns was definitely getting through security with this one giant disgusting lopsided dreadlock that was now my whole head of hair. I guess I hadn't really looked in the mirror for a few days with the whole not-feeling-well thing. Anyway, I don't know how we got on and off that airplane, but we did. We landed in New York, went straight to the dope spot, back to our apartment, and were shooting up on the couch before we even had our coats off.

Whew! That was a nightmare! Let's never do that again!

Then I noticed my arm felt kinda sore, hmm. I took off my coat and looked down at a bulging abscess the size of a golf ball. Shit. So we shot some more dope for good luck (in the other arm) and went to the ER. The nurse looked at my arm and looked at me: "Good thing you got here today. If you waited until tomorrow, we'd be amputating your arm." I have played that tape over in my head a few times, a few different ways, the one where I *didn't* get on that plane with the singular-dreadlock hairdo. Sindi always said I was like a cat with nine-plus-elevendybillion lives. And yet, enough was never enough.

SINDI: I can say exactly when I started worrying about Squid's using. We were in Europe. I remember getting there, and she was out of commission for the first two days. We did all of the interviews and press-related stuff without her. She knew she was going to have to kick on the tour, so she took tons of pills or whatever she did, and she shut down. We were left holding a sack. The only reason she didn't get kicked out of the band at that time was because we were so tight, like a family.

SQUID: Touring was becoming a logistical nightmare. I was around people who wished I was dead because junkies are annoying and I was ruining their lives. I'd be kicking dope in the van every time we left NYC, or I would be trying to rush into bathrooms at every gas station to get high. In every sense of the word I was useless. It sucked. I couldn't move fast enough and struggled to carry my bags and gear. Everybody hated me. *"Pick up your shit, LET'S GO!"* The girls were damned if they were going to move my shit because I was dopesick.

It was hell, especially in a foreign country. I was living my dream in every capacity, and I wanted to die. I would be so sick I could not stand up during sound-check. But no matter how close to death I felt, the instant we started playing, I didn't feel sick. It was gone, replaced by a numbing wall of sound. And the instant the music would stop, it would all come rushing back like the Black Death. Theo would be talking to the crowd between songs, and I'd be like, *"Oh my god, hurry up I'm gonna shit my pants staaarrrt already!"* because the pain would be crushing me. As soon as I heard *"Onetwothreefour!!!"* I was okay, popped back into the happy rock 'n' roll white light.

THEO: It's very painful to watch your friend go through that and become a junkie. When she first started using, I noticed she was high at a rehearsal. She promised up and down that it was the last time. It was so innocent, though. I felt like, "Oh, she can make that decision and have control over it." Well, maybe she could have, but she didn't. Junkies are messy. We had a gig at the Middle East in Boston, and she disappeared after soundcheck. Showtime came around and she still wasn't there. Turns out she had gotten busted for shoplifting around the corner. She tried to steal a pair of pants. In order to get through a flight to Europe, she took so many Valiums on the plane that we practically had to carry her off of it. Then for all the press and interviews we had to do upon arrival, we propped her up like a rag doll. I was so angry, but I loved her so much and had a naive hope that she would get out of this somehow. So we all continued to put up with it.

SINDI: I always felt that Theo and Squid had this unconditional allowance. Squid could get away with anything, and Theo was gonna accept it, even if it was bad and hurting her. It was still going to be all right. I didn't have that unconditionality with Theo, and that was fucked up and it made for problems down the line. That imbalance of what's okay and what's not okay pissed me off.

I was never scared for Squid. I had a few friends like that; they could do the worst shit in the world, but they're gonna land on their feet and be all right. They weren't going to be the ones who died or got raped or whatever; they're gonna be okay. Even though you would think, "This is the end of the line for them," it never was. Squid was a very good friend, but I didn't like her then. It was sad, and it really did affect what we were doing. We had to drag a bag of fucking rocks with us through life sometimes when it should have been a good time.

CHAPTER 20

CHIP ENGLISH

When Becky was out, we had shows booked that we needed to honor, so we asked our friend Kate Schellenbach from Luscious Jackson to fill in. We adored her. She was even-keeled and caring, considerate, fun, professional . . . Kate was a dream. She wrote us a letter after the tour, with a section and a haiku for each of us. Kate was loyal to Luscious Jackson, otherwise we would have kept her forever.

We eventually found The One, though it took a minute. We auditioned drummers all day and were getting so bored. In between auditions, we decided we'd switch instruments and make a racket. When we were done, we walked out of the room and saw a note on the door that said, "Sorry, your music just isn't my style." They heard us playing so badly that it scared them off! Hilarious.

Fate's a funny thing. Early on, we auditioned Chip English, who was playing in a bunch of bands, including the very awesome Tomboys. We really liked Chip—and what a great name!—so we said, "Come join our band!" Chip said no. Ha! So we were like, "Well, why did you audition if you didn't want to join the band?!" Maybe we weren't good enough because we were just starting out.

CHIP: I did audition for them the first time, but because of all
the other bands I was in, I decided not to stay with the
Lunachicks, only to find out that they were doing really

well and touring. That was a big harrumph for me. Then years later, they needed someone to fill in on their next European and Japanese tours, and so that was me.

I was born in Kingston, Pennsylvania, in 19something-orother. I've got two sisters. One sister is about fourteen months older than me, and my other sister is five years younger. Both my parents are from Pennsylvania. My father, Don McCloskey, was Lithuanian. He was deaf from age sixteen and went to the School for the Deaf in New York City. He excelled at lipreading, so his deafness wasn't a hindrance on his life or career. When we spoke to him, we would over-enunciate the words. We also learned what I think is called the Boy Scout sign language—which is just the alphabet, not the Helen Keller kind of signing of words—so I never had any issue talking to him. He was a photographer for King's College and the local newspaper, the *Times Leader*, in Wilkes-Barre, Pennsylvania. I grew up with a huge darkroom/photography studio in my basement and would help my father print pictures.

My mother, Doris McHenry McCloskey, was Irish Scottish and a real stunning beauty. I mean, she had movie-star good looks and won the Mrs. Wilkes-Barre beauty pageant. I guess I'm proud. She was a stay-at-home mom and had dinner on the table every night when my father got home.

Their parenting gave me complete self-worth. My father taught me everything I know: He showed me how to change the oil in the car, check and top off the transmission fluid, stuff like that. And we would wrench on things, and we'd take apart and fix stuff. He would introduce me as his son, which made me so proud because people always said to him, "You have three daughters, wow!" but he would say, "Well, Chip is my son," and then he'd go on to explain all the things we did together.

The name Chip comes from when I was ten. We used to hop the fence on Saturdays at the football stadium down the street. One day, I had a running race with a friend, tripped over a step, and slammed my face on the concrete. I ran home and my mom was horrified to see my blown-up lip and my front tooth cracked in half. After that, I was known as Chippy because of my tooth. When I got older, I thought Chippy was too kid-sounding, so I decided to go with the more mature-sounding Chip.

I had a really relaxed, idyllic childhood. I always called my neighborhood "Brady Bunch land": main street, red lights and stop signs, house/driveway/house/driveway/house/driveway. We had a big backyard, and I rode my Sting-Ray bike or minibike three and four towns away every day. On the last day of the school year, my family headed to a campsite and we lived there for all three months of summer vacation. Then for two weeks, we would pack up the campsite and have a vacation at the Jersey Shore. Unfortunately, my father died when I was thirteen and everything changed. My mother was only around forty, so of course she needed to have some companionship. Naturally, because we were teenagers, that didn't sit well with us. Things got pretty strained between me and my mom from about age thirteen to seventeen. We reconnected as adults, and I got to spend several years with her before she died.

Growing up, I wasn't very social, but in a good way. I didn't need the acceptance of anybody. I was my own kid and mostly hung out with guys and had mad crushes on my sisters' girlfriends. I barely remember anybody from my childhood and can't name a single person I went to school with. I just didn't care. I was fully comfortable being with and by myself. I never had a need to be accepted, even though I always was accepted. Oddly enough, it always seemed *not* caring drew people to me. I spent a lot of time riding minibikes, building stuff, going out on expeditions looking for snakes and lizards by the river, playing baseball or football with friends, just running around the town like a wild animal. I remember riding my bike around the block several times with a pet rat on my head, that kind of thing.

I did not enjoy school whatsoever and referred to it as jail my whole life. To this day, Labor Day depresses me because it reminds me of going back to school. I'm thoroughly horrified by the back-to-school commercials on TV in August. I went to a technical high school, but I quit in eleventh grade and got my GED a couple years later. Jennifer Lawrence also quit school and has a GED, so I feel I'm in good company.

In the summer between sixth and seventh grades, a friend of mine stole (or more likely borrowed) my bike. I searched him out and beat the living shit out of him on the front yard of somebody's home. During the beatdown, several girls that I'd be going to school with that year walked by. They saw the whole thing. My reputation was set.

My neighborhood had its fair share of juvenile delinquents. In high school, all the JDs would always call me over to their lunch table to sit with them, but I didn't care. Actually, the hallways would part whenever I walked down them. I'm not bragging; this is just how it was. I did bully one or two people once or twice, only because that's what I thought I was supposed to do, and I completely hate that. I wish I could go back and change that. I really, really lament that part of my life.

The summer I was fourteen, a massive flood completely devastated my town and the whole surrounding area. So me being fourteen and it being summer meant there were

For the last time: FASHION.

Nurse Kogan will see you now. Squat and cough.
BJ Papas

Spinal pap: The sustain . . . listen to it.
Gina, 1996.
BJ Papas

Jew-wish: Squid.
BJ Papas

Sindi making plans to knock out the fool in the back who just threw that pint glass.
BJ Papas

Is this thing on?: Chip.
BJ Papas

Jam out with your clam out.
BJ Papas

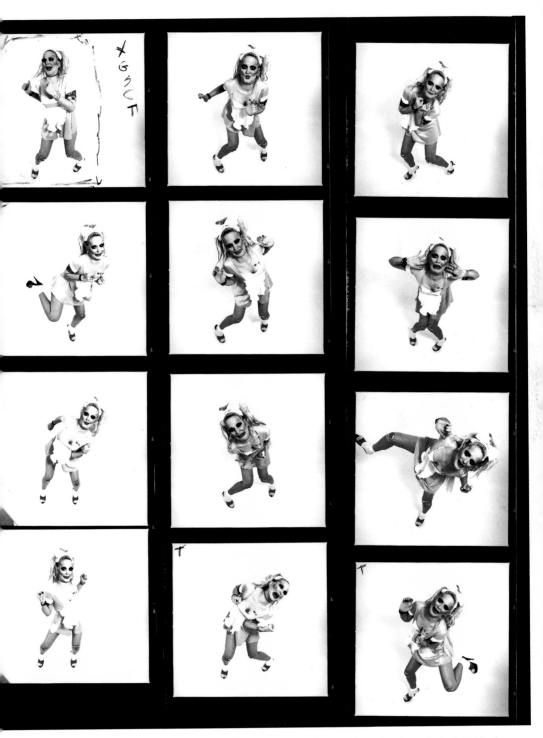

Theo Kogan, clown princess: Outtakes from *Jerk of All Trades*.
Michael Lavine

Wild Wacky Party.
Katrina Del Mar

Another day at the office, live in Vegas.
Julie Gunther

We will follow you onto the bus.
Bob Mussell

GOOD OL' BOYS '93

Halloween: The official Lunachicks holiday.

PINK LIGHTNING '94

LUNA SKINS '95

HAGS FROM HELL '96

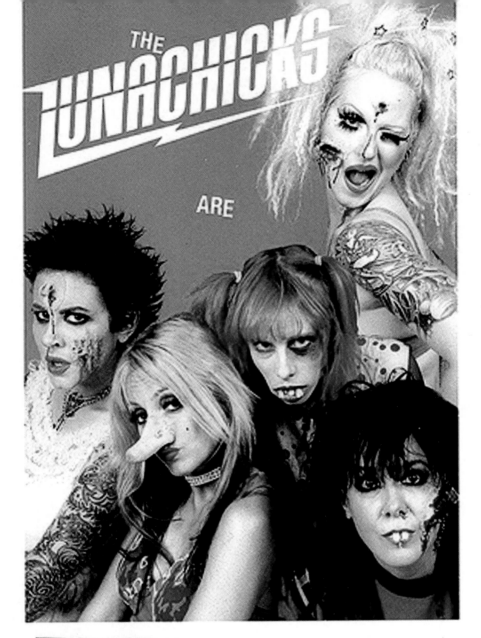

The world is her trampoline: Theo live at Tramps, NYC.
BJ Papas

On the Williamsburg waterfront, 1995.
Amber Sexton

I see London, I see France . . . Squeezebox at Don Hill's, NYC.
Mike Leach

Available to play at your wedding, retirement, and bris. Cash only.

Theo: Always a lady.

Meet and greet with Chip.

We can be worster: Gina and
Squid, 1999.
Somadream

Theo.
Greg "G-Spot" Siebel

Gina.
Greg "G-Spot" Siebel

Squid.
Greg "G-Spot" Siebel

Attack of the fifty-foot Lunachicks.
Brooklyn, 2019.
ad photo credit: Chris Boarts Larson

Business as usual: Lunachicks, 2020.
Michael Lavine

no laws, so we did things like hang out on the roof of our front porch with the turntable blasting Jethro Tull's *Aqualung*, Black Sabbath, and Led Zeppelin. A lot of guys started to hang around my sister and her friends, so we became a group of pot-smoking, lawless kids. Eventually they all paired off as boyfriend and girlfriend. Being closeted, I was always the odd person out, sitting there while everybody went off to make out in their parents' bedrooms. Once I got out of that stage, I never wanted to look back. That was probably the worst part of my teenage years. But I always had music.

My sisters and I started off listening to 45s of the Beatles, Turtles, and Monkees, and then my mother's best friend brought her a reel-to-reel tape recorder, which played tapes of things like Brasil '66, samba music, jazz, that kind of thing. At around thirteen or fourteen, I discovered metal. I always commanded the stereo at parties and would crank up the volume as loud as possible at certain parts of songs. Music was a constant part of my life. Everything grabbed my attention. I listened to all the classics: Sabbath, Zeppelin, Grand Funk Railroad, ZZ Top, you name it. I was a Beatles fan and thought that made me slightly superior to the people I was hanging out with. See, the Beatles were something older kids listened to, but I was drumming along to them in my bedroom and could easily decipher what the drums were doing in those songs. I'd also listen to "Stairway to Heaven" nonstop. If you're a musician, you have to know all the basics and the beginnings and everything about music.

I know this sounds weird, but I didn't connect listening to music with playing the drums. I just started playing the drums because that was something I wanted to do. Then I met this girl named Rita who was in a band and she asked me to audition. I remember thinking, "Wait a minute ... I'm playing the drums *and* I could play in a band?" I might've been a little dumb because I didn't put two and two together.

I was fixated with drumming since I was a little kid and would watch as the town parades went along the end of our street several times a year. My mom loved the marching band and was especially excited when the drums got nearer and nearer. I could feel them in my body! I got hooked. I started taking lessons at around nine years old with a great local drummer, Angelo Stella. Every Saturday, my parents would drive me to Angelo's and the whole family would then patiently sit in the car for an hour until the lesson was over. In seventh grade, I took band in school. The two other drummers in band had full drum kits, but I just had a pitiful little snare drum to play on. A year before my father died, he bought me my first drum kit for Christmas—or maybe it was from Santa Claus.

I think the first live band I saw was KISS in Wilkes-Barre. I also saw Uriah Heep and caught a drumstick! Then my cousin Dan started dragging me out to shows. I saw Peter Gabriel and Cheap Trick, Todd Rundgren, UK, and Fleetwood Mac, even Chuck Berry. It was all good. I'm really not the kind of huge fan who needs to see everybody or needs to know all the names of all the musicians. I keep my music and my drumming to myself. I'm not putting down anyone who is a huge music fan; it's just not what I do.

I wasn't really into punk rock either. In the suburbs, we were listening to metal. Once I was introduced to punk rock, it wasn't as inspiring as you might think. To me, it was so basic. I wanted complicated parts, and punk rock drumming can be just machine-gun style. I listened and played absolutely everything—I was in a country-rock band, a bluegrass band, a Texas swing band, and when I was sixteen I even sat in with a polka band with forty-year-old guys on New Year's Eve. You could say I discovered punk rock with the Lunachicks.

I had grown up my whole life wanting to leave Pennsylvania, so I used to buy the *Village Voice* and scan all the ads for bands looking for drummers. I found a band that was doing an East Coast tour. They were a show band, so I auditioned for them and got the gig. I left Pennsylvania saying, "SEE YA!!!" So that's basically when I left my whole family and didn't look back for about ten years. Not that things were horrible between us, but they weren't great either. So after that show band broke up, one of the dancers was moving back to her apartment on Fifty-Fourth Street in New York City. There was no way I could've ever gone back to Pennsylvania at that point, so I moved in with her, which also worked because she was my girlfriend. I remember getting into her apartment and looking out the front window. Down the street, there was a sign for Studio 54. I knew I was making it.

I can honestly say I was in easily seventy to one hundred bands in my life, though nothing really worth noting (although the other band members might say differently). It was just years and years of thinking every band I was in was going to make it. But in my mind, to make it you have to record and you have to go on tour. While I did a lot of recording, the only time I fully felt I made it was with the Lunachicks because we toured the world.

When the Lunachicks called me to go to Europe with them, I was already in a band called 1-900-Boxx with

Cynthia Sley from the Bush Tetras, Steph Paynes from Lez Zeppelin, and Carla Olla from Blondie. We were doing our thing and getting recognition, but when you're asked to go on a European tour, there's no way you can say no! So I left my band behind, and actually they were mad at me for some time.

I remember feeling that the Lunachicks were doing what they did exactly the way they wanted to do it. I kind of came from a background of always trying to figure out what the next big thing would be and what it would take to make it in the music industry. There was something cool about seeing the Lunachicks doing their own thing.

Turned out they were a natural fit for me. When I was filling in on that first European tour with them, Gina was on the phone getting confirmation for another tour, either in the States or Europe. She stood there telling the other girls where the gigs were, and I was just chomping at the bit. I needed to be in this band! It really meant everything to me because I'd been working to be a professional musician virtually my whole life. You see, when you're in a normal New York City band fighting for your place at CBGB's and getting twenty to forty people at your gigs, it can be very disheartening if that's all you get to experience. But with the Lunachicks, it was nothing but sold-out standing-room-only shows and tours. It was instant fame, and I really needed that to complete my journey of being a professional drummer.

CHAPTER 21

BIG IN JAPAN

Lunachicks was essentially a manifestation of our sisterhood—our friendship directly led to the band. Not too long after, a shift took place and the band was what nurtured our friendship. The art and songs became the spiritual glue that bonded us. One way we honored each other and ourselves was by committing to be the best players, songwriters, and performers that we could possibly be.

GINA: The time that Syd, Theo, and I put in to learning our instruments and writing songs can't be overstated. (Chip was already fucking great.) Syd was really serious about her bass playing, and she practiced a lot and kicked fucking ass. And Theo worked on her voice so much. She took lessons and practiced every day and did whatever she could to perfect her voice and take care of it. It was important to us, not only because we were musicians and we wanted to be good at our instruments, but also because there was an extra pressure: people expected us to suck because we were women. I was not going to get up onstage and do a dinky little shitty lead—that's exactly what people expected. Fuck that. I wanted to blow people away.

SQUID: Having chops was about power and being in control. I want you to fucking lose your teeth when I play. That was driving much of my desire to be a good bass player. I cared about perfect execution and writing the perfect song, to tap that perfect feeling, and harnessing the power to carry that hotness to the people. The Lunachicks were like an elite force of mutants, each with their own superpowers. Taking the stage together was like jumping into a street fight with Green Berets by your side. I never felt competitive with them; they made me want to be better. My job was to hold the line alongside them, in the impenetrable wall of unfuckableness.

THEO: I had been going to vocal coaches for years, took my role as singer very seriously, and worked very hard at it. Staying quiet during the day, drinking tea and water, getting sleep, doing my warm-ups religiously, not drinking or staying out late. I slept in when we were in the big European cities I had always wanted to see because being in good shape for the show was the most important thing. If I couldn't perform, the whole thing was fucked. It was a lot of responsibility on my shoulders. When I got sick on tour—and there were plenty of those times, be it from a flu or menstrual cramps of death or stomach viruses—I would be as sick as I had ever been all day and then somehow I'd pull it together to get onstage at night. I was a firm believer that the show must go on.

SQUID: Theo sacrificed so fucking much. She didn't talk for a week before tour. She drank disgusting tea all day. She warmed up alone before every show and disappeared again after. She went to bed early while we were all hanging out, smoking cigarettes, and drinking. She really, really sucked up so much shit to make it work. She was 100 percent. It was so hardcore.

All that hard work was about to pay off in a big way. Japan was our dream. The ultimate. We wanted to be like our heroes, all of whom had live albums recorded there: the Runaways, Cheap Trick, KISS. They went there, so we had to go there. That was our logic. We were determined to get there one day.

Sometime after *Binge and Purge* was released, we were playing a show at CBGB and a man and a woman, Shisaka and Hiroshi, came up to us and said, "We want to bring you to Japan." Uh, yes, we want that too! They said they'd act as our promoters and bring us over. And they did. Three times! In 1993, after wrapping up a tour in Europe, we flew directly to Japan.

In true Lunachicks fashion, as soon as we landed, we went to a gas station and spent like $300 on snacks. We had just been in Europe eating all their weird candy, but then we got to Japan and it was stuff that we absolutely never imagined existed. There was a soda that had a marble that would spin around when you drank it. We found vending machines on the street that sold cans of beer and hot coffee. Hello Kitty–everything you could think of. *Dehydrated snow peas?!? Holy shit, this place is incredible!* Taxi doors automatically opened and closed; the first time it happened, Theo screamed. Everything that was traditionally American was like campy theater. We drove by a town square that had two dozen Elvis impersonators holding court. There were T-shirts with bizarre American words that didn't go together, like "Kitty Muffin" with a picture of a shrimp. Hotel rooms were so tiny, with odd-looking little tubs and green-tea makers. The hotel gave us robes and slippers, so the minute we got there, we all got naked, put on our robes, and walked around the hallways. Everything in Japan is built vertically, so we'd go to a restaurant and it would be on the sixth floor of an apartment building. Even the venues we played at, we'd ride an elevator carrying our guitars with people shopping at the mall—fifth floor, lingerie; seventh floor, menswear; tenth floor, rock club.

We were struck by how polite and reserved the fans were during our sets. They would barely move and then they'd clap. People followed us around. We felt like the Beatles. We would get off a subway and a crowd of people would be there. We were like, "What's going on?" and we realized they were waiting *for us*. We'd be walking, and a block later, we'd turn around and there'd be two girls following us. Three blocks later, we'd turn around and there'd be five girls following us. And then we'd turn around, there were ten girls following us. They kept multiplying. Whenever we'd turn around, they'd politely giggle. That actually happened—*to us*.

CHIP: The Japanese fans were very generous. They gave Theo makeup from a super-famous high-end store, which I thought was so cool, and through the years, they've sent me birthday and Christmas presents. I always wondered how they knew it was my birthday. The thing I remember most is one time when we were leaving Japan and were walking through the airport and heard all this yelling and crying. We looked up at the mezzanine right above us and there were maybe twenty, thirty Japanese kids yelling "Lunachicks! Lunachicks!" and crying. We got on the plane, flew home, and got dropped off at our apartments. Then the door shuts behind you and there's just deafening silence. It's really quite strange.

It was the most famous we'd ever felt and it left us with such an incredible buzz. After our gigs, we'd be taken to dinner at classic Japanese-seating-style restaurants. The bottles of Sapporo and Asahi would be all over the table; things would get sloppy pretty quickly. You have to take your shoes off when you get into the restaurant, so Chip, who always wore lace-up boots, would always be the last one at the table. Japan was always throwing us little curveballs like that.

THEO: Our merch didn't make it through the mail, so we quickly ran out of T-shirts to sell at shows. No merch, no money—that's the whole point. Time to DIY, motherfuckers! We drove to the art store, picked up dozens of white T-shirts, and set up a makeshift assembly line in our hotel room.

GINA: Theo and I were drawing with puffy paint, shouting out designs like, *"Now I'm going to make one of a girl squeezing a pimple on her ass with boogers coming out of her nose!" "YES, DO IT!"* Squid's job was to use a hair dryer to dry the shirts. Our hotel room transformed into a mini T-shirt factory with Theo and I furiously churning out as many as we could. Handmade shirts covered the walls and were strung from each corner of the ceiling. Every single design was different. It was so very Lunachicks.

A whole other surprise was waiting for us. We thought we were in Japan to tour, but Shisaka was like, "Hey, we happen to have two days booked for you at a recording studio!" We were like, "Uh, okay!" The result was the EP *Sushi a la Mode*. We recorded a cover of Boston's "More Than a Feeling." Theo sang the guitar solos—*neer, nee-ner ner ner*—and changed the lyric from "I see my Marianne walkin' away" to "I see your derriere walking away." (Sorry, not sorry, Boston.) The EP was never released in the States, but at least the cover art is great.

CHIP: The name *Sushi a la Mode* came to me in a dream state. Back in NYC, Gina and I went to Chinatown and bought a huge red snapper and brought it to the prop house where I worked. We set it up with ice cream, sprinkles, and whipped cream and photographed it for the cover.

The best part of recording was the bathrooms. The toilets were heated and had a plastic wand that would wave over the seat to disinfect it after each use. Bizarre. And there was a bidet. You pushed a button and wooooo-hooooo! We were in the bathroom whenever we weren't recording, each of us in a stall, like, "Fuck the record, check this out!!"

Bonus surprise: the tour arrangements. We were shoved into a large van with a Japanese Rasta driver and the other bands. That's when we found out Japan's drug laws were insane. We were told we'd be thrown in jail for ten years if they caught us with a joint. And they were super-serious when it came to tattoos. We were told back then that tattoos equaled the yakuza, the Japanese mafia. Theo, Squid, and Chip had a bunch of tattoos by that point.

> **SQUID:** We were sitting on the floor in a restaurant with our entourage and a bunch of fangirls, and somehow it came up that I have kanji that I tattooed on myself one day when I was bored at work in the tattoo shop. "Ohh, very nice, can we see? What does it say?" to which I proudly replied, "It's my zodiac; it says Scorpio!" As I peeled back my sock to display it, the whole table burst out laughing and pointing. "Sheep! Sheep! It says 'sheep'! Bwahhhahhaaa!" Oh, whoops. My band never let me live that one down. I had to go back and tattoo the word for *black* above it to save myself.

Theo, Squid, and Chip got tattooed while we were there. They wanted to tattoo *Lunachicks* in Japanese lettering. Theo asked the artist, "How can you write that?" Well, there's no word for *chick*. It's either *bitch* or *girl*. So Theo, Squid, and Chip got tattoos that translate to "crazy moon bitch."

> **CHIP:** Shisaka said it could also be interpreted as "crazy moon female ninja," so once when I was at the bar Crazy Nanny's in downtown New York, somebody asked me what my tattoo meant, and I said, "Crazy moon female ninja." A blonde girl next to me looked at it and said, "That's not 'female ninja,' that's 'bitch'!" Apparently she lived in Japan for years, so now it will always be crazy moon bitch.

CHAPTER 22

THEO: THE ROAD TO MENTAL HEALTH IS JUST AROUND THE CORNER

Around 1993, my mental health was becoming an issue I could no longer avoid. I suffered from depression for as long as I can remember, but I didn't really know this because I was so used to the feeling. My baseline was a light melancholy—that's what I knew. Maybe it was taught or maybe it was in me, the Russian/Ukranian immigrant depression DNA carried over from the actual Depression and passed down to me from my grandparents and great-grandparents. Nature/nurture? Fun fact: a great-grandmother of mine on my dad's side had been given shock treatment back when they were doing that for depression. Can you imagine? I guess our band name came with more truth than anyone really knew. But then as a teen and in my band, I felt unstoppable. Infallible. Strong as hell. Most of the time.

My skin erupted into cystic acne in my early twenties after I went off the birth control pill, which can happen and it sure did. We were touring a lot, and it was so awful to literally show my face to the world. Around that time, a friend shot a video of the band during the day in the desert while we were on tour. I was fucking horrified, couldn't look at any of the footage. So on came the drag. Thank goddess and science for Dermablend, which is a very thick pancake concealer/skin abrasion makeup that can cover up any and almost all imperfections, including beards, cystic acne, and tattoos. The drag queens used it, so I learned from them (as you do) and on it went. It covered my acne pizza-face and made me feel like a pretty drag queen/clown. I was miserable without it. Also, I had cut my hair short and it was in an awkward growing-out phase, which did NOT help matters. It was a pretty ugly time for me. I realize these are luxury problems, but it still sucked.

The band's makeup began to take a greater and funnier and more extreme path, which coincided with my worst acne years. We wore pounds of makeup to make each other laugh, but for me, it was also a mask. Squid was right, I was completely enveloped in drag culture and that's where my glamour came from. I saw myself as a drag queen. Pimple-faced boy Theo during the day, woman-ish Theo during the evenings (or when I felt like it).

These feelings were made worse by the fact that I was the subject of so many people's attention, both as a singer and as a model. A big part of both those jobs involves being looked at, and the thought of that was terrifying. In the modeling and acting work I did apart from the band, everything was based on my exterior. That fucked me up, but I fed on it all like a starving baby. I knew the girls hated all of it—my modeling and acting. The friction it caused made me so uncomfortable. They didn't want me to be too "pretty," but I wanted to experience that part of me—a pretty drag queen—so there was definitely tension about this for a time.

All of this was like being a child star without being a child star. We started as teenagers, for crying out loud. I was hired because I looked a certain way, whether it was funny or pretty or whatever. I started to wonder, "Am I actually good at singing? Or acting? Or even modeling? If my Lunachicks persona goes away, then what's there?" The fans who showed me so much love while I was onstage didn't really know me at all. If anyone really knew me the way I knew me, would anyone like me? Without the persona I hide behind, would anyone care? Did I have worth in the world without this role? Fun fact #2: I feared that I would be sent home from every single modeling shoot I went to. Never. Happened. Hello, impostor syndrome.

It reminds me of how I used to try to shrink myself as a child. Even though my grandfather seemed like the boss, the women ran the show. My maternal great-grandmother was the family matriarch at that time. When she lost her mental faculties, my grandmother took over. And in our house, my mom was boss. Us kids were loved, and to my maternal grandmother, family was the most important thing, but I felt I had to be smaller than all these women. In some ways I did this with my bandmates too—I dulled my own light so they could shine brighter.

If I wasn't distracted from about twelve years old on, I found a way to be self-hating. And I had some help with that. During my teens and part of my twenties, I was in and out of a few relationships with some jerks—tough guys or mama's boys who had violent outbursts and were always looking to pick a fight with anyone they could. None of these boyfriends ever hit me, but they did abuse me in other ways, belittling me to the point where my self-esteem was wrecked. It was heartbreaking. These types of relationships were torture, but torture was what I was looking for at the time, apparently—an all-consuming distraction from myself and more fodder to hate myself with later. Nice job, Kogan. Thank you, therapy.

It all came to a head in Japan. I realized, "Wow, this was my dream to get here. Now I'm here and I don't feel like I'm on top of the world—I just feel like shit." It was one of those revelations: all your dreams can come true, but if you're not right within yourself, you're not going to be happy no matter what happens. Japan was my true awakening, probably because it felt like a dream realized. Depression got a hold of me, as it does, at what should have/could have/would have been the time of my life. But there were other things that weren't celebratory then: my crumbling relationship with my boyfriend, and Syd's addiction.

I was a ham that wanted everyone's approval and love, and I found it. The high I got while playing live was love like I never felt before. I became that ballerina and clown that I'd always fantasized about being as a small child. I was even in a tutu, just in a really different way than I had imagined. Part of the euphoria came from the audience's love and attention, but a big part of it was also the rush I got from tapping into this inner power source I carried around with me but hardly ever got to take full advantage of unless I was onstage. There was a bigger, brighter self inside me. I wasn't following a script someone wrote for me. I created this . . . I can't even call it a character, it's more like an alter ego.

One of the best, most bizarre moments was when I was invited to Keith Richards's private solo album release party around 1992. Iggy Pop showed up. I started talking to him and ended up giving him a Lunachicks demo and one of our bat-woman pins. Cameras were flashing, and the next thing I knew I was in a Keith-and-Iggy sandwich getting my picture taken. I have never seen this photo. If anyone reading this has it, please let me know! A year or two later, Iggy saw us play at a Rock for Choice show in LA and said we were one of his fave new bands. Now I am dead. Later in the decade, Gina and I played in a Blondie cover band, and who was in the audience but Debbie Harry and Chris Stein. NO PRESSURE. After the show, they came into the dressing room and Debbie said, "You're brave. VERY. BRAVE." I choked out a thank-you and smiled nervously. MY CHILDHOOD IDOL IS TALKING TO ME. Then she said, "We should do a duet sometime." ANYTIME. I wrote down my number, thinking I would never hear from her. A couple of weeks later, the phone rang and guess who it was? I recorded backups on a couple of songs on Blondie's *No Exit*. I left the recording session feeling so elated and high, if I was to get hit by a bus right then, it would've been okay with me. Then there was the time Joey Ramone said we were one of his new favorite bands . . . my life was complete.

The highs were life-affirming, but the lows were even lower, especially when we got home from a tour and I got what I like to call post-tour depression, or performer's postpartum. It's the worst. One day I'm onstage in front of two hundred or fifteen hundred or fifteen thousand people, feeling fulfilled and like nothing could break me, the next day I'm just another face on the subway. For some reason, I couldn't access that power source inside me once I stepped off the stage. It was like that Theo was one person, and everyday Theo was someone else. Kinda like Superman and Clark Kent. But we were one and the same. I just couldn't integrate my two selves.

As much as I loved performing and enjoyed the surges of what was perhaps faux self-esteem, it came at a hefty price that I paid over and over again. I spent so many years keeping my shit together so I could sing, all while watching everybody else around me have fun. There'd be times we'd be sleeping in a room above a club in Europe, and I'd have to go to bed early to the sounds of *boomp-boomp-boomp* all night. Everybody would be running around, getting fucked up, and smoking and laughing, and I was trapped in hell. I wasn't even on drugs! At least that might've been fun! I went into a chrysalis state between each show, just watching and waiting to come out again. I'd get offstage and go somewhere and be catatonic. I was very lonely, but I was holding it together for everybody. I had a job to do and took that very seriously.

Even at my sickest, tripping with fever dreams all day in the van, I would rally and get my butt onstage. Pure adrenaline helped me do it. In Europe, I had terrible bronchitis and people still smoked everywhere so every breath I took while singing was a gulp of secondhand smoke. I sang my lines and then turned around and hacked up a lung during guitar solos. I only ever had to cancel when my vocal cords were swollen in 1995 after a big tour with the Offspring or Rancid, or maybe both back-to-back. It was bad. I stayed totally quiet for two weeks and wrote notes to communicate, to the point that a neighbor thought I was deaf. Talk about a lonely two weeks.

I knew I was the singer and had that level of attention being paid to me, but I don't know if it was that I didn't feel deserving of it or if I felt that Gina and Syd were so much *more* than me. I was jealous of them: their talents, their coolness, their bodies. I always felt like an outsider even with my best, closest friends next to me. I felt kinda like a nerd, all in all. I was constantly comparing myself to them. I thought everybody loved Syd, that she was the fan favorite. Gina was the hot shredder with the hot legs. And mama Sindi, she was cool as shit and tough as nails. And I was the singer, like the *honk-honk wakka-wakka* clown-dork. As everyone got older, we became more unified and more confident performers, which helped me to not focus so much on personal shortcomings. We wore matching costumes and felt more like an army at war not with ourselves, but with the world. It was like "we complete us," but each of us alone was another story.

At twenty-three, I put myself into therapy. Even though I had lied my way through family therapy with a pig-nosed therapist as a teen, I now saw the value in it. I was ready to be honest and real because I was so deeply unhappy and recognized that I shouldn't be. I took myself to Washington Square Institute, which charged on a sliding scale. This, plus years of performing in my superhero alter ego, eventually helped me become stronger in my regular life. But I was also trained to be strong by my mom and all these boss-women who surrounded me. My band made me laugh, of course, and it's not like I didn't have a total blast a lot of the time, but I hid my depression pretty well. The girls had no idea. The first time they heard about any of this was when we were writing this book.

Mental health is as important and serious and real as anything else. If you have appendicitis, you take care of it; if you have cancer, you take care of it. If you are depressed or anxious or want to die, you have to look at it the same way. I am not sure why it has been such a shamed illness, but I am here to tell you that if you need help, don't be ashamed—go get it.

CHAPTER 23

SQUID + DRUGS, PART 3

SQUID: I was so sick in Japan. I got lost. Try being dopesick and lost in a country where there's not even letters on the street signs. I was on the sidewalk, sick and starving and by myself. I could see food through the glass of a restaurant—*I just want a fucking sandwich!*—but there was no way I could figure out how to make that happen. My nose was running and I could barely walk or talk, let alone think and navigate a menu in Japanese, so I gave up. I remember having that feeling, and I knew it, like, "This is the greatest thing that could ever fuckin' happen to you. And you. Are. Fucked." This was my wildest dream come true, and there I was; at that moment, I would have been happy to get run over by a bus. It was so shitty. I don't know how I found my way back to the hotel. I don't know how I wound up alone. Maybe I went off by myself. But the band might have ditched me, honestly, because I was so sick and slow and they kept walking faster, trying to get away from me.

CHIP: When we were in Japan, I remember walking by Squid as she was sick and lying on a bench by a bathroom that reeked of fish pee. When we got home, I either thought to myself or said to her directly that she didn't even know she had been in Japan!

SINDI: I had personal experience that nobody else had of losing people close to me to the call of drugs. I adored Squid, and I saw that I was losing her, that *we* were losing her. I have no problem with drug use, but heroin was something that I always steered far clear from, and for good reason. I had my lines. This is where recreational drug use ends, and beyond that is not the place to go. I saw her go there. I knew that it was only getting worse. To see Squid falling down that hole was sad. Most of my anger came from sadness of the loss that I could see and feel.

SQUID: I got off the plane from our Japan tour, and within hours I was in a record store on St. Marks Place with X where he used to pawn all our shit for drugs. I looked at the cashier and noticed a bunch of Lunachicks singles and records on the wall above his head. My first thought was "Oh, that's so cool he has all those rare Lunachicks singles." Then slowly through the fog, the pieces started falling into place—those were *my* copies, my *only* copies, my personal collection of all our recordings. My life's work hanging up on someone else's wall, hocked by X for a few bags of dope. A day earlier, I was playing with my band, living my dreams, shouting "HELLO, TOKYO!" to a sold-out crowd of screaming fans. And now I was headed to a dope spot on Avenue C, having cashed my life in for a shot of junk that I didn't even want. But what was I gonna do now, not get high? That's the hook. The more your life turns to shit, the more you can't face living in it. By the time we were done in Japan, I had probably been clean for two months, I was finally coming out of it, finally feeling good again. And it only took forty-eight hours for my big, bright, shining star to come hurling back down to earth in a shitball of diarrhea flames. I'm thinking, *"What the fuck is going on? How is this even really happening?"* And then I got high, again, just like I always would, 'cause I was so mad or I was so sad. I think this happened approximately a hundred thousand times.

There is no glamour in addiction. It's just depressing. For starters, I was a junkie with a job. I was tattooing the whole time I was strung out. It sucked. I had to be straight to function, and I needed drugs to get straight so I could go to work to get money to stay high and, you know, do all the other things that regular people have to do like clean the toilet and pay the bills. Having to keep up a normal life *and* a drug habit is like having two concurrent nine-to-five jobs with overtime. I was beholden to everyone. I always paid my rent. I'd get high, go to work, get high at work, leave work, go home, get high, go to sleep, wake up, get high, and go back to work, infinity. I don't think anyone ever understood how fucking hard I worked to maintain a drug habit. I had like three full-time jobs being a junkie and everyone acted like I was on fucking vacation. Annoying.

X was a little devil. Boosting shit, selling drugs, and lying to my face four out of five days a week. He was a shameless thief. Every room this kid walked into, something went missing. At one point, he was climbing up the fire escape of our building and regularly robbing the apartment upstairs. I had gotten my friends the apartment! One time, he was boosting steaks on the corner. Who the fuck buys raw meat on a street corner from a junkie? I still can't figure that one out. He tried to rob the Dominican deli down the street from us in the middle of the afternoon. A seventy-year-old lady in a housecoat and slippers was working the counter and she beat him out the door with a broom yelling, "Bad man! Bad man!"

I started shooting coke more regularly, and I was really into speedballing. There's only so much coke you can do before your heart explodes, and there's only so much heroin you can do before your heart stops. So in combination (this is a theory), it's the most fucked you can possibly be, without killing yourself, hopefully.

Shooting coke is so mentally insidious. I would cop blow from this old '70s weirdo at the Chelsea Hotel and try my best to get outta there, but I couldn't get down more than one or two flights of stairs before I'd freak out and have to duck into another bathroom to keep slamming shots in my arm—my ears are ringing, I'm having a heart attack, and I'm panicking that once I leave the hotel, I'll have to wait to get back to Brooklyn to shoot up again. It would take like an hour to get out of there! Then I would get home, sit in my shitty little bathtub in two inches of lukewarm water, with an egg timer and my pile of coke. I'd shoot the coke—bells and black spots and blinding numbness—and set the timer because I wanted to make sure the timer would run out before I shot up again so my heart wouldn't explode (that was me erring on the side of caution). Over and over. Till it all ran out. And god help us all if I didn't have some heroin to kill the bone-crunching crash of coming down off all that shit. That is some I-don't-want-to-be-here shit. FYI, cokeheads make dopeheads look like upstanding model citizens.

I OD'd on more than one occasion. One minute everything was going fine, the next, my eyes were struggling to focus as I heard voices and realized there was a fireman or a paramedic sitting on top of me in my apartment accompanied by a handful of cops. Narcan is a shot used to save people from OD'ing. It instantly reverses and blocks the effects of any opiates in your system. Ask any junkie, "Which do you like better: dying or being thrust into instant crisis-level withdrawal symptoms?" and you might get feedback around fifty-fifty. The latter is akin to something like being hurled off a giant cliff. Everyone knows about that shot. You do *not* want the shot. This is the mentality of a junkie: imagine you're nearly dead and there are people trying to save your life, and you're struggling to wake up *not* because you don't want to die but because you don't want to get the shot. All those good drugs would've gone to waste. Forget that you almost died! If you did enough drugs that you fuckin' OD'd, that meant you had a decent stash and a pretty good day. You don't fuck that up and start from zero.

I'd be coming to, completely out of it, but I knew something was going on because all these uniforms were in my house. They'd be resuscitating me, and inside my head I'd hear this voice: *Syd, just act normal, be casual, act normal and no one will know, offer them coffee.* "Anybody want coffee?" I never got the shot. I talked my way out of it with the coffee thing every time.

I managed to get a black eye from OD'ing one time, still unclear how, probably from someone smacking me around trying to revive me. I got questioned on that one (obviously) and told my band, "I slipped in the shower." How their eyes are not permanently stuck upward in their sockets from rolling backward I have no idea. Shit got so out of hand so many times. There were too many moments where I thought, "That almost went so irreversibly wrong." Getting robbed at drug spots, almost getting stabbed in the neck by a mad crackhead with a screwdriver, the dumbest shit you can imagine, not to mention the fact that I almost killed my best friend.

1964 is supposedly the first year Chevy installed seat belts, but as luck would have it, my Nova had none. One evening, Theo was in the passenger seat. I was super-high and driving us back to Brooklyn. As we approached the bridge entrance, I was asleep and hit the median. In any other circumstance, this would've sent Theo—my beautiful best friend, and her model face—flying through the windshield, but by some miracle, I hit a ramp-shaped part of the cement and it flipped the car up onto two wheels. I must have felt it because my eyes popped open in time to see us sailing sideways toward the bridge at a 90-degree angle. I never forgot about that. I almost sent my best friend through a windshield.

X got arrested a few times for selling drugs, and I had to make a bunch of trips to Rikers Island to go see him. He was locked up there for a while, more than once, and eventually had to do a year. I was lonely, so I took up hanging out with one of his old drug-dealer buddies who by lucky chance was living up the street from us. She was a dope dealer and her hubs was doing federal time, so we became besties. She'd have literal piles of uncut heroin sitting out on the kitchen table. "Yo, chica, try this!" I wanted to be her best friend every day of the week. She was under FBI surveillance and knew it. She'd walk out of her house and flash her tits to the cameras. She also told me she had recently been released from a mental hospital as a diagnosed schizophrenic and had to take her pills or else she might stab someone because she heard voices and thought people were trying to kill her. We were a good fit.

Then, on tour, I realized I was pregnant. Whoops. This was not feeling like the optimal time to start a

family. I had no money for an abortion, so I got someone to front me the cash. When the tour ended, I came
home and went to visit my girlfriend. For some ridiculous reason I was carrying my abortion money around
in my pocket in an envelope. I left her house and realized the money was gone. Somehow, I lost $700 worth
of $20 bills in a three-block radius. It vanished. So
I went crazy retracing my steps, freaking out, looking
everywhere. There I was, on all fours crawling under
a car looking for my cash, when all of a sudden a car
with two guys in it pulled up alongside me, and I heard,
"Hey, Sydney, what's the matter? You lose your drugs?"
And that's when I learned the FBI knew my name. "No, I
didn't lose my drugs," I said, "I lost my abortion."

My band tried to get me help so many times. They
would call my dad and urge him to intervene, but he was
in such denial. He would invite me over for dinner; I'd
be shooting up in the bathroom. "Oh, you look great!
So skinny, like a model!" Absolutely clueless. My mom
called me one time because I guess word had gotten to
her. I was sitting on the couch getting high, and she
was saying, "I just want you to know that I know that
you're strong, and you'll always land on your feet, and
I'm not worried about you." I had a belt around my arm
and in my mouth. I was like, "Uh-huh." Yeah, I got it.
I'll land on my feet. Thanks. *Click.* That was the only
time we ever spoke about it.

I guess Theo or Gina was calling my dad, and then he
would call me and ask, "Are you doing drugs?" and I'd
be like, "No!" and he'd say, "Okay! Talk to you later."
Then my band would call him three months later, like,
"You better fuckin' do something." This went on for
months. Those women endured such hell. As my using progressed, their patience with me wore exceedingly thin.

They wanted to kill me. I was useless, and I couldn't get anywhere on time. I couldn't get anywhere, period, and forget about getting anything done when your only priority is getting high.

Band rehearsal was a nightmare. One time, I kept leaving the room to run to the bathroom to shoot coke every fifteen minutes. After a bunch of trips back and forth, I went to open the door to the rehearsal room and walked straight into it. The band locked me out. I was like, "Guys! Hey, guys! The door's locked!" Those poor women.

We were asked to be part of an Iggy Pop tribute album, *We Will Fall*. I was trying to leave my house to get to the studio to lay down my bass parts for "The Passenger." I knew I couldn't shoot up at the studio, so I'd say to myself, "I just need one more shot before I get on the train!" I probably left the house six times and then, "Ooop! Just one more!" and then ran back upstairs. Needless to say, I never made it. Gina had to record my bass parts. Shameful moment.

One night, we played a show on the Frying Pan, which is a boat in the Hudson River on the West Side of Manhattan. I was getting high with friends before the show, sharing needles of course, just as an example of where my priorities were at. I could barely play the show. I was so gacked out. I was frozen. I couldn't move. I really fucking blew it. It was horrible. The worst. So embarrassing. Joey Ramone was there. I just remember my band looking at me. It was sheer hell trying to get through the set.

Being in a junkie marriage wasn't really conducive to me living my personal best. There was so much torment surrounding our codependency and the guilt I felt for introducing him to heroin. The combination of the codependency and the drugs was toxic. I felt responsible, and I couldn't get over it. That's why I let him get away with so much shit.

I'd come home from tour, I'd be clean, and he'd have sold damn near every fuckin' thing in the apartment. My clothes would be gone, my jewelry would be gone, my records would be gone. One afternoon, I was walking down the street behind a cute girl, spacing out, staring at her leather miniskirt. It reminded me of a skirt I got on tour with the girls in Amsterdam at this cool outdoor market. I noticed a little bit of the lining was hanging down off the bottom of her skirt. Huh, weird, my skirt had a little bit of the lining hanging down too ... heyyy, wait a minute.

This was my life. I was twenty-five.

I tried kicking so many times; I really was trying to get clean for so long. I wanted to be rid of all the weight and sadness and misery, and I was just so beat up at that point. I'd see this little old Puerto Rican granny who lived up the block from me in slippers, a housecoat, and shower cap, walking down the street with her little dog, and I would think how great her life looked, how jealous I was. *Ugh, if I could only be her, she's so lucky, my life sucks.*

There was a time when drugs were fun, but my life was ending. I was completely, deeply wrecked. Everyone hated me, and I hated myself. And it went on forever.

CHAPTER 24

DON'T WANT YOU

After *Binge and Purge,* Safe House didn't offer us another album, not that it broke our hearts. Around this time, music critics kept referring to us as riot grrrls in their album reviews, and we couldn't figure out why we kept seeing those comparisons. Someone finally told us it's because our press release called us riot grrrls—the label was trying to capitalize on that movement. *WHAT?* First of all, what's a press release? Second, *WHAT??* Squid called Safe House to complain. Loudly. It went sort of like this:

Label person: I sent you the press release. You knew what it said.

SQUID: IF I HAD WRITTEN THAT YOUR FATHER FUCKED YOUR SISTER AND THEN FUCKED YOUR MOTHER AND THEN FUCKED YOUR BROTHER, YOU WOULD FUCKIN' REMEMBER READING THAT! I DIDN'T READ THIS THING! THERE'S NO FUCKIN' WAY I WOULDN'T REMEMBER SOMETHING LIKE THIS!

And that was that. We were free agents, but by then, the game had changed. The punk rock underground was more or less upended for good in the mid-'90s. Of course, a counterculture still exists, and scrappy little bands will continue to put on house shows and keep the spirit of punk rock alive, but there's no disputing the fact that the climate of that era was very, very different from when we were coming up.

In our little microcosm, the turning point came in 1994, when Green Day's *Dookie* was released on major label Reprise Records, after the band's first few albums were released on Lookout! Records, a well-loved punk label out of Berkeley. That set off a chain reaction, and nothing's been the same since, really.

Bands that went from indie labels to majors got slagged as sellouts. Certain fans (and bands) saw the move as greedy, a slap in the face to the whole punk rock ethos. But listen, *all* of the bands in our circuit wanted to get signed. Even if they didn't say it, they were hoping for it. Think about it, getting signed meant you had real money for the first time in your life. You could quit your shitty day jobs and make money doing what you loved and were passionate about. That's the American fucking dream!

We made many attempts to get the attention of labels in the hopes of landing a deal, but each one either passed on us or didn't even bother responding. We didn't know what to do. It was a weird transitional time period, a gray area. Charcoal, more like it.

Here's a telling metaphor. While driving from one gig to another, we realized we'd be very near the Grand Canyon. We figured we couldn't pass up the opportunity to experience this incredible sight because even with all of the touring, none of us had ever seen it. The drive took forever, and by the time we arrived, it had just turned dark. We all ran out of the van, hoping to get a glimpse of the Grand Canyon—and it was completely dark. Couldn't see shit. It was so Spinal Tap. In true Lunachicks spirit, we posed for pictures, knowing it was pointless, but it made us laugh our asses off. All that glorious scenery was surrounding us, and we were able to say we were there, even if we couldn't see a goddamn thing.

GINA: I put together a package for Epitaph, for Sub Pop, a bunch of labels. At the time, several of our peers had major-label interest, but we were being told, "We have our one all-female band; we don't need anymore, we're good." I was depressed about it.

SINDI: We don't begrudge any of our peers their success. But there was no fathomable reason why we weren't also participating in that. Why weren't we along for the ride? All our dues were paid with interest. All the pieces were there. It didn't make any sense. The only thing that was different was that we were women. Was that it? Was it because we were from New York? We weren't from California, and we weren't a bunch of dudes. Was that really what was holding us back?

CHIP: We recorded a single and had local friends of ours that were big, hairy, truck-driving-looking guys as our body doubles. We photographed them wearing tutus and bras and panties and high heels. Then we cut and pasted our heads on top of their bodies. My body was that of my dog, a Doberman/Rottweiler, Magnus! Some douchebag balding-white-male record company executive saw the cover and thought we were men—but that didn't help us either! It's almost like we couldn't win.

GINA: According to Greg Ross, the reason Warped Tour founder Kevin Lyman was so reluctant to put us on Warped was because he saw that cover and thought we were guys who dressed in drag. He didn't think it was funny, even if still, to this day, we howl in laughter looking at that cover. We crack us up.

Compared to other bands of the time, we were a bit more slippery. On top of our music, we were horror movie creatures *and* we were cartoons *and* we were political *and* we were feminists *and* we were a punk band. No box existed for us.

That's not our opinion either; it's what we were told. We heard it so many times: "None of the labels want to pick you up because they don't know how to market you. They don't know where to put you. Are you punk? Are you metal? What do we do with you?" There was no compartmentalizing, no peg for us. It literally wasn't worth their effort to take us on. We were a commodity, nothing more. Did it surprise us? Not really. Labels are in the business of making money. How do you earn a profit when you can't perfectly package your product, give it a definitive label, put a bow on it, and sell it?

In hindsight, it makes perfect sense in every way. The core part of us was always about not fitting in, and in order to be financially viable, on some level you have to be able to fit into something, somewhere. From day one, we were all about *not* giving people what they wanted or expected. It wasn't premeditated; it was just who we were and still are.

Some bands that shared a similar aesthetic to us *did* have success. On a mainstream level, artists like Alice Cooper, Rob Zombie, and Slipknot were allowed to be weird and scary. On an indie level, the Dwarves had a naked guitar player in a gimp mask, and Gwar wore giant latex monster-alien costumes with four-foot-long dicks that sprayed fake cum and blood on the crowd. So it's not like we were the only band doing something freakish. Even though the Dwarves and Gwar never reached megastardom or commercial success, they got signed by big-deal, reputable independent labels (Sub Pop and Epitaph, and Metal Blade, respectively). Was it because they were dude bands that they had more permission to be undefinable? Meanwhile, we had friends and supporters who worked at almost every big label, but even they couldn't get a single executive to take an interest in us.

SQUID: If I had a dollar for every person who worked inside of a major label that would come up to us and be like, "I fucking love you guys, you're my favorite!" We had hardcore fans inside these major labels that wouldn't fuckin' touch us. If everybody was like, "You guys suck," I'd have been like, "Okay, fine." But it wasn't like that at all. That's the part that was always weird.

THEO: I met with a guy from Atlantic Records in a big fancy music building really early on with our very first demo tape. He was an old-timer; he probably dealt with Motown bands and was almost at the end of his career. I walked into his hotshot office with our demo cassette tape and played it for him. It was one of those things where he looked at me like, "Let me try and find something positive to say but, um...good luck." Like, "Yeah, no." I could almost hear it through his ears and felt like laughing out loud as he was listening. It was kind of him to sit down with me, truly. I knew how preposterous the whole moment actually was. But that's okay; in the end, we did it ooooooouuuuur waaaaay.

GINA: The rejections made me doubt our value and ability. If you look at it through the lens of sexism, it makes me realize how many women experience feelings of self-doubt because they can't find success within a system that was never built for them.

But us being who we were (and still are), all those rejections could never shut us up. Pfft. We had a LOT more to say, and there was no fuckin' way we weren't gonna say it. Maybe we were too illiterate to read the writing on the wall, but we believed in us even if everyone else thought we weren't talented or marketable. Our band was built on a cocky, oblivious teenage promise that we were awesome and we would keep getting more awesome. That never left our brains. Gotta be the New Yorker in us.

CHAPTER 25

GINA: LOOKS LIKE I PICKED THE WRONG WEEK TO QUIT SNIFFING GLUE

I always had this nagging feeling that my *Instructions to Life* manual might be missing a few chapters. It's a perpetual scramble having to piece together whatever information I'm missing and try to catch up to everyone else. The end result being a timeline of my life that looks like a first grader's macaroni-and-glitter collage Frankensteined together with staples, glue, and chewing gum. "Hey, look what I made!"

Most likely this is a result of the fact that I live inside my head much of the time, daydreaming and getting lost in the imaginary stories spun from my "Abby Normal" brain. And also 'cause the moment I hear the words "Pay attention," ya know, to be informed of the important stuff that everyone kinda needs to know, is when I tune out the most. Or maybe that's just a gentler way of describing undiagnosed ADHD.

My band will be the first to tell you that I drove everybody crazy because I had lots of opinions on how I thought the songs should go and how the artwork should look. I'm filled with creative visions and ideas, and I'm passionate about all of them. I have catalogs of songs that never made it past my bedroom, stacks of sketchbooks with pages full of drawings that will never turn into paintings. Spiraling into the abyss of possibility is one of my greatest talents. The biggest obstacle to getting my ideas out was always the lack of confidence to execute them all—that and trying to hold the same thought in my head for more than two seconds.

It's difficult to describe, but sometimes it feels like I'm carrying around a secret. An inexplicable secret, but one I can recognize in other artists. It's like an invisible pixie that whispers into my psyche. A silent roommate that I forget is there sometimes—dependable, loyal, but also chaotic and dysfunctional. It's the thing that helps me create. When I look at my work, I feel a sense of pride, but not for myself—it's for whatever it is inside of me that creates these things. It's a feeling of great fortune and wonder.

Growing up as a shy child surrounded by woods, I had my very own Narnia in my backyard. I spent a lot of time alone wandering through the trees. I was obsessed with dioramas, like the kind we'd make for a school project. These mini worlds built inside shoeboxes dazzled me, entire planetary systems contained within the cardboard walls of an Adidas box. In creating my own little habitats, I discovered a safe space of retreat. I painted murals on my bedroom walls, mosaicked with my extensive collection of rock posters and show flyers.

The fabric I hung from the ceiling and draped around my bed in high school made easy cover for me to silently slip out of the apartment at night after my mom had fallen asleep—vegetable oil on the front-door hinges also proved to be quite helpful. I would meet up with neighborhood kids to explore the city at night, trekking through Central Park and running barefoot through the grounds of the Metropolitan Museum of Art.

As an adult (and I use that term loosely), my room habitats grew even more elaborate. I built an entire ocean over my bed: I covered the ceiling with reflective blue Mylar and strung up hundreds of plastic sharks overhead. My plastic shark collection was unrivaled. Scenes were shot in my room for both the "Don't Want You" video and our *Naked* home video. It's no wonder I went into working on sets for film and TV. Even the one time we had a tour bus, I made sure to bring along some fun fur and other decor to deck out my bunk; the sharks, sadly, stayed home.

Here's the thing, I'm an introvert by default who's had to dig out the extrovert in myself—because I also have that in me too—but sometimes it's an effort to really drag it out there. I can only live in my little bubble for so long before I start to crave interaction. I actually love being in groups; I love being around people and having lots of friends. I need BOTH. There's a duality to me, and I noticed it while working on this book. I'm like, my answer is *this*, but also *this*. Yes to both! I'm always of two minds, and two opposing things will usually possess equal amounts of truth in my brain. Absolutism has never been my bag, I guess. Typical flaky artist. Probably explains why I never got tattooed. Permanency— yikes. Choose a design? Impossible!

A lack of self-confidence has always been the thorn in my side, my low self-esteem often derailing social interactions. Being around other people was sometimes a good opportunity for me to feel like I wasn't enough, and having to go onstage and reckon with that was a process for me. In the context of Lunachicks, these fearless and fierce sisters of mine, it was easy for me to feel invisible—not that I really wanted the attention, but I did crave some acknowledgment for my part in it all. A lot of the time it felt like I was in the shadow of Theo and Squid. Theo was a natural star, gorgeous and in control. Squid was the cool, tough badass. And I was the weird, nerdy chick. So I plugged away and did all the books and wrote music and did the artwork and managed the shit and booked shows, proving my worth by grinding the gears behind the curtain in order to make up for what I felt I lacked while I was in front of it. I always felt a little disconnected from the role of performer, like I was never sure if I actually belonged there. I didn't have the magnetic personality, the good looks, the tattoos, or the cool factor. When you're onstage, that's half—if not all—of it. I might have had the talent, but I didn't feel quite equipped with all the rest. I never did create a Lunachicks character for myself. I didn't have a punk rock name, and I didn't build a persona. To this day, I don't know how to be other than just kind of . . . me. Of course, I had on all the makeup and funny clothes, but if you were to ask me to define my stage character with personality traits, I'd be at a loss. Mostly, I was concerned with just keeping my head down and my mouth shut, my tube socks up, and rocking the fuck out (along with trying not to trip and fall off the stage).

Often I would step toward the background. I put my hair in my face and, with my big Roman nose peeking out, would hide from the audience. Although one time, some jerk in the crowd screamed out at me, "Geddy Lee!" (the hook-nosed singer from Rush). SERIOUSLY?! Mortifying! God, I hate that band. Reality is, there is no hiding when you're up onstage. Nose slander aside, experiencing that level of full-on self-expression is beyond exhilarating. Performing with the Lunachicks made me feel powerful, even when it sometimes was a struggle feeling so exposed.

Later on fronting my own band, Bantam, those feelings of exposure were challenged to the next level. At the first Bantam show, I thought I was going to have an actual heart attack in the dressing room. Now that I was the singer (and the guitarist), I was completely panicked about having the spotlight solely centered on ME. As soon as I stepped out onstage, I had to fight every urge not to run backstage and dive under the couch. But I had learned so much from playing with the Lunachicks and all those years of touring that being in front of an audience eventually became second nature, just like any other job: I know how to do this, and I'm here, so I'm going to do it. Once I was onstage, I could flip that switch and be like, "All right! It's on!" And just like in Lunachicks, it became something that I actually loved to do and was totally worth fighting through all those feelings of awkwardness. I love to play music and I had a kick-ass band that I was really proud of and, truthfully, being onstage and playing live is super fucking FUN! There really is nothing else like it—in fact, try it. No joke, go start your own band right now! You're welcome.

There was also a lot of gender stuff that I was very aware of throughout our career, which was a bit of a minefield to navigate. Squid, Theo, and I would talk about how we measured ourselves against each other because we knew everybody else was. We felt that. We'd all look in the mirror together as we were putting on our makeup, inspecting each other's faces and comparing flaws because we knew each other so well that we had become the standards for each other. "Do you have wrinkles there? What about cellulite? I have this weird thing on my ass," etc., etc. Maybe that happens with male bands too, but the gender component really reinforces this for women. It always felt like there was a societal push to define each of us by some sort of Spice Girl–like archetype character. There's always the pretty one, the cool one, the tough one. Are you the babydoll-dresses-and-combat-boots-type girl? Sexy-black-catsuit-and-wild-haired minx?? PUKE. I so wanted to get away from all that. I could give a shit what little label was going to get slapped onto me. But if you call me Geddy Lee, I will come down there and kick you.

Look, trying to figure out the identity thing is tricky enough for most twenty-somethings, but then add a sprinkle of anxiety, a few bouts of low-level depression, and a dash of OCD into the mix of public performance, and *blam!* It's a hot, boiling mess of feelings to sort through. Yay! All I knew was that I was on a mission to kick ass. When we had a good show and I came off the stage knowing that we had killed, it was the most satisfying feeling.

Much less fun was trying to maintain relationships when I was on tour half the year. Some of my boyfriends were not crazy about me being away for so long. They were either jealous because their band wasn't also touring, or just impatient and couldn't stick around until I got back. Honestly, I never pictured myself married with kids anyways 'cause commitment, and also because I was determined to experience as much as I could in my young life. I had a major case of FOMO, which helped land me in some questionable situations (usually involving large amounts of alcohol), like winding up drunk on the back of some dude's motorcycle doing 120 mph down the FDR Drive, or climbing into a stranger's van high out of my mind on pills in a foreign country where I didn't speak the language. Bad decisions—yup, they happen . . . but hey, stay in school, kids!

And speaking of staying in school, punk rock don't pay the rent, at least not for most bands. Only a few peeps we knew made a living off of their music, which gave me some hope, but in the end, out of all the things we did make, money was never one of them. Sadly, I don't know of that many women in rock who have had financial success. I'll never forget the night Squid and I got to share the stage with Sandy West and Cherie Currie of the Runaways to play a full Runaways set as their guitarist and bass player—AH-MAZE-ING!—but when I asked Sandy about her life, I was shocked to hear her say that she spent most of her days working odd construction jobs and worrying about money, just like the rest of us. That was when I realized that this was a long haul and that "success" was really how you chose to define it. For me, it was just an endless string of odd, dumb day jobs, and I would die a little inside every time that world collided with my Lunachicks notoriety. I'd be bartending and someone would come in and say, "Hey, you're Gina from the Lunachicks. I love your band, you gals are the greatest! Can I get a lime in that Corona?" Ugh, kill me now. We just sold out Irving Plaza! Don't forget to tip your bartender! #@$%! I hated that, I guess because of my own expectations of where I thought I should be, which was onstage with my best pals rockin' out to screaming crowds. Jumping back and forth between touring-superhero-rock-'n'-roll-dream-fantasy-come-true and ordinary life was always a rough reentry.

I never really did find myself another career to support my music habit, which would have been the responsible thing to do. "But what about health insurance?!" my mom would plead. Ugh, I just couldn't do it. Basically, I would rather be broke and have more time to make my art and music. It's still kind of that way, though I continue to tell myself I'm gonna get a real job one day. Ultimately, time has always been worth more to me than money. I just want time to crawl into the safety of my world and create. When I'm in that mode, I'm like, "Maybe I'm not such a weirdo after all. I'm fine. All is well." But as soon as I'm seen within the context of other people, and especially in the context of being a performer, all those feelings and issues of self-esteem and self-realization arise, and I question everything about myself. I wonder if I'm able to keep up. "Am I fitting in? Is this human suit looking right?" Because at some point somebody's going to be tipped off that really I'm an impostor who is playing along and trying to blend in with the crowd. They're going to find out that I am an alien.

CHAPTER 26

WE CAN BE WORSTER

Our good friend Jane Gulick knew a guy who was starting a label named Go-Kart. Gina called the owner, Greg Ross, and told him we needed a label, and he said, "Well, we're just starting up and we have one other band, but what we can offer is our undivided attention." That was all we needed to hear. Back in business, baby!

We wanted to name our next album *I'm with Stupid*, but we found out through the industry wire that Aimee Mann named her album that and it would be coming out around the same time as ours, so then we wanted to name it *I'm with Stupid Aimee Mann*.

GINA: I have a picture of my dorky neighbors from when I was a kid, and one of them is wearing the classic '70s "I'm with Stupid" T-shirt that points to the guy next to him. It would have been the perfect image to go with that title.

THEO: We also wanted to name an album *The Brown Album*, then Primus got to it first.

We decided to go with *Jerk of All Trades*. We made it with Ray Martin, a huge guy with long hair who was the brother we never had. He's an asshole, but somehow charming. We wanted to murder him, but we also adored him.

SQUID: I wanted to punch him in the face, but I loved him at the same time. We'd be driving with him, and he'd be like, "I fuckin' hate girls that are pigeon-toed." And I'm like, "You're four hundred fuckin' pounds! Shut the fuck up! Stop talking!" Fuckin' Ray. I'm still fighting with Ray Martin!

GINA: He loved to say things to piss us off, but out of all the people we worked with, I trusted his ear more than anybody's. He really knew what he was doing. We recorded in a studio he worked out of on Twenty-Second Street. We got a deal there by recording during off-hours, nights and weekends, and last-minute cancellations.

THEO: There were so many shenanigans with Ray. He did such a great job, but we would get in fights. I got thrown out of the control room for popping bubble wrap, so I went into the waiting room, grabbed the phone, and kept calling Ray from the waiting room, popping bubble wrap over the phone. He kept hanging up, and I kept calling. It was total stupidity. Ray is a large man, and at some point he said something that annoyed me so much that I kicked his roll-y chair across the room with one foot while he was sitting in it. Not in a mean way, but I sent him flying. Even he was shocked. We ended up getting along really well.

For all the ridiculousness, *Jerk* was when we honed our sound, and who we were as a band. Having Chip be so on point and steady was amazing. We all thought, "Wow, this drummer is fucking pro." Everyone was always impressed by Chip. *Jerk* feels like when everything came together. It was a high point, the album that everybody loved, the fan favorite so far.

Everything clicked and we finally became what we thought we should have sounded like way back when we were jamming away in each other's bedrooms. It reminded us of those times in Studio A when we'd tell each other, "No, we don't suck!" In our rattled teenage minds, we thought we sounded just like KISS. "No, really! Really! We do!" Except now the five of us were so in sync and the songs were actually solid. Lyrically, Theo outdid herself.

THEO: 1994 and 1995 were up-and-coming years for me personally and also for the band. I started modeling more frequently and did a Calvin Klein CK Be campaign. The legendary Richard Avedon shot the photos and commercials, which were written from interviews I did with the incredible Doon Arbus, daughter of Diane Arbus, who is one of my most favorite photographers. It was epic, truly. I was a guest on *The Jon Stewart Show* the same day as our album release show at CBGB. It felt like a pinnacle time. Then the fucking album cover with me goofing in a waitress costume made by David Dalrymple. It was so ridiculous, it was perfect. I remember people saying, "Who's the ugly chick on the cover?" Oh, that's me. But honestly, I was also going through a hard time. I finally ended it with my boyfriend right before we went into the studio. A lot of the songs on *Jerk* were fueled by that breakup.

We had exactly zero patience for guys who stepped out of line, especially when they were dating one of us. They should know better. One band member—who shall not be named in order to save her the embarrassment—was dating a real know-it-all. This guy was in the van with us one time during a heated band debate when he made a fatal mistake: trying to speak for his girlfriend, our sister. He was like, "Well, *I think* what she's trying to say is . . ." and we all turned and looked at him in utter and complete disbelief. Aliens could have landed outside the window and we wouldn't have been more dumbstruck than we were at the fact that this guy was (a) inserting himself into our conversation and (b) presumptuous enough to speak for one of us. Ho-lee shit. We were like angry apes. As if there weren't enough fucking opinions in one place!! Our eyes shot out of our heads. "What? He is *really talking??* IS HE REALLY HERE? Get the fuck out!" We almost drove the van off the road. We were like, "OUT! OUT!"

So yeah, Theo immortalized some of those idiots on *Jerk*, and she did it brilliantly. "Drop Dead" was the epitome of our "fuck you, you fucking motherfucker" message:

> Walk in front of a car, at the mall
> Trip and fall in the hall
> Smash your head against the wall
> You want to die, I can see it in your eye
> Rob a bank, tip the boat, sell yourself
> Break the law
> I like you better, when you're deader
> Don't you fuck with us
> We will follow you onto the bus
> Fart right in your face
> And watch out because
> Should've worn Tussy like your mama said
> Then maybe you wouldn't be dead
> We can be worster!
> Drop dead! Drop!

SQUID: I don't even know how to talk about Theo's lyrics. Too genius. Every time I start listening to those songs, it's like getting sucked into a crying-laughing K-hole. So fuckin' funny.

Two of our best feminist anthems are on *Jerk*: "Bitterness Barbie" was about smashing beauty standards, and "Fallopian Rhapsody" was about being pro-choice. Then there was "Brickface + Stucco," about a transgender couple falling in love.

CHIP: I think Theo's lyrics are what set us apart from all other bands. They are political, intelligent, funny, clever—things that nobody else was writing about. I'm very proud of her lyrics. Sometimes we'd get fan mail from kids who were questioning if they were gay or transgender, or we'd get letters from girls who were in bad relationships and took steps to get out of their abusive situations after hearing our songs and Theo's lyrics. We knew we were making a difference in those fans' lives, and each of us personally wrote back to every single letter.

THEO: Except for the creepy ones, obviously.

Of course, we included some ludicrous songs too.

GINA: I had written a riff that became "Fingerful," and Theo was like, "I don't know what to write about. Give me some subject matters." "How about fetishes!!" So she came up with that one, genius as always. Also can't forget "Buttplug"!

THEO: "F.D.S. (Shit Finger Dick)" came from Dean Kennedy, our English tour manager. He was yelling about somebody, "Buh buh buh shit finger dick." We fell over laughing. It was a saying, I think. But FDS is "feminine deodorant spray"—vagina perfume that actually exists. Just a letter scramble/inside joke released into the world.

GINA: FDS had the same letters as the words *shit finger dick*, but they weren't in the right order, which we thought was hilarious. So we kept it.

SQUID: The lyrics I wrote for my vocal part in "Shit Finger Dick" were heartfelt:

Only want what you can't have and babe
and what you can't have is me

I don't care who you are
What the fuck you want from me
Dis me once, dis me twice
I don't think it's very nice
Fuck you in your stupid face
I shit on you and it feels great!

SQUID: I wrote it for Jimmy from Murphy's Law, who I know will be flattered. We had been friends for a long time, then a little more than friends. Then he started sleeping with someone else, which was whatever, but didn't feel like telling me because men are cowards. Ha! But then he stood me up on my birthday! I was in the Music Building in a shitty rehearsal room waiting for him, and fucker no-showed. I was so pissed, waiting for him to call me or meet me but he never did. So I was there by myself writing music, and those words floated down like I was Moses on the mountain. Be warned, mutherfuckers: that's the risk you take dating a songwriter. I never lost the pleasure of singing that part with all the girls in the crowd who jumped to the mic to join me. I guess I'm not alone in my sentiments. Love you, Jimmy! Thanks for the mammaries.

If you listen all the way to the end of the album, you can hear us cracking up and trading burps on the phone with Lady Bunny, the drag superstar whom we love so much. We wanted her on the album but didn't know what she would do, so we called her up and hit the Record button. Perfection.

Jerk was so much fun to make, and we toured like mad to support it. We were getting progressively bigger and bigger gigs—except for that time we played to a crowd of one in Geneva. We stood onstage and wondered aloud, "Where is everyone?" The lone attendee must've felt bad for us because she yelled back, "I'll call my friend!" which brought the grand total to two people. But really, *Jerk* put us back on the up-and-up, thanks in part to the popularity of West Coast punk. The first half of our career was really centered on the European markets because that's where we were initially famous and developed the first wave of our following. We played here and there in the US, but it felt like we had actual careers in Europe. Then we hooked up with West Coast powerhouse and BOSS booking agent Stormy Shepherd, who later became our manager as well, and gave our band a second incarnation. It's almost as if there were two parts of our career: before Stormy and after Stormy. Once we had her leading the way, we started playing better-fitting bills and amassing a new and younger fan base.

> **THEO:** I was introduced to Stormy in the early '90s by my then-boyfriend. We were both in Hawaii in August 1995, and I ended up crashing in her hotel room for the duration of that trip. We became close friends and remain so decades (and countless hotel rooms) later. Stormy is an anomaly: a Mormon from Salt Lake City who is a punk rocker on the top of her game, booking many of the biggest punk bands of all time. She flipped our fan base from college age up to all ages. I trust her implicitly and eternally. Love you, Stormy!!

Part of that also had to do with the fact that when punk music hit the mainstream and got rebranded in America, kids could go into stores like Hot Topic and buy punk records. We started touring as the opening act for enormously popular West Coast punk bands like Offspring, NOFX, and Rancid. They were similar to us in that they had all been friends for so many years and had intense histories with each other. They were teenagers together, and had stories about growing up and forming a band to hang out and have fun. Suddenly, we were in their world and playing for their fans. We went out on tour with the Vandals and Offspring in 1995, when Offspring were huge. A couple of years earlier, those guys opened for us on tour.

GINA: We were getting ready to go on a US tour. Stormy sent me one of their CDs telling us, "These guys love you and really want to open for you." They were absolutely unheard of at the time, but I thought their CD was pretty decent so we figured "Why not?" and brought them on tour. After the first few shows, we were like, "Who are these jock-y guys?" Our audience wasn't particularly kind to them, but we wound up becoming friends with them because it turned out they were great guys. Within a year, maybe even six months, they dropped *Smash* and became international rock stars. They didn't have to take us out with them, but they did. Three times!

Offspring always remembered that we were good to them back then, and they repaid our kindness with their own. The joke was, if you open for us, you *will* get a major record deal. It was incredible, but it was also bizarre.

GINA: For so long, we were THE opening band. We joked that we should cover the Grand Funk Railroad song "We're an American Band," but change it to "We're an Opening Band."

THEO: Years later, Lady Gaga opened for my band Theo and the Skyscrapers at our last New York show.

SINDI: I think all the successes of bands we had grown up with affected the other girls strongly. The Offspring, who had opened for us in the early days of their band—I have a picture of them sleeping side by side in the back of their van—were suddenly millionaires, and we were opening for them in arenas. Of course that sucks! They're on a luxury bus and don't have to load their own gear and they have catering. It was frustrating as hell, even for me who cared less about that stuff. I will say, those other bands treated us well when they had success. They all shared with us. They were great. When our van broke down while we were touring with them, Offspring sent their bus to pick us up so we could make it to the gig. They even had someone stay with our van while it got fixed. Nobody was like, "See ya!"

THEO: After the shows, Offspring would shower and then get on their bus and drive to the next place, so they would let us shower and sleep in the fancy hotel rooms that were already booked and paid for. It was so nice of them. Hotel guests would leave their leftover room service in the hallways, and if it was vegetarian I'd eat it. I scored a delicious Indian takeout meal on a tray in an Offspring five-star hotel hallway. Thanks, guys!

GINA: They had a chef who toured with them and cooked for them. One night, the chef made dinner for me but I was feeling so sick that night and couldn't eat. He was actually of-fended: "I made you this big dinner and you didn't even show up!" I felt bad: "I didn't know you cared!" But it gave us a sense of what major financial success felt like (even if it wasn't our own), and bands like the Offspring were super-generous in sharing that with us. It was a very different reality from our indie punk venues to the arenas, luxury hotels, buses, and catering.

SQUID: I remember they had socks and underwear on their rider every night. I was so confused. Apparently, it was cheaper and easier to ditch their clothes than launder them. Wow, that blew my mind. My parents used to cut the mold off food and feed it to us. This became the new hallmark of rock 'n' roll famedom—brand-new socks at every show, wow!

It was a huge coup to be on that bill, and we lived it up. We'd never been on a tour of that size, and we quickly learned that every sound-man's hard-on is Steely Dan. There is no band we collectively hate more than Steely Dan, but for some reason the mix on their albums is the standard by which soundmen equalize their mixing board in arenas. We endured consecutive soundchecks to Steely Dan blasting away. Ugh, we hated it so much.

One bonus of those big tours was the roller-skating. There's a video of Heart roller-skating around a big venue while soundchecking with wireless guitars. We were like, "We need roller skates so we can be like Heart!" One night after the show, Theo was wasted and decided to get her roller skates. She tied the skates, stood up, and wiped out.

THEO: I had been drinking Goldschläger and Jägermeister—I never drank! I had been skating every day for hours, no problem, but that was when I was sober. I put the skates on and barely stood up. Down I went. I fell on my thumb, which got bent backward, like in the wrong direction. All I said to myself was, "No hospital." I sat down, put my thumb on our buddy Dave's leg (he was one of the Offspring's roadies), made a fist with my left hand, and slammed my thumb back in place. Needless to say, Dave freaked out. He screamed, "I never felt something like that in my life! You are so fucking punk!" Whatever, I just didn't want to go to the hospital. I put ice on my thumb and didn't feel so good, so we all left to go back to the hotel. I was wearing shorts, a full face of stage makeup, fake eyelashes, and glitter. I hailed a cab and got in the front with the driver, holding my hand over one eye because my vision was so blurred and I didn't want to get sick in the cab. My thumb was the size of a soda bottle. The driver was talking to me: "Oh, you've never been to Milwaukee? Let's do a tour!" Noooooo!!!! I got back to the hotel and started pounding on doors. I got into the right room, and luckily the girls were there.

SQUID: The night ended with Chip holding Theo by the hair over the toilet so her face wouldn't fall in. We were all vegetarians, and I could hear Chip saying all this meaty shit to Theo, like, "Chicken-fried pork fat!" and Theo puking so hard. "Pigs' feet in gristle!" *Bluurrrgg-hhhh!* Theo was puking glitter from the Goldschläger all over the toilet.

THEO: I had a full mouth of glitter from my makeup too, but I didn't know any of that happened because I was so wasted. Chip taught me how to stop the spins: put one arm and one leg over the side of the bed. I have never forgotten this tried-and-true method. The next day my thumb was giant and swollen like Fred Flintstone's feet.

CHIP: The best part was the next morning, when I went in the bathroom, there was glitter at the bottom of the toilet and lipstick on the toilet seat. If that ain't punk, I don't know what it is. But for me, it was really quite lonely on those arena tours because it was just dudes, dudes, dudes: lighting dudes, sound dudes, grips dudes, roadie dudes. The girls had a blast, but I found myself without anything to do or anybody to talk to, so I would often go out into the van and watch movies by myself to kill time. It wasn't that I wasn't happy, I was just very bored. I can only be around dudes for so much.

GINA: I think for a lot of male bands, it was refreshing to have us around. Just like Chip was saying: dudes 24/7. It was always such a sausagefest that I think part of the reason bands took us out—aside from knowing we were every bit as fuckin' awesome as their dude-musician friends—was to just get a break from all of that.

Everyone had so much fun the first time, Offspring invited us back on tour. One night, both bands stayed at a hotel and partied. The guys were running around the hotel, moron-drunk, pranking each other. Somebody stole the guitar player Noodles's glasses and colored in the lenses with black Sharpie so he couldn't see. He was super-drunk and flipped his shit, trashing everything in the hotel room. He tried to pull the TV off the wall and throw it out the window, but it was bolted in.

SQUID: I thought he was gonna kill himself trying to rip that thing off the wall. Total rock-star fail. Everything in the room was smashed. It was like rubble. Theo and I were in bed giggling. The only thing left that wasn't broken was a lamp. So finally, I was like, "Okay, time to go to bed. Turn the light out." Theo grabbed the lamp and smashed it. We laughed ourselves to sleep in the dark.

THEO: After the first big Offspring tour, a roadie pal who had a crush on me invited me to Hawaii for a big music festival. So I went. Didn't sleep with him, but it all worked out—he wound up meeting the girl who he would marry! I hung out with all the Rancid guys on that trip. We had played with them previously, but we really started to bond. Turns out the guitar player, Lars, always wanted to be a clown too. New friend for life! After that, they brought us with them for their huuuuge ... And Out Come the Wolves Tour. I loved watching their sets every single night. Squid tattooed "Rancid + Lunachicks '95" on me, Chip, Lars, and the bass player, Matt. Rancid is still a favorite band of ours.

The one drawback to opening for some of those West Coast bands was the audience they drew. While there were a lot of awesome die-hard punk fans, there was also a component of straight-up fratty jocks that didn't exactly appreciate a bunch of freak women blasting out their eardrums. They weren't sure if it was cool or okay to like us. Was it okay to be fans of women? Some sets were amazing and some just felt like a battle. At one show in Minnesota, an entire arena of douche-boys was chanting, "Show us your tits! Show us your tits! Show us your tits!" We were shell-shocked, appalled. This wasn't like the old days, where we were in some punk club and could pick out the one or two drunk dummies and sock them in the face. This was a fucking ocean of Neanderthals who wanted us offstage to make way for the headliner so they could start a mosh pit and beat the shit out of each other. Theo reached between her legs and, in a nod to our sister Donita Sparks of L7, pulled out her tampon and threw it into the crowd of fifteen thousand people. We all looked for it afterward but couldn't find it, which means someone either threw it out or took it home as a souvenir. GROSS! During another show on that tour, a super-violent mosh pit broke out—people were getting hurt for real. Theo stopped the whole show and had the venue bring up the lights and got security to march the cavemen offenders out of there.

Other crowds were more receptive, much to our surprise. Our good friend and mover and shaker Cyndy Villano worked at Interscope and helped make two tours happen that really broadened our audience. No Doubt took us on an arena tour during the peak of their popularity. It was massive. We had absolutely no idea how their crowds would react to us, seeing as how we were not at all the polished Top 40 pop stars that No Doubt were. Not only did we win over the young girls in the audience, we also won over their moms! Playing for two generations of women screaming for us night after night was mind-blowing.

A similar thing happened when we were the opener for Marilyn Manson's Smells Like Children Tour. Depending on which of us you ask, it turned out to be a winning bill. What stunned most of us was just how receptive the audiences were, especially considering we weren't in the same musical genre as Manson. We'd been busting our asses trying to connect with the pop-punk crowds who theoretically should've been into our music, but it turned out we had a huge and almost immediate appeal to dark-and-creepy goth kids. Our connection to Manson's crowd transcended music to also include the shared outsiderness and displacement we all felt as freaks. It was beautiful. And so a hearty "FUCK YOU" to every narrow-minded music industry moron who told us they had no idea how to market us or who our audience could possibly be. We play for the misfits and weirdos—and they are everywhere—but those suits had no foresight to connect the dots.

THEO: That was one of the best tours we did. It was a very good match in terms of freakiness, and the crowd was won over much more easily. It was chubby boys in dresses and makeup, just staring at us, and me thinking, "I get you." We were used to playing in front of frat boys all the time and having to basically fight our way through the set. But for this tour, the fans and us could *see* each other, we *got* each other.

SQUID: Manson was the first gender-bending bill we were ever on, and I have to say, I really was aware of it. Those were our freaky people. They were very responsive.

GINA: I had such mixed feelings about that tour. They were the one band we toured with that we didn't become tight friends with. I don't remember ever going out together after shows or bullshitting in the dressing rooms with them. But I will say that their audience was great. These strange, arty kids all dark and brooding were the kind of kids I could have hung out with as a teenager. In a way, I felt more at home with them than I did with some of the macho crowds of the bigger punk bands.

SINDI: I thought Manson's crowd hated us the most out of any tour we ever did. It was a super-goth audience, and we were a thousand different colors thrown up all over the place. We'd take the stage and look out, and the room was a sea of black clothes, black hair, black eye makeup, and totally sullen. Then there we are, goofball box of Crayola 64.

CHIP: I liked Marilyn. During that tour, I stopped being vegetarian and was always very hungry since we had a vegetarian rider. I must've complained a little too loudly because after Marilyn's set, he came to our dressing room and stood in the doorway with big cuts on his chest (he used to cut himself with glass during the show) and said to me in a very motherly way, "Chip, we have some extra fried chicken if you'd like?" It was very sweet. And then one time I went to Deb Parker's Beauty Bar on Fourteenth Street in New York City just to hang out, and when I came in, Marilyn was sitting there with about twelve girls fawning all over him. He looked uncomfortable, and when he saw me he was like, "CHIP! Hi!! How are you! Come on, let's go to the bar and do some shots!" I think as a way to get away from the fans staring at him.

At one old, famous club on that tour, there was no bathroom backstage, not that there weren't any facilities per se.

THEO: There were litter boxes. We peed in them. Litter boxes backstage were part of Marilyn Manson's rider.

GINA: What?? I do not remember that.

SQUID: WAIT, THE CAT BOXES WERE FOR THE BANDS?

GINA: NO.

THEO: YES, YES, YES. I peed in the cat boxes because the cat box was there to pee in. I swear to god. Actually a pretty smart thing to do in a pinch if you have people to go to a pet store and buy a litter box and litter for you. Ha!

CHIP: Theo definitely peed in a litter box backstage—a couple of times. You see, when you're in the dressing room almost ready to go onstage, the last thing you wanna do is walk out into the middle of the audience and head to the bathroom.

We must have made some kind of impression on Manson, though. He and the band left the tour for a minute to go make a video for "Sweet Dreams," and wouldn't you know, Manson's in a tutu in the video. We saw the video on MTV right after we got home from tour with them and were like, "He totally stole Gina's tutu look!"

> **GINA:** Who doesn't love to wear a tutu, come on? Even saying the word *tutu*—it's so good! Speaking of stealing, one time we played a show with a band called the New Bomb Turks. After we got offstage, we hung up our stank-ass, sweaty, wet stage clothes to dry in the shared dressing room, as per usual. At the end of the night, our clothes were gone. Jerks took our stage outfits. Sue me for libel, but somewhere, some dude is out there lookin' real cute in my tutu. Perv.

Our little New York City scene happened to be experiencing a surge in popularity right around the time we were writing and recording *Jerk*. A new glam-rock party called Squeezebox popped up downtown at a club called Don Hill's. It was created by our good friend, the amazing clothing and jewelry designer Michael Schmidt, as an antidote to the gay clubs that played nothing but dance music. Squeezebox was the first weekly punk-rock drag party in New York City. We played opening night, April 15, 1994, and basically became the mascots of that scene. To us, that meant we were part of the signature of what that crew stood for. It was a shared subculture of creativity and color. No rules, no uniform, no inhibitions, everyone flying their freak flag. There was none of the sexism or homophobia or jock-y boys' club bullshit of other music scenes. It was a complete 180-degree turn from the hardcore matinees of our youth. In fact, some of the hardcore guys would hang out at Squeezebox because word traveled fast that it was the most fun, most anything-goes, most rock-'n'-roll thing the city had seen in ages. It was such a mixed crowd: rock 'n' roll people, gay people, straight people, go-go dancers, all of the freaks we considered to be part of our extended family. While then-mayor Rudy Giuliani (jerk) was choking the fun out of our city, Squeezebox preserved it by giving our arty downtown crew a place to let loose.

GINA: It was our own version of a rock club. On tour, we played our share of rock clubs that were full of testosterone and angst, dudes posturing and fighting. Who needs that crap? Nope, not us! I played guitar every week in the Squeezebox house band, having the awesome experience of backing some of NYC's most amazing talent like Lady Bunny, Jayne County, and Justin Vivian Bond. One night I backed up Jean Hill, who played Grizelda Brown in *Desperate Living*. I have a picture of me and her. She came on in a vinyl catsuit with her oxygen tanks. I was in awe.

SQUID: At Squeezebox, you had to go far out of your way to stand out in that crowd. People were getting blown on staircases, there were tons of drugs in the bathroom, go-go boys/girls danced onstage, every size, shape, style, and theme—the crazier, the stranger, the funnier, the better. I danced there too. It was so much fun. And there was straight-up boy-on-boy fucking being projected onto screens throughout the club. It was the hottest punk club in town, and it came with the most awesome sense of pride. It was a total takeover, like, "YES! WE WON!" No one dared pull shit in that place.

CHIP: Squeezebox was our second home next to CBGB. I remember the whole club stopped to watch the O. J. Simpson Bronco chase on the TV while somebody was getting teabagged at the bar.

THEO: I felt very comfortable there in a way that I never felt anywhere else—certainly never in a straight bar. I still feel that way if I'm in a very "straight" place—I feel very uncomfortable and unsafe, but that just goes to my otherness and PTSD. I have always felt somewhat like a gay man trapped in a woman's body—a general "queer-do" by today's standards.

By 1994, I had already started go-go dancing. The whole club-kid era started shortly after we became a band. There was a kind of synchronicity between what those kids were doing to nightlife in the post-Warhol years and what we were doing to music in the butt-rock hair-metal and hardcore years—we threw a wrench in it. In the Warhol era, everyone wore designer clothes, went to exclusive clubs like Studio 54—all very posh and fabulous and glamorous, celebrity-centric. Then these no-name kids showed up, made their own outrageous, cartoony costumes and makeup, and started throwing their own parties and became downtown celebs themselves. Meanwhile, the OG nightlife people are like, "Warhol's dead, nightlife is over," and they really didn't care for these new club kids. Music didn't have much to do with it. It was all about expression through your looks, and being as ostentatious as possible. Lots of shaved eyebrows. It was yourself as the art medium, which I really could relate to.

My first go-go gig was in the basement of Webster Hall at my close friends' Miss Guy and JoJo Americo's party called She. Each week there was a different theme. Squid and I both danced there—not topless dancing, just theme dress-up. They spun all our favorite records; it was heavenly. Gina DJ'd there a few times too. One night I dressed as Debbie Harry, and Squid was Wendy O. Williams. There was a *Carrie* theme, where we were covered in fake blood. It was a gathering of eccentric types. When She ended, Squeezebox started at Don Hill's. The club had just opened on the West Side, near Canal Street. Drag queens used to lip-sync, but at Squeezebox they sang live with a house band, some for the first time in their lives. It got pretty glamorous, very rock 'n' roll. The Toilet Boys formed there, Hedwig came out of there. I go-go danced there every weekend that I was in town and sang with the house band all the time. It's where the real honing of my becoming a drag queen took place. It was the *Cheers* bar for queers and allies. I was Norm.

SINDI: I never had tattoos or piercings. I was pretty strait-laced, comparatively! But I never felt any weird vibe at Squeezebox because I wasn't, say, outrageous. But, like, in San Francisco, I always felt like the red-headed stepchild that nobody was interested in. I never felt that way at Squeezebox. Everybody was accepted.

THEO: There was so much dancing. Nobody got hurt. Squeezebox also did the first live broadcast on the internet.

SINDI: We opened for either Debbie Harry or Joan Jett for that broadcast. Both of them were there that night.

THEO: One night, Green Day was playing some big multi-band show at Madison Square Garden, probably for a radio station or something, and they invited a ton of Squeezebox regulars to dance onstage with them at the Garden. It was me and a gaggle of drag queens including Formika, Jackie Beat, Sherry Vine, and Miss Guy. I was like, "I'm onstage at Madison Square Garden!!" That's where Jackie Beat deemed me an honorary drag queen. (SIGH, dreams really do come true!) The afterparty was at Squeezebox, and a bunch of us got tiny star tattoos on our wrists that night. There's about thirteen people with identical tattoos. Every now and then I'll run into someone who has the star. So many people came to Squeezebox through the years: Laverne Cox, John Waters, Anohni, Desi Santiago, Kristofer Buckle, Joey Arias, Liv Tyler,

Waltpaper, Angie Bowie, Bridget Everett, Marc Jacobs, Boy George, Pete Burns, Anna Sui, Drew Barrymore, Natasha Lyonne—everybody came through there if they were around.

SQUID: We all grew up thinking we missed New York's heyday, like Max's Kansas City and CB's in the '70s. We were doing anything to entertain ourselves in the space that came after that. But Squeezebox really was a moment, a great scene, and we were part of it. The kids today have something, somewhere, so good for them. You don't know what you've got till it's gone.

These years were a really special time for us. We were well known, joining great tours, and getting praise from all over the world. Our fan base kept growing and was enthusiastic to an extreme degree. Of all the crowds that came to see us, arguably our favorite was at an event called Rockfest at Gallaudet University in Washington, DC, in 1996. Gallaudet is a school for students who are deaf and hard of hearing. There were bands, circus performers—it was so much fun. All the bands played in a really deep cement loading dock, like a metal-and-cement horseshoe. The soundperson turned us up super-loud so the vibrations carried really, really strongly. There was a live sign language translator for the lyrics. The people went bananas for us. It was next-level in terms of letting go. In between songs, it was silent; to applaud, they would raise their hands, wiggle their fingers, and wave at us. They loved us. We loved them. The school newspaper said we were the favorite entertainment act of the festival, such an honor. The paper also noted that we had an impressive list of food requirements. Yup.

When you add it all up, we had so many life-affirming, fuck-yes moments as a band that helped balance whatever gripes we had with the music industry, which, irony of ironies, turned out to *not* always be great for business. Many bands we knew got signed to a big label only to get dropped shortly after. These hopeful little punk rock bands would sign contracts, record an album, and then the label would lose interest and shelve their album for god knows how long. AND they couldn't get out of the contract because majors have big-money lawyers who will litigate up the ass.

We weren't about to let that happen to us. As far as our brains can piece together, back when we were with Blast First, the label didn't want to release *Babysitters on Acid* in the States—Paul Smith might have decided he didn't want to pour any more money into it. That might have had something to do with why we wanted to cut ties with him. Who can remember? But we were adamant about getting our masters back, which meant we had to steal them. Master tapes (two-inch tape reels) are about the size of a cymbal, and they weigh a lot. It's not like you could put a thumb drive in your pocket and take off.

Anyway, the actual stealing of the tapes is like the Three Stooges version of *Mission: Impossible*. We hatched a plan. Blast First had an office in SoHo. We (Theo, Gina, Squid, and Sindi) all met outside, went over our little scheme, and proceeded to walk into the building. Two of us distracted the employees while the other two rifled through all the master tape reels stored on giant shelves that took up one side of an open loft-style office. That was the plan. We put the reels under our coats and walked out like, "Oh, here! Look over there! Lemme show you something! Look out the window! Byeeee." We seriously stole our shit while the whole place was fully staffed.

Great story, right? Well, in true Lunachicks fashion, we have no idea where the tapes are now. That's right: we lost the master tapes we stole. How we lost a stack of reel-to-reel tapes is a separate mystery; it's not like they could be under the couch or in the back of someone's closet.

GINA: I have an unidentified half-inch reel in my apartment. Because why would there be anything written on it?!

SQUID: We probably stole Dinosaur Jr. masters or something.

As a result, when Go-Kart decided to rerelease *Babysitters on Acid* in the US, they had to bootleg it because the masters were gone. Theoretically, all of this would be a big legal fiasco—if only there was a contract.

That's right. We have no idea where the original contract that we signed with Blast First is. Nobody does. As such, we're able to tell this story without the threat of being sued. Um, or not . . .

We had a contract with Go-Kart for each album, except, of course, none of us seem to know where any of the signed copies are. That was one of the many benefits of working with Greg (aside from him becoming like family to us). He would offer us one-offs with the option of doing a next album so we didn't feel trapped. That is not typical of a label. Usually you're stuck with them for a few albums. But Greg was really rooting for us and doing whatever he could to help us move forward. He also didn't interfere, and let us put out the kind of music that we wanted. Through the grapevine, we heard that certain big labels would restyle a band's music in order to make it more attractive to a broader audience. It certainly *did* work for some bands, but there was a price. One band that we were close to that blew up would complain that they couldn't get laid once they got big because all the girls in the audience were thirteen. They got super-famous super-quickly, and went from veritable nobodies to basically teen-pop crushes. It just seemed like we were all striving so hard to get to this place, but the place wasn't always what we'd envisioned.

The fact was we were scary, we were funny, we didn't give a fuck, and nobody could tell us what to do, least of all a label person suggesting we be more appealing in order to sell more albums. We'd have been like, "Pfft!" An attempt was, in fact, made to make our music more commercially viable. Imagine how that turned out.

CHAPTER 27

WE LEFT OUR FARTS IN SAN FRANCISCO

Jerk of All Trades was a success. Not that it went gold or anything, much less bronze, but tours sold well, and we got (mostly) favorable international press coverage, and more importantly, the fans really dug it. When it came time to make our next album, we wanted to take advantage of the momentum.

We decided Fat Mike from NOFX was going to produce our follow-up album, *Pretty Ugly*. We had toured with his band, had a blast, and all became good friends. Mike produced a bunch of great albums, and we really liked the production of NOFX's *Punk in Drublic*, which was engineered by Ryan Greene. We figured if we could get our album to sound like that one, we'd be golden. Plus, having Fat Mike's name on it wouldn't hurt. (Mind you, he never offered to put the album out on his very popular label, Fat Wreck Chords.)

And so, this meant we'd be making the album in Mike's neck of the woods: San Francisco. We played one of the most magical shows of our career out there with the Del Rubio Triplets, may they rest in peace. They were three seventy-something-year-old Dolly Parton–ish rejects playing ukuleles. Genius. Whoever promoted that was brilliant. That city was so queer and fun and felt like its own universe. It became our second home, where we always had huge audiences and always felt welcome and adored, plus Gina's sister lived there. We had never gone anywhere to make a record before! Hey, look at us! We were flying to California to make an album!

> THEO: It felt glamorous to go away and record. I was trying to be cool about it, "Yeah, we're going to San Francisco for a month to record our new album, no biggie..." All blasé and shit.

We spent two weeks in a Victorian house on Divisadero Street, allegedly where Anne Rice wrote *Interview with the Vampire*. The opening of that book is the vampire looking out the window onto Divisadero Street. We were sleeping in that room. There may or may not have been a ghost in the house.

Pretty Ugly was a fun record to make, we laughed *a lot*, but it was also trying at times on a number of levels. We showed up at the studio, which was in the basement of the vampire house, with most of the material written and ready to go. Mike had other plans for us. We played him the songs, talked about what we were going for, the usual process. He explained that his whole philosophy was to rip everybody off. If you liked something that someone has done, just rip them off. So he asked us who some of our favorite bands and songwriters were, and we of course said, "Buzzcocks!"

At that moment, Mike declared that he hated Buzzcocks and thought they sucked.

Oh boy.

We were stunned. Was this guy serious? That is the punk rock equivalent to saying the Beatles suck. Even if it's not your cup of tea, you can't say those aren't good songs. That was so weird for us to hear—and also sort of terrifying, given that this guy was *making our fucking record*. As if that wasn't unnerving enough, Mike had his own music theory that he wanted us to adopt.

> THEO: Mike's signature vocal style was that every song should end on an up note. If you think about Buzzcocks songs,

like "What Do I Get?" or "Ever Fallen in Love (With Someone You Shouldn't've?)," they don't do that. The blues didn't do that, and the blues were the beginning of rock 'n' roll. Well, guess what? Neither did we. The most famous band I can think of that often sings with that ending-on-an-up-note is the Beach Boys. I was NOT a fan of the Beach Boys. Surprised?

SQUID: My most hated band ever is the Beach Boys. I. Despise. The Beach Boys. Those songs give me hives.

GINA: Mike definitely had criticisms about our song structure. He liked things his way, and I remember butting heads with him a lot.

SINDI: I listened to Mike. Musically, he and I were on the same page, so I was ready to go down his road. It wasn't that I was gunning for commercial success; I really agreed with his ideas. I knew everybody didn't feel the same way.

The OC scene was very popular. That whole sound was Mike's world, and some of those bands were making shit-tons of money. Like a businessman, he thought he knew why we weren't selling more albums. He saw an opportunity to reimagine our entire musical approach. He wanted us to be more pop.

He would always say, "People don't like songs that are fast and then slow." Many of our songs have tempo changes in them. Our song structures include weird parts that would throw off the mosh pit during a live show. We dug that. But that was a big criticism of his. He is a formula guy. In terms of his own band, he found out what worked and he continued to do it and he thought that was what was best for everybody. He kept trying to push a similar formula into our songs.

Here's the thing: we were approaching our album as artists first, businesspeople second. We weren't about to compromise our own vision for the sake of sales. Were we?

THEO: Mike wanted me to change my vocal melodies to meet his formula. I mean, we were there for the ride, but as history has shown, it didn't matter who was telling us how to do our thing, we were still going to do it our way at the end of the day. I was willing to bend a bit to meet his ideas because he was so successful. He made a lot of money with this sound of his and his record label. We had done things our way; why not try something a little different? Yet ...

SQUID: He wanted you to sing like Gwen Stefani.

GINA: He wanted Theo to sing like a little girl. I was not feelin' it. He said, "I want you to sound as young and girlie as possible." I was bummed.

SQUID: There's one track where we were in the mixing booth and Mike was really pushing Theo to do it his way, encouraging her to do that young-sounding voice. It was strange. But I also remember thinking, "Well, I want to sell a hundred million records, so fuck it. Whatever. If Theo's fine with it, I'm not going to stand in the way."

GINA: I remember being the difficult party in that discussion. I got into a disagreement with Mike and Sindi. Theo was upset with me.

THEO: At some point, I just left. I had had it. Everyone was trying to tell me how to sound. "Sing like this!" "Sing like this!" "Sing like this!" Finally I said, "I AM GO-ING HOME." I left the house and was like, "I am walking home, right now, from San Francisco. I wonder how long that will take." I left in a rage and was walking toward the highway. Not even kidding. I ended up at Rainbow grocery store, got myself some snacks, and walked back to the house. Maybe I was just hangry?

GINA: At the time, I felt like there was an attempt to manip-ulate our sound and change us into a poppy band, but when I look back on it, that's not really how the album turned out. It was no great leap from what we were doing previously. Although *Pretty Ugly* may not be my favorite Lunachicks record, there are still several great songs on there, for sure.

SQUID: "Mr. Lady" opens with one of Theo's best lines: "My brown eye's blue from so much lovin' / Gettin' another lovin' oven." Theo needs her own special place in this world.

THEO: "Mr. Lady" was inspired by the time I went to Japan with the Squeezebox crew, which included some of the most incredible drag and genderqueer performers ever: Joey Arias, Sherry Vine, Mistress Formika, Jackie Beat, and my BFF Miss Guy. I was the only cis girl invited to sing. I felt like, "Yes, I made it!" While we were there, we went looking for crazy shit to entertain ourselves with, and someone found the movie *Mr. Lady* at a theater, I think. It's a real movie! That's where the song came from. Having been in the drag scene and being the club kid that I was, I was around drag queens and trans women on the regular. I remember when Amanda Lepore and Sophia Lamar both got their sex changes. I think we were all modeling the NYC designer Maja's clothes at a rock 'n' roll/fashion VH1 event where we had to stand on a giant rotating record player, and the two of them were running around naked showing off their new vaginas. They were so excited; it was a beautiful moment. Some of the other girls would travel to Mexico to get boobs, but there was also a local lady uptown who would do silicone injections out of her apartment—butts and lips and cheeks and things—but it was all silicone and silicone would move around. Some of those injections did not go well. I mean, it was sketchy. The first boobs that some of the girls got were practically at their collarbones— they took a bit of time to drop into the right spots. I remember the first really nice ones I saw. I was invited to feel them. The girls were so happy, and I was thrilled for them. The thing is, back then, transgender issues were not at all as openly discussed as they are now, but the downtown scene was a spectrum of gender identities, and that crew was extended family to us. They always will be.

SQUID: For the final song, "Missed It," we got Mike to be the guy at the end of the song who yells, "'Free Bird'!" and we used Prince's live album for the crowd noise. I remember being in the control room, and you could hear the jets flying over the crowd. YES, put that on our record! Perfect! That is the stuff I'm most proud of, ripping off Prince.

Pretty Ugly was also the last album we made with Sindi. We could kinda see the writing on the wall. It was probably a long time coming.

THEO: She just wasn't around for that album.

SQUID: I forgot she was there.

GINA: I was annoyed with Sindi because she insisted on putting her rhythm guitar parts down first. And once the first guitar goes down, the second guitar has to follow it, so I usually do the initial tracks. But she wanted to go hang out with her friends. She put down her tracks and then split. She was never really as involved musically. She was always, "Whatever, you guys." She didn't do backups or overdubs and wasn't involved in the mixing. I'm the control freak when it comes to the creative process, and recording is my most favorite thing ever. Put me in a recording studio, and I am the happiest girl in the world. I love everything about it. I get super into it when it comes time to get to work. Sindi and I were opposites in that sense. I was like, "This is OUR

LIVES!!" Yeah, I know. I'll own it, I'm a passionate paisan, what can I say? Sorry, guys!

SQUID: We weren't moving forward together anymore, so I guess we had to move apart. She was miserable, and she was making us miserable. It wasn't a good time.

THEO: It was very, "If mama ain't happy, ain't nobody happy." Sindi and I were roommates for about a year in the early '90s, so we had lived together on the road and at home. I knew her very well, how she thought, how she operated in her life. I got her. She was smart and a shrewd businesswoman, but also—and she probably won't like me saying this—she was sensitive. She'd put up a wall and shut down when she was no longer having fun. We all felt it, and it was very uncomfortable.

GINA: I guess maybe it was a long time coming. She had almost left a tour in the middle of it, a couple of times. I remember staying up all night and talking her into staying for the rest of the tour. We were in Italy, and she and Theo had a spat over something that happened during the set. Sindi threatened to quit the tour. I spent hours convincing her to stay. In the morning, Squid and Theo said to me, "Why didn't you just let her go?" And I thought, "I dunno why." I guess because I could not fathom doing this with one of us being gone, but maybe I should have just let her go. One time in Europe while we were on a ferry, she casually mentioned that she always kept enough cash on her to get her home from no matter where we were in the world. She always had a way out. "Wait ... what?" ... it blew my mind. It was unthinkable to me to just up and leave. To me, there's no out. You're here. We're all here, together!

SQUID: It's like when you're married and everyone's like, "We're a family, do or die," except for one person who doesn't completely share that sentiment. Theo, Gina, and I weren't sophisticated enough to walk out on each other! We didn't have any money! We were kids! This band was everything we were living for! Because Sindi was older, she sort of had an adult life, and we just didn't get it.

GINA: It never occurred to me to have a backup plan in place. But looking back at it now, I totally get it.

THEO: Sindi, knowing her how we do, was very intent on surviving and taking care of herself, no matter what. She had that mechanism that we didn't. She was prepared because she didn't know what shit was going to hit the fan. Thinking about that now, I can feel much more empathy. But back then, I was like, "WHAT?" The three of us were in it together, do or die, perhaps to a fault. And, plus, we had no money.

SQUID: She also never needed the band the way the three of us needed it. She had an identity and a grown-up life. We were so young; we formed our lives and identities dependent on one another. There really was no "us" without the Lunachicks, not at that point.

THEO: I think she was like, "I'm going to do this until it's no longer fun." And when it wasn't fun anymore, she wanted to walk. I get it now. We weren't making tons of cash, so why would she want to stay if she was unhappy?

SINDI: Being on tour was very different in the early days than the later days. Obviously, the being onstage part was the best part. Early on, it was all fun. We were the best of friends and made a party out of everything—every truck stop, every pee stop was entertaining. We took pictures and laughed and enjoyed each other's company. Even sitting in the stupid van could be fun. I did a lot more, you know, loading the van than some of the other people did—that was fine. I was happy to do it. I liked the work, you know. I did fewer interviews because I was always going to go get paid or load

the van. Everybody kinda had their roles that worked
well for a long time until later when maybe ... people
started to get a little more snippy with each other and
then you could use that: "Uh, how come you're not doing
the interview?!" Because I'm going to squeeze the money
out of the promoter. You wanna switch? So, yeah, that
was less fun. But the time onstage made all the other
hours worth it, even in the bad times. Almost. In my
end times, the good and bad weren't balancing anymore.
The stage time wasn't enough anymore because the karma
wasn't as good. I don't think there was a moment where
it stopped being fun—it was definitely a progression of
fewer and fewer moments of fun.

I found that I was distancing myself from the rest
of the band more during the last tours we did together.
During the bigger tours with the Offspring, I was riding
on the crew bus. The crew had adopted me and I would
help them break down after the show. I would get on
the bus and show up at seven o'clock in the morning
with them, and the band would roll in later. I did that
a lot because we weren't really enjoying each other's
company anymore. I thought, "Okay, well, that's one
less body there for them, one less person in the hotel
room, one less seat taken in the van." I thought that
would be a good thing, although I don't know if it was.
I think they might not have been happy with that even
though in my logical thinking they should have been
happy with that, but I can't speak for them if that was
a good thing or a bad thing. For me, it was a necessary
thing. For me, I was still in it to have fun. I didn't
care as much about succeeding, about making it, about
whatever the things you're supposed to care about.
From day one, I was in it for the fun. So I was pointing
myself to wherever the fun was for me. I related much

better to the crew. Always. I never hung out with the other bands we toured with that much. The crew were my people. They worked hard, they had no glory, they woke up early in the morning, busting their asses so that the stars could go on, and then they busted their asses all night and had a great time on the bus on the way to the next gig. That was fun. That's where I should've been all along—being a rigger or a roadie or a sound-person or whatever. But that's not where I ended up. Those were some really good times for me, as long as I wasn't getting flack from the band for it or could ignore any attitude that they might have been giving me. But there was definitely a divide growing and getting wider and wider. It was gradual because those big tours made everybody happy. We were able to still have a lot of fun together.

As time went on, those times were less and less frequent, and that was sad. I was looking for the fun, and also it was heartbreaking to see how relationships were starting to deteriorate. To me, the whole purpose of the band thing in my mind was "It's us! And here we are! And we're seeing the world together!" And my desires and dreams didn't progress in the same direction as everybody else's, where they were seeing "Oh, these people are succeeding" and "These people don't hafta ride in a van anymore" and "These people don't hafta hustle when they're not on tour." I was not really as concerned with that. Touring was great when you're on tour, and when you weren't, it was nice to be home too. That also made the divide bigger. Then came the divorce. The hurt was real. We didn't have the same goals. What they thought was important wasn't what I thought was important. I got a very definite sense that they were looking for a reason why the success wasn't coming our way, and they scrambled to find where the problem was. At some point, the finger was pointed at me. Because my musicianship wasn't developing fast enough, I—fair enough—could be sloppy onstage. I did not spend my free time noodling on the guitar, you know, because I thought I was in a punk rock band, and that's not what you gotta do in a punk rock band. An attempt was made to give me an ... *ultimatum* might be a bit of a harsh word, but they wanted me to tighten up my musical act. I didn't want to! I just didn't want to.

THEO: Squid, Gina, and I were always on the same page when it came to our commitment to music and art. For the past few years, we were each focused on learning more, being better, pushing our creative selves. Sindi felt differently. She didn't want to play guitar; she just wanted to hang out and go on tour. I remember saying to her, "You need to get your chops up, practice more, and maybe take some lessons." I think she didn't speak to me for years because of that. I was profoundly distressed and felt like the one Sindi blamed most for her exit. Yet there was also a sense of relief because I knew she would ultimately be happier without the stress of dealing with the band and us. It still hurt a lot. We were sisters. I always loved her.

SINDI: I cared about them all so much, and still do, that if I had had the slightest belief that I was the thing that was keeping us from making it, I would've practiced day and night. I would've done whatever it took. I could have. There was nothing stopping me. But I didn't believe there was a need for it. I was a great stage presence. I was as important as everybody else in that band. My musical influences and my musical input were as important as everyone else's. I believed that. I knew it wasn't me, but if they were going to believe or insinuate that it was me, I didn't really wanna do it. I didn't wanna be there.

GINA: We started out as a scrappy and loose doesn't-matter-if-you-can-play-an-instrument-or-not kind of punk band, but over the years we got better and faster and musically more complex. We couldn't force her to hold those same values; it's just not where she was at.

SQUID: We were giving her a way out, basically. We were like, "What do you want to do?" And she was like, "No." We were in Gina's kitchen. It was horrible, tension-filled. She chose powerfully. She was over it.

SINDI: Any joy that was left then was stabbed in the heart. I think that we all agreed to part ways. Although it wasn't messy and sloppy and mean, it was a deep cut and it took a long time to heal. But it was the right thing, I guess, for all of us. For me to have that satisfaction, like, "Look! It wasn't me!" ... I don't know if they had any regrets or thought it was better without me. It was time for me to go. I was a little older, I was sick of the life, I had a nice place, I liked being home. I didn't like being on the road all the time anymore, especially since we hadn't really progressed to more favorable touring conditions. It was the right thing to do, but it wasn't super-amicable. I didn't talk to Syd and Theo for a while after that. I distanced myself pretty well. But I wasn't scared, like, "Oh my god, now they're gonna make it and I'm gonna miss out on all of it!" I thought it had run its course and we had taken it as far as it could go. As soon as the fun was out of it, why keep pushing it?

SQUID: Sindi leaving the band did destroy our friendship for a time. That breakup was touchy. We didn't see her for a while. I had no idea how it was going to play out, but it was the right thing. But, man, it sucked.

GINA: It was painful losing Sindi. We were a family, and we had spent our formative years bonding over all of the incredible experiences we got to have together. We were sisters through and through. It felt like a divorce.

The pain went deep, and it would be years before we could truly mend our friendship. Getting older definitely has its benefits. Back then, we had piss-poor communication skills and coping mechanisms while we were trying to coexist in a creative endeavor that also functioned as a business. Being back in each other's lives has been a gift. Sindi is our sister forever, and she will always be a Lunachick.

CHAPTER 28

INTERVENTION

THEO: Worrying about Squid consumed so much of my life for so long; I lost years of sleep over her. I loved her so much it hurt, but I couldn't take it anymore. The thing about a band—you are dependent on each other to show up, to play properly, to be a team player, to be respectful, to do your part. It's like being on a rock 'n' roll mission of survival. And I was fed up and angry and hurt (as if her addiction had anything to do with me and my feelings). She was and is one of the strongest, most willful people I have ever and will ever know, and yet she was powerless to a stupid drug! It was too much for me. I knew she could get clean if she wanted to, but did she? I didn't know, but what I did know was that if this went on any longer, I had to walk away.

GINA: Theo and I didn't know what to do. It was getting worse and worse. We told Squid, "We can't even go onstage with you." So we decided to "kick her out" of the band just for one show and had our friend Greta play bass in the hopes of scaring Squid into getting clean. She was so sad. She told us, "That's fucked up, you can't play a show without me." But ultimately it didn't get her clean. I remember saying aloud, "I don't know what else to do about this."

CHIP: We'd come home from tour for a week or two or three and then go back out on another six-week tour. The first couple days of the tour, Syd would be very sick but she always seemed to pull it off for the gigs. At one point, I said to the girls that I was fed up with the constant three, four days of Syd being sick at the beginning of every tour. I put my foot down and said we have to do something.

SQUID: My band reached a point where they couldn't take it any longer. The other girls were finally fed up with me.

THEO: This was one of the pre-final final straws: we let Squid stay in the band under the condition that she enter an outpatient program, get drug-tested weekly, and bring in the clean tests to rehearsal. She didn't seem clean by any means but would show up to rehearsal with what looked like Xeroxed and re-Xeroxed papers stating that she had a clean urine drug test. At some point, I called the drug counselor to try and find out what was really going on. I couldn't get a clear answer. The counselor wouldn't tell me if they had even seen her! The amount of times these drug-test reports looked Xeroxed was fishy as hell. I called her dad, Gary, and told him my suspicions, but he said, "Well, she's getting tested and the tests are clean." And that was that.

SQUID: My downstairs neighbor had three little girls, and I'd try to get them to pee in a ziplock for me. A lot of days they wouldn't want to pee in the bag. I could hear them from outside of the bathroom: "No, Mommy, no I no want da go pee-pee in da baggie!" GAHHHH ... Fucking kid, I'm late for group therapy! I guess I achieved the goal I had set for myself when I was eleven. I'd said I wanted to see it all. I saw enough. I was going to get kicked out of my band, fired from my job, lose my apartment, my friends and family were cutting me off, and X was stealing everything that wasn't structurally attached to the earth. It was the perfect time for me to get the fuck out. All aspects of my life came crashing down at the same time. Thank god.

THEO: I read a book called *Intervention* at this time that told me you had to speak your truth, make a real ultimatum, and stick to it. So I followed that advice and hoped that the threat of my being out of her life might help her get clean. I called Syd's dad again and said, "Gary, it's for real this time." And he finally heard me.

GINA: It was Theo who said, "I think we should do an intervention." We knew a girl whose father was a well-known drug counselor, Lou Cox, who had gotten Aerosmith clean. It was Theo who called Squid's parents and said, "We'd like to hire this guy. Will you pay for it? Will you get involved, because we don't know what else to do." Greg also played a big part. He helped set up the intervention and got an organization called MusiCares to pay for some of it. It was all thanks to Theo and Greg.

SQUID: Theo called me and said she never wanted to speak to me again. I finally heard her words through the phone: "You're nothing but a junkie." Ooof, that hurt. I felt like she couldn't see me at all anymore. Looking back on it, I totally understand. I learned a lot about what people can handle and how they can handle it. Everybody has their own threshold. For Theo, I think my using was really personal. She was hurt and freaked out. Gina was calmer about it. She was angry, but she was pragmatic. She said, "You're out, and that's it. But I know you can beat this." I never forgot that. She believed in me more than I believed in myself at that time.

GINA: I never thought Squid was gonna die; I even told her this in the intervention. I am one of her biggest cheerleaders; I really think she is like nobody else I know. I believed that as bad as it would get with her, she would find a way out. She's a resourceful, resilient woman who is one of those people who can do anything when she puts her mind to it. I told her, "I know you and I know that you can do this."

SQUID: Part of the reason getting clean was so hard was because I felt like I was giving up my personality—drugs were so enmeshed with who I thought I was, I couldn't see myself apart from using. Getting clean seemed like losing the war, surrendering to boring, beige, and normal. But thank god for New York City, once again. There was a cast of characters so off the charts of normal who really showed up for me during this time—creative weirdos and legends of the downtown music and art-freak scene, walking the walk, leading by example, and showing me what was possible, waiting for me to get out and hold my hand on the other side. I followed them. I did what they did, went where they went, and stayed clean.

THEO: I was so nervous that day. It was a mission: save my best friend's life. Her dad was there, her mom and her sister flew in, the whole band was there. Every most-important person in her life was there to face her, along with some friends who had been clean for a while that we knew would be a good influence for her and give her a light at the end of the tunnel. I was so afraid she would walk in the room and see us all and do a reverse loop and walk right back out.

GINA: As soon as Squid walked into the room, she realized what was happening. She opened the door and the look on her face when she saw all of us sitting there ... she went, "Ohhhhhhhh."

SQUID: I got tipped off from a friend who knew the intervention was about to go down. I sent X to cop me enough bags for the long drive to wherever I was going, I didn't even care at that point. By the time people came for me, I was so ready to go. I was so shattered. Out of gas.

During an intervention, people figure out what your argument is going to be and they find ways to remove the roadblocks. X was a pretty big roadblock, and everyone knew it. Every day I vowed to get clean, and every day X would do some crazy shit like disappear the TV or the stereo or my guitar, and I'd be in such a rage that my skull was gonna blow off the back of my head. I thought I would kill him, and then he'd come skipping through the door with a smile on his face and enough drugs for me. I fell for it EVERY time. Imagine: he boosts MY shit and then proceeds to get high on MY couch while I'm watching him nod out and drool as I sit this one out stone-cold sober. Good thing I got high or I'd be doing time for murder. I just wanted the nightmare to stop, even if it was for a few hours of numbness where I could pretend everything was all right. It was living in real-life hell, and things were deteriorating fast. At some point, I was sleeping with my money and dope under my pillow. One morning he went for it and I pulled a knife on him. I mean shit was getting weird. It was over.

But I wouldn't leave him. Addiction is like being at the bottom of a well, with smooth, tall walls all around you and no way out. Add codependency to the mix, and you feel like you're holding this person's fragile life in your hands at the same time. Now try to climb out. It's an agonizing conundrum with no visible escape. And the hardest part about it is having to face the actual truth: it's all bullshit. No one's saving anyone. We're all hiding behind something, and we're all selfish to the core. But I was years away from being able to admit that. We all blamed him. By the end, my band wanted to fuckin' kill X. They hated him.

GINA: We made it known that the biggest problem was Squid's husband, and it wasn't going to work unless he was out of the picture. We had to make specific arrangements, so we told Squid, "You'll be escorted by your dad, and you've got a half hour to pack your things, and you can't see X." I felt like she needed the right opportunity and she needed to get away from her husband.

CHIP: Each person was asked to say something. Everybody was saying stuff like, "I love you, let's do this, you're going to be strong, I love you, I love you, I love you ..." But when they got to me, I wasn't in that headspace; I was like, "Syd! Are you aware that you lost two motorcycles, all your leather jackets, and wedding rings?? They were all pawned or sold by your husband for dope while we were on tour!!" I guess I just wasn't in the poor-baby-I-love-you frame of mind. I was more like, "It's time to shape up."

SQUID: I couldn't wait for it to be over. "All right already, save your breath and get me outta here! What took you so long!" Rehab was paradise. After what I had been through on my own, kicking on the floor of a cramped and filthy cargo van, going to rehab was like kicking in the Waldorf. I was surrounded by people who understood that I didn't feel well and were going to help me instead of yell at me and want to kill me. The doctors put me on meds. I slept for four days. It was heaven. And I knew it would never be that easy again. Not that it was easy, but it was luxury compared to what I'd been through.

Years later, Theo's daughter would be born on the same date I got clean, and now it's both our birthdays.

It was really hard for the first few years, I can't minimize that. I had feelings again. I almost had a nervous breakdown on tour in New Orleans. It was my first year of being clean. We were soundchecking on-stage at the House of Blues and I couldn't stop crying. I went into some kind of psychosis. I wasn't sobbing, but water was pouring out of my face. I started freaking out: "There's something wrong with me, water won't stop leaking out of my eyeballs, I can't stop, there's something wrong." Greg Ross had to talk me down for hours. I was like, "I-have-to-go." I could barely form sentences. I wanted to leave on the spot. Greg was shitting his pants that I was going to bring the whole tour down. After all that! I guess I just became super-sensitive because I wasn't high anymore. It's like I had no skin, I was totally raw, like a broken tooth with a missing cap. I had to learn how to experience emotion without slitting my wrist or killing somebody. They say whenever you started using is when you stunted your growth and stopped learning how to process feelings. And since I have a visceral memory of being ten and being like, "I can't deal. Every time I get upset, I'm gonna smoke weed," well, I have my work cut out for me.

I need to make this very clear: I never cared about anything more than I cared about my band. I always knew that if I lost my band, there would be no coming back, there would be nothing left for me, nothing left of me worth fighting for. The Lunachicks were the only thing that got me clean. I was fighting my way back to them, and I would not have made it without them. I have always known that to be true.

SHIT·FINGER·DICK
(F.D.S) ©LUNACHICKS 1993

LIGHT AS A FEATHER
(STIFF AS A BOARD)

SPECIAL THANX 2 - EDDIE, MIKE, JUAN, CHET + MAGNUS

LUNACHICKS
532 LAGUARDIA PL #345
N.Y. N.Y. 10012

PRODUCED + MIXED BY VIN CIN + LUNACHICKS

CHAPTER 29

CUMMING INTO OUR OWN

By the time the late '90s rolled around, we were headed into our late twenties and were growing up. Things really felt different. They felt good.

THEO: We were definitely on a high in terms of our artistry; it felt professional and right like it never had before. The energy and enthusiasm within the four of us bubbled over like a freshly opened bottle of champers.

GINA: Sindi had left the band and Squid got clean—those two things happened around the same time. I remember feeling more, well, adult-ish. We made a concentrated effort to step up our game. Live-wise, we were killing it, and we were tighter than ever.

SQUID: At that point, we were a machine. We reached that place where we were just locked in.

The city itself was changing too. Even though it was gentrifying, there were still tons of new artists creating, bands playing, and film festivals happening. New venues and bars were opening up all over the Lower East Side and Williamsburg, Brooklyn, and rock 'n' roll parties took place almost every night of the week. Jessie Malin's Coney Island High opened up on St. Marks Place, and we played there regularly. We felt so at home on that stage that we went on to record our live album there in 1998. So many great bands were also playing around: Miss Guy and the Toilet Boys and D Generation were making a big splash. Theo's modeling and movie career was going well, and she got a part in a Scorsese movie! And because of Theo, we got asked to play live on television at the CFDA Fashion Awards honoring Betsey Johnson in the Armory on Twenty-Fifth Street and Lexington Ave. We were also asked to be in the Troma Entertainment movie *Terror Firmer* and write the theme song, and Theo starred in an indie film called *Potluck*, which we also made an appearance in.

It was truly a magical, electric time. Around the summer of 1998, there was a feeling in the air of the city that something awesome was burgeoning, although maybe in hindsight it was just collective anxiety about Y2K. Whatevs, we were having a freaking blast! We staked our claim as the queens of our great city. We walked into whatever club we wanted, free of charge, drinks on the house. The Lower East Side was our playground. Our records were selling (still not enough to pay the rent but . . .), we were getting great press, we were filming a home video, and we were invited to do cool things like movie cameos and guest DJ spots at radio stations. Our fan base was growing by the day, and it just felt like shit was happening.

Greg got to fulfill his dream of having a record store. He moved Go-Kart records out of his little West Village apartment and rented a space on St. Marks Place. Record store in the front, label in the back. He even offered us the basement to rehearse in and store our gear, which was amazing because it meant never having to go to Midtown after a gig again. Yes! Score! There was one caveat: the basement had to be cleaned out and set up for rehearsing.

Chip being the master carpenter and Gina being the willing assistant, they went down to the basement with two-by-fours and drywall and got to work. They didn't get far, though, because the basement was infested with water bugs—giant cockroaches to those of you non–New Yorkers. These things are freaking huge, like nightmare-bad-PCP-trip-holy-shit-kill-me-now kind of huge, and some of them even fucking fly.

GINA: Chip was getting super-annoyed with me dropping lumber and screaming bloody murder every time a giant roach came crawling out from the depths of hell sent by Satan himself to eat me alive. Obviously, we weren't going to get anything done like this. Chip picked up a bunch of Raid bug foggers, and we planned to set them off and come back the next day when all the bugs were gassed to death. We set them off, closed the door, and went upstairs to tell Greg that we'd be back tomorrow. I remember being happy for Greg that day because as we were walking out through the store, there seemed to be a good amount of customers shopping and browsing through the bins. Go, Greg! This place is a hoppin'! As soon as I got home, the phone rang. It was Greg and he was pissed. "What the hell did you dooo?!" Water bugs were crawling all over the store, in the bins, up the walls, all over the records, and onto the customers who had all run outside screaming in horror. "It's like goddamn *Creepshow* in here now! I had to close the store!" Oops. It never occurred to us that setting off the bug bombs would result in a roach tsunami that would engulf a crowded store full of unsuspecting customers. Sorreeeeeeee, Greg.

It felt like a new beginning, and we were chomping at the bit to move on to the next chapter of our crazy lives. We had released our live album and spent the summer touring in Europe, sharpening some kick-ass new material. Just before Christmas of '98—a little more than one year left of the first millennium—we started to record what would be our last studio album, *Luxury Problem*. During that particular time, everybody had different tastes in music they wanted to explore. There were a lot more opinions on what the album should be like—many more than ever before. The wild and freewheeling teenagers who started this band had, by that point, established distinctive personalities and creative leanings. We all felt a strain on the collective songwriting. None of us is a pushover, and there was a lot of pushing. But we were also at our peak.

Once again, Theo's lyrics ignited us on a molecular level. Her evolution as a writer just kept unfurling in the most thrilling of ways. The album opens with "Less Teeth More Tits," a commentary on the Miss America pageant.

Miss Demeanor, a Misstake
A Misshap, oh I implore you
It's no mystery I don't wanna know you
But Miss America I can't ignore you
You can't wipe out all our progress with your little cotton ball
Slice and dice your face to perfection
Slip up a word and down you fall
Teeth are capped and lipo-sucked
Hair is set and nose is contoured
Tummy's tucked and boobs are lifted
Uncross your legs and your pantyhose shifted
Am I smilin' enough? Am I smilin' too much?
Am I tucked in and buckled, do my tits touch?
Hi, how are you, how high are you?
Less teeth and more tits
It's never enough
You'll never be good enough
You got less teeth and more tits
What a bunch of hypocrites tryin' to change the world
Bonded tooth smiles travel so many miles
How you gonna change the world?
I wanna see something else
You put the extra in ordinary
You add the minus to the plus size
You put the blues into my brown eye
You put the "turd" into Saturday
You can't wipe out all our progress with your little cotton ball

Slice and dice your ass to perfection

Slip up a word and down you fall

Am I smilin' enough? Am I smilin' too much?

Am I tucked in and buckled, do my tits touch?

Hi, how are you, how high are you

Less teeth and more tits

It's never enough

You'll never be good enough

You got less teeth and more tits

What a bunch of hypocrites tryin' to change the world

Bonded tooth smiles travel so many miles

Whatcha gonna do now?

Something different and meaningful

That makes your smiles not seem so evil

When that crown falls off your head

Will you still feel better off dead, yeah?

I wanna see something else

Why won't you show me something else?

I want so much to see something else

On the other end of the spectrum, we closed with "Down at the Pub," our demented tribute to the English punk scene and our beloved UK fans. It begins with an enormous burp (courtesy of Chip) and all of us bellowing "Oi! Oi! Oi!" We couldn't help but laugh our asses off until the literal last second of the last song of the last album we made together.

GINA: I loved recording that album. I just felt so much more confident in the process, in the studio, in the engineer and producer, and in myself. We all did, I think. We were professionals, finally. We may have been more fragmented in writing this album, but there was no denying that the material was strong no matter which one of us wrote it—some of the best we'd written yet. It was more sophisticated and sharp, like a solid roundhouse to the groin. We were at the top of our game, and we were pumped.

We finished the record in January 1999. Gina had just started working in film production and wanted to set up a shoot for us in a junkyard. Some of her film buddies helped us rent a bunch of furniture and drag it out to the middle of a scrapyard in Maspeth, Queens. We got all dolled up and fucking froze our asses off shooting the album cover in the middle of winter with barely anything on. Worth it! Major props for our muscly pal John who braved the frigid temps in nothing but a banana hammock and baby oil. We were so proud of the album and the cover.

That summer, we toured with the Go-Go's—a blast. Those women were just so cool to hang out with, and we loved listening to their stories of what it was like for them as one of the first chart-topping female bands. They were our big sisters, and it was hands down one of the funnest tours we've ever done, but our summer was just getting started.

CHAPTER 30

WARPED REALITY

The Vans Warped Tour—a huge summer festival of pop-punk bands, skateboarders, and BMX riders—invited us two years in a row, 1999 and 2000. Those two tours get blurred together, but it was a pretty big deal for us both times because we were among the few, if any, women on the main stages. It was like getting a leg up, a promotion, being included in these lineups with bands who were way bigger than us, who had radio hits and videos running nonstop on MTV, and now we were there too. One of us! One of us!

Knowing the kinds of scrutiny we were going to get as women on this sausagefest made us want to go out there and kick ass. And we did. It was empowering to know that we could be as good as and as important as every other band on the bill.

THEO: It was the traveling carnival that I had always dreamed of when I was little. I was once again a clown in a tutu in the circus for real! Waking up every day on a different plot of land or field or pile of dirt or cement parking lot full of buses and stepping out into a world of tents and excitement and music and snacks and people and peers. Watching BMX bikes flying in the air, seeing SO many of our favorite bands play daily, trading merch (the swag alone was incredible), all while sweating

299

buckets of Gatorade and glitter. It was fabulous and joyous and fun as shit. I felt like we had arrived all over again. It was great except for when we had to go for our first pee in the morning in the disgusting sun-baked Porta-Johns that all the dudes already dumped in. Aside from dealing with the poop, I felt loved and respected by most of the bands, if not all of them, testosterone et al. It was a personal career high-hurdle for this show pony.

We were touring in an RV, which, for the record, is a deathtrap. Somewhere stuck to the RV there's a tiny label that says passengers are supposed to be buckled in the seats at all times while it's being driven. Pfft. Yeah, right. Only after it's parked is it safe for you to lie down to sleep, or move around in it. On top of that, one of our drivers was a hazard in and of himself.

SQUID: I was woken up in the RV by someone jabbing me in the ribs and pointing to our driver. So I sat up and looked at him through the rearview, and his eyes were fuckin' shut. He was on speed the rest of the time. He'd been up for, like, four days. I thought we were gonna die. After I got clean, it finally dawned on me that dying might be scary. Tears were pouring out of my eyes. I was having sober panic attacks thinking, "I'm gonna fuckin' die." Come to think of it, I'm pretty sure both me and Theo were lying in that bed crying, like, "Goodbye, old friend, this is the end."

THEO: Oh yeah, I was crying. Tears falling into my ears, crying myself to sleep with Syd across from me because we were stacked three-deep in that bed. It felt like we were in a cardboard box. It would've taken the smallest thing to go wrong, and we'd have been squished flat like

bugs in a roach motel. We agreed to let this particular
kid be our driver because he wanted to come along on
Warped and see Green Day. He promised to sleep during
the day, but then he wouldn't! So he'd be up all day and
then drove us while half-asleep through winding roads
all night in this flimsy, flying box. Terrifying.

There were six or seven of us packed into this thing, one of whom was
a last-minute addition that turned out to be way more hassle than she
was worth. She was a reporter at a major network who wanted to do a
story on us while touring (or so we were told). Greg said it would be great
exposure for us and we really should consider taking this woman on the
Warped Tour with us. After much groaning and eye-rolling, we finally
conceded, although there was no room in the RV for an extra person,
so the reporter had to double as our T-shirt seller. Turned out not only
was this supposed "reporter" a terrible merch person, but also an incredibly annoying presence in the RV who drove an already-irritated Chip
even more irate, making for many long and uncomfortable drives. She
had little to offer in the way of companionship and whined about pretty
much everything to do with being on tour. Obviously her main priority
was getting her story, so needless to say our merch booth was often left
unmanned while she ran around trying to rub elbows with the bigger
bands on the bill. She also had the maddening habit of disappearing just
as we were about to leave for the next city, making us all wait as Andrea
(our super-hot seven-foot Amazonian take-no-prisoners tour manager)
hunted for her in the tented backstage areas. In the end, we never did get
to hear the piece she did, but we did get wind that our name wasn't even
mentioned once in her story, which apparently was solely focused on her
running around backstage at Warped. So much for exposure.

Our first set was somewhere in the desert, maybe Arizona or New
Mexico. It was 100 degrees in the shade, and we played in the middle
of the day in black-and-yellow vinyl costumes, with Theo in her wigs
and giant black boots, in the blazing sun. Why it didn't dawn on us to

consider the weather while brainstorming stage outfits for the tour, we don't know. It was like performing on the surface of the sun in a full plastic clown suit and makeup every single day.

> **CHIP:** Sometimes we'd have to play at noon, and because it just felt so early, the standard situation was for our roadie to have at least two cans of beer waiting for me. He'd be like, "Okay, here you go," and hand me my beers. I'd shotgun them, let out a thirty-second belch, and get onstage.

> **GINA:** Playing in broad daylight under a high-noon sun was a new experience for us. All I remember was that I was having a hard time lifting my feet because the rubber soles of my Converse high-tops had actually started to melt onto the scorching-hot black stage!

> **SQUID:** Aside from the headliners, the lineup of remaining bands was chosen at random (or so we were told) each morning. So you never knew going to bed at night what god-awful time you might have to play the next day under the blinding sun. Sometimes you'd win and sometimes you'd lose, as in being jolted out of deep sleep: "Get up! You're on in an hour!" Gahhhhh noooo helllp COFFEEEE!!! Smearing glitter and clown paint on your face while trying to pee and brush your teeth. "Good morning, Tucson!" Vomit.

We got a lot of respect from other bands like Black Eyed Peas, Mighty Mighty Bosstones, even Eminem, who wasn't particularly embraced. (When he was onstage singing, "My name is, my name is, my name is," the whole crowd would yell out, "ASSHOLE!" That shows you the tone.) We even had a dance party on the Black Eyed Peas' bus. One time, we were walking past all the band tents, and Kim Hill, the singer from the Black Eyed Peas (the one before Fergie), saw us and yelled out, "Hey, Dixie Chicks!!" *ACK!!!*

CHIP: I guess that's who we were, the proverbial girl band among dude bands who could be mistaken for the Dixie Chicks. But when I think about it, we really held our own. My drum tech told me a lot of drummers from the other bands would gather behind me backstage to watch me play, and he said they were always commenting on the speed of my kick foot, so I guess I had some moments to live off of.

One of the highlights of Warped was the continual reminder of just how many awesome fans we had. Because Warped was all-ages, it gave many young punks, misfits, and geeks a place to be themselves. These kids were so cool, so fierce, and hilarious, and they came out in droves for our sets, even in the cities where we didn't know we had a following! It really was punk rock summer camp. Playing to a bouncing, screaming crowd that sings along to your lyrics is one of the most gratifying and memorable experiences you can have in life.

Some fans would come bearing homemade gifts: drawings, customized action dolls of each of us, Lunachicks lunch boxes. Our favorite Japanese fan, Chilli, made us Lunachicks hand towels. It's abundantly clear to us that we wouldn't have had any music career to write about in this book if it weren't for our fans, but on top of that, we fucking love that they're interesting, creative weirdos just like us. We've made lifelong friends with many of the people we've met at our shows. The freaks shall inherit the earth!

Of course, there were always a few dicks in the audience who wanted to disrupt our mojo. A few times, what we were literally hit with reminded us of our first show in England, where people were hurling pint glasses at our heads. Some of these Warped bros began throwing nearly full bottles of Gatorade (the large size) at us. The sentiment was clear: "Get off the stage so the dude band after you can play."

As annoying and sometimes painful as it was to get hit with giant bottles, it didn't make us want to stop. Initially, it only made us angrier. *Fuck you, we're gonna get through to you.* We knew we earned our spot on the bill and could turn at least some of the other bands' fans into our fans. It was a kind of ego thing, this need to win over the haters. Obviously, not everybody was going to love what we do, but we didn't expect such vitriol from a bunch of people who came to see a skate-punk tour. It's not like we were so outrageously out of place. Or were we?

A large element of the Warped scene was a big ol' boys' club. On one hand, Warped wanted to include women, which is partly why they invited us, and there were also more musicians of color on that festival than any other that we had played, but there was also a handful of conformist jocks with guitars trying to get laid—everything punk rock was born out of hating—whose behavior incensed us. One rap star would routinely get onstage and shout, "Which fourteen-year-old girl am I going to get pregnant tonight?"

SQUID: This fool seriously got onstage before our set and tried to shake my hand. Like, right after he said that shit, he wanted to be all cool with us and show us props. How's about you show us how fast you can GET THE FUCK OFF OUR STAGE?

One of the other mega-bands, Blink-182, would get onstage in city after city and instruct the girls in the crowd to show their tits. In between songs, they had a little shtick acting like proverbial mega rock stars and saying things like, "Who's gonna give us blow jobs after the show tonight? Who's gonna lift their shirts for us?" And while we could kinda get that they were trying to be tongue-in-cheek with it all, the irony and sarcasm just weren't there. The lines quickly blurred to just plain creepy as they attempted to point out the ridiculousness of hero worship while at the same time seeming all too comfortable in the role. Their request for sexual favors from their teenage female fans was a "just kidding" but really "not kidding" little gag, and more blatantly to us, a not-so-subtle reminder to these young girls of what their role at the festival truly was.

GINA: At some point, one of the guys in Blink came up to me in the parking lot and said, "Hey, I hear you don't appreciate our little joke onstage. Well, I just want you to know that I love women, I love my mom and stuff, and we don't really mean anything by it." I went into my whole long spiel about how much power they wielded over these young women and what kind of message they were sending, what it's like for us women going to shows and having to constantly battle gender stereotypes. His response? "We'll just cool it for now while you guys are still on the tour. Oh, and by the way, tell your bass player that she is the hottest chick I have ever seen." Wait, what??? Did you not listen to a word I just said? His only self-reflection from our criticism was to put their blatant misogyny on pause for a week—and that our bass player was hot. Get the fuck outta here!

THEO: More than once, in between our songs, I yelled at the crowd, "Whatever that dude band on that stage over there is telling you to do, DON'T DO IT. Girls, keep your shirts on!" I also warned against anyone groping girls who were crowd-surfing. NOT ON MY WATCH. I was the proverbial big sister, and there were freakin' thirteen-year-old girls being told by Blink-182 to show their tits. No. Just no.

These weren't harmless, joking statements (and they weren't even remotely funny). The words had consequences that we saw with our own eyes. There were *actual* underage girls at these shows—a lot of them. And a lot of them would, in fact, pull up their shirts and flash their boobs at the band and wait diligently backstage after their set. It pissed us the fuck off, and Theo used her power at the mic to mercilessly make fun of the band and call them out on their shit. We came offstage to much applause by the female festival crew and staff members who had been on the entire tour (we were not) and had to endure their set for weeks on end. *"Thank you! God, it's been awful having to hear that shit every friggin' day!"* We did what we could to combat it, but it never, ever felt like we did enough.

SQUID: I regret not sneaking onstage and head-butting one particular singer in the nose in front of ten thousand people. That would have been awesome.

THEO: I was worn down near the end of the tour. Burnout, I suppose. Some days I felt like, "I'm going to make everyone LOVE us. I am going to do my fucking best and kick ass and have the best show!" And then the next day I was like, "I don't care! I'm not going to change any of your minds and I don't give A FUCK." It's hard, because it's my job! But some days my job really wasn't fun, and I'd get fed up. We all would. It's not so fun when you feel like you're in a diamond-encrusted Liberace tuxedo fighting your way through a daily heat wave and sandstorm. One day, we all decided to wear our pajamas—we still wore full makeup and loads of glitter, but we didn't bother with our black-and-yellow outfits. When I read about the accusations of sexual harassment on the 2015 Warped Tour, it got me so hopped up and angry. Sexual harassment and abuse are always fucked up, always wrong, always annoying, and we would ALWAYS push back on it with our words, our music, and sometimes our fists! It makes me bonkers. Yeah, rock 'n' roll is fun and sexy and alluring and mysterious and dangerous and full of reckless abandon, but as a human you still have the responsibility not to be a fuckin' asshole.

Even though we had such a great summer playing the Go-Go's and Warped tours in '99, Chip seemed moody and unhappy, and just started to disengage. On the way home from tour, we spent the night at a motel.

Theo asked Chip to turn off the TV. Chip said no. They exchanged "fuck you"s and went to sleep. We *never* spoke to each other like that before. There seemed to be a culmination of minor grievances that Chip had, which eventually piled up too high to reconcile.

GINA: When it came time to register the *Luxury Problem* song-writing shares into our performing rights organization, I asked the band if, instead of splitting things up evenly the way we usually did, it would be okay if I asked for just a little more of a percentage for some of the songs that I had spent a lot of time on. I had been doing all of the books, tour managing at times, creating artwork, and taking care of all the little shitty details that no one wanted to think about. On top of all that, I felt I had worked really hard on writing music for the album, as we all did, but still I felt a bit like I was carrying a heavier load and I wanted to be acknowledged for it somehow, even if that just meant it was written on a paper somewhere that no one would ever see. In hindsight, it was a mistake to conflate those two things as they were completely separate issues. Monetarily, since we never made any money on publishing royalties, it would make no difference to anyone. I didn't see it as an unreasonable request, but to my surprise, Chip very much did and blew up in a rage at me. I was in shock. Chip was my buddy, we were pals, and I cherished our friendship. I had never seen Chip so incensed.

CHIP: There was a disagreement concerning songwriting credits, which would've left me to be the least-paid member of the band. I'm "all for one and one for all," so that stung pretty bad. I wouldn't want our fans to think that we resorted to such pettiness as money in the end—all the TENS of dollars! But I didn't quit the band over songwriting. It came to a head when the band sat me down at a Starbucks to have a meeting before our gigs with Buzzcocks, and I was reprimanded and told not to be grumpy around the boys. I just felt they were more concerned about Buzzcocks' feelings than mine, and it certainly didn't feel "all for one and one for all" at that moment. (By the way, I do take full responsibility for my grumpiness—my loneliness misinterpreted as grumpiness.) I have no idea if it was a week or three months between the songwriting summit and the Starbucks summit. Anyway, we were a good seven or eight years into this, so emotions can sit a little high, yada yada yada, snap decision, Bob's yer uncle ... and I walked away.

It was clear that Chip was over it—over being surrounded by dudes all the time, over being alone in a sea of testosterone, over feeling like there was no place to stand in such a staunchly binary environment like the Warped Tour. By the end of the summer, it was obvious to all of us that the fall tours we had lined up would be untenable unless we made a change. That was really hard, like losing-a-limb hard, and it was scary too. We were so bummed about it, but we were also all aware that if we didn't take some kind of action, we would have imploded and that would've been the end of the band.

CHIP: We've always gotten along incredibly. I thought we got along better than any band I'd heard of. We know we're amazing. You don't get this a lot of times in your life. Most musicians never experience this degree of four musketeers.

SQUID: Chip was great, and we were great together. No one wanted that split. But we were having déjà vu: this person is unhappy, and it's making us all unhappy. We weren't willing to go down that road yet again. Once the "fuck you"s start flying, it's pretty hard to turn back the dial. I remember hearing a story that each member of the Rolling Stones had their own private jet to get to and from gigs. I mean, that's how you stay a band for fifty years! Not sitting in a goddamn van all day where you can feel the razor stubble of the arms and legs of the person sitting next to you. Being in a band is an unfair and unnatural test of any relationship.

GINA: When we were asked to play a show for the closing of CBGB in 2002 (little did we know, the club didn't actually end up closing until 2006) after taking the year off, we just naturally got back onstage with Chip. I don't even remember having a discussion about it; it was just, "Chip is our drummer and we're gonna play a show," kinda like an old married couple who got back together after separating and couldn't remember why they had parted in the first place.

THEO: There wasn't a second thought as to who would play with us at CB's in 2002; it was a no-brainer, a natural reflex to ask Chip to play. Water under the bridge was never so true a metaphor, so much so that we forgot about the bridge. Where's that confounded bridge? (Led Zeppelin quote for you rock nerds out there.) Chip is, was, and always will be our drummer.

go-kart PO Box 20 Prince Street Station New York, NY 10012 phone/fax: (212) 673-3380 email: gregross@panix.com

CHAPTER 31

FAST-FORWARD TO PAUSE

The new millennium hit, and we achieved a huge career milestone: Australia. We had so much fun, we practically had to be dragged out of the country, but we had to come back because we were once again playing the Warped Tour. It was especially fun that year because we had so many friends in the lineup: NOFX, Green Day, the Muffs, and Bif Naked, whose backing band included our beloved old friend Gail Greenwood of L7 and Belly. We watched Hot Water Music and Zeke crush it every day. When Chip left, we recruited a heavy-hitting drummer prodigy, eighteen-year-old Helen Destroy (now Gus Morgan).

GUS: My band at the time, Cattle Axe, had opened for the Lunachicks at Coney Island High the night they recorded *Drop Dead Live*, so that's when they'd first seen me play. After meeting them, I helped out drum tech-ing for Chip and doing merch at local NYC shows. Then, in September of 1999, I got the phone call from Gina. It was very much a movie-type moment that seemingly comes out of nowhere and changes your life forever. I was shocked and surprised and totally honored! Imagine being asked to join your favorite band?! I also knew I had big shoes to fill, but it was incredibly exciting, and I couldn't wait to get out on tour!

GINA: I'll never forget when the NOFX drummer broke his thumb during the 2000 Warped Tour. The next day, NOFX asked all the drummers from the main stage bands to come in and play two songs in lieu of a replacement for their drummer. So the drummer from Green Day sat in and played two songs, the drummer from T.S.O.L. played two songs—all the drummers from all the big bands had their turn. Then comes our teenage-girl drummer who fuckin' blew everybody away and was hands down the best player on that stage. I just thought that was so cool.

SQUID: All the bands crowded the stage to see their drummers pitch in on this all-star lineup. To see all these dudes slack-jawed in awe of this girl just destroying the drum set was a sight to behold. At least one of the bigger rock-star drummers (who will remain nameless) was visibly pissed and annoyed as the rest of the bands and crew onstage just doubled over pointing and laughing at him while this teenage girl quite obviously blew him out of the water. She was better than all of them and they knew it.

GUS: My time playing with the Lunachicks was nothing short of a musical education, life lesson, and leap into adulthood, all in one. I wouldn't have called myself a professional musician before joining the band. Having this intense on-the-job training was something I've learned from and put to use. I was glad to have that high level of trust and faith put in me, that I could show up and execute and do the music justice with my playing. I'm truly honored to be a part of the band's history.

Warped practically broke us in half and marked the last big tour we ever did. One of the things that started driving us insane was strictly the lack of privacy. It was the opposite of solitary confinement, and we could barely sleep. We didn't even have privacy to be in a bad mood or feel our feelings. It was fucking grueling and ultimately became one of the catalysts that led to the beginning of the end-ish.

GINA: That whole summer, I had it in the back of my mind that maybe we should end the band, but then it really started to nag me even more during the Warped Tour. My main impetus was that I really wanted to start my own band and time was running out. I was so afraid of turning thirty. *Oh my god, my twenties are over!* I was really freaking out about it and feeling old, which is so funny to think about now that I am truly old. Really? I was worried about thirty? You asshole. You thought thirty was old?! Wait till! So we turned thirty, and I knew if I didn't start a band then, it was never gonna happen. Months later I formed Bantam with two amazing dudes, Pete and Doug. It felt like all of my identity was tied to being in the Lunachicks; up until that point it was the only thing I had known in my entire adult life. I wondered what else was out there and if I could even exist outside of the band. And mostly I wanted to sing and write my own weirdo, quirky songs. I remember being in the RV, mentioning something to the effect of "Well, eventually, this band is probably going to come to an end, don't you think?" I even said, "I want to do my own thing." To my surprise, Theo said, "Yeah, so do I." I didn't know she was also feeling that way. Squid was a bit shocked because she didn't see that coming from either of us, and she got upset. She was like, "Wait, what? What are you guys talking about ... really? You would leave, really?" And I said, "Yeah, I've been thinking about it." And Theo said the same. Knowing that Theo had similar feelings and aspirations to move in different directions solidified it even more. I remember thinking, "Huh, this is really gonna happen."

THEO: It was all so hard toward the end. I was exhausted and burned out. Sometimes when we got offstage, I'd be completely drained. I wanted to move on, but I was too codependent to do it. I kept worrying, "What will everybody do if I quit?" It was a caretaking thing. I was also so constantly afraid of losing Squid, like if she gets clean and then I leave the band, what if she dies? That fear consumed me for a while. I have to give that woman credit. Getting clean and coming back, she really fought to stay in my life in a way that I never expected. When Gina said, "I can't do this anymore," I was like, "Finally!" I was so glad it wasn't me who initiated it, even though it probably should have been had I been healthier. It was almost like being in a troubled relationship and waiting for the other person to break up with you instead of doing it yourself. When it was a unanimous decision at the end, it was such a big relief.

SQUID: It was *not* unanimous. I was newly clean and just getting my life back together. At that point, the band was our entire adult lives. None of us had ever been a grown-up in the world in any other fashion. I didn't have a fucking clue what my life would look like without the band, and I didn't want to know. It was terrifying. We're not even talking about the end of the band here, we're talking about the end of my whole life because I barely survived up to this point, and the only thing strong enough to keep me from killing myself was the Lunachicks. Maybe it was because I was young and we were all so naive, but I never saw us not being together as a band; I mean, I didn't really think we would be playing "Buttplug" onstage together at sixty-five or anything, but I just always thought things would sort of magically work out. Like one thing would lead to the next, creatively, and I'd always have a fabulous next move. But the day came, both Theo and Gina had a plan, and I did not. I. Couldn't. Handle it. I felt as if they were both like, "This sucks! On to the next!" I was angry and so jealous because they were excited and I felt like I was going to die. It never ever ever ever dawned on me that one day it would all just stop. I couldn't see what was next, and nothing scared me more than having nothing. I had no other identity, no other way to mirror my self-worth. Losing the band was like getting saddled with a giant hunk of kryptonite. Where are your superpowers now, bi-otch?! I knew it was going to be like getting clean all over again, starting from nothing. *Guhh, what thaaaafucccck killlll meee.* I don't really remember being asked. I wouldn't have done it, but thank god I didn't have a say. I would've hung in probably forever and endured anything just because I didn't know what the hell to do next.

GINA: Another reason I had for wanting to stop was that music started to change. It was 2000, and we were a '90s punk band, but it was a new millennium and all this incredible new music started to come out. The 2000s are still, to this day, one of my favorite eras of music. The '90s were very poppy-punk and then all of a sudden everybody was going into this more offbeat, dark area, which is where my heart is. People were emulating Gang of Four, one of my favorite bands, and looking to the new wave and post-punk eras for inspiration. It was a creative cross-pollination of styles that I was ready to tap into for myself, but we still had tours to finish, so for the rest of the year, we kept plugging away in our yellow-and-black outfits. I feel like a dick saying this, but I felt like maybe I had grown out of being a Lunachick. I didn't feel so crazy or funny. I didn't want to wear silly dresses and glitter anymore.

THEO: This was cute when we were teenagers and in our twenties, but we were thirty and it wasn't so cute anymore. It was like I grew out of it. The experiences I was having weren't as fulfilling, and definitely felt more pressure-filled. "Okay, now we have to make another album. Is it going to be as exciting as the last one? What do I have to say?" Knowing myself as an artist and the way art flows through me, I needed to take a little left turn. And I've taken many left turns since. Art is so developmental in that way. When we began, I was like, "I want to be in the spotlight, I want to be the ham." It's almost like I went from that to needing to retreat inward like a caterpillar. From our teens to age thirty, the band was something I needed, then it was like, "Hmmm, this is not working anymore." If we were to have made another album after *Luxury Problem*, there would have been a lot of arguing. Gina was into Jesus Lizard, and I was more into weird electronic dance and metal. So when the band was over, I made a metal dance album. Actually, three metal dance albums.

GINA: Yeah, I know, I'm stubborn. I knew what kind of music I wanted to make, and I guess I just didn't want to have to compromise on that anymore. I wanted to do my own thing. I was listening to PJ Harvey and Queens of the Stone Age all the time. I wanted to be playing more than just three-chord punk songs—which I love, which is fun, but it wasn't a challenge for me.

SQUID: In truth, creatively, we hit a wall.

THEO: I was tired of making punk rock songs. At that point, it felt very automatic: *I am a robot and this is what I do onstage. These are the songs I sing. I jump around and I wear this hair.* It was a job, but it wasn't financially practical—the band was never anybody's only source of income. We just weren't successful enough to

tell ourselves to keep trying. The lack of greater success definitely contributed to our decision to end the
band. We couldn't be in our thirties and lying three in
a bed. We needed space. Not that we didn't all love each
other, but there came a point where we couldn't do that
anymore.

GINA: It was apparent to me that we weren't going to get to
the next level. We all put our heart and soul into this
band, and maybe we shoulda made it along further, but
for whatever reason, we just were not able to, and of
course I had some disappointment about that. I believed in our music, but I knew we were oddballs who
didn't write the kind of songs that appealed to a mass
market. Or maybe it just wasn't in the cards for us.

THEO: I hate to think about being competitive and jealous of
other bands, other women in bands, and other women in
general, but it *is* real. It exists. I have to be truthful. I was jealous when other female bands got signed
to major labels in the '90s and we didn't. I now see
why, and I get it—we were a different animal not to be
domesticated—but it *did* hurt. I feel it is my duty as
a feminist to talk about this. When a certain pop star
who was very familiar with us (who we may have toured
with) started wearing her hair and makeup and clothes
like mine, I felt like I was going insane, like my soul
was being stolen and I was the only one who saw it. I
didn't want to call out the person, plus I figured I was
better than that and no one would care anyway. We all
copy someone. When other people started noticing the
similarities between this pop star and me, I knew I
wasn't insane, but I was still pissed as hell.

SQUID: I'm horrified to talk about this and almost don't wanna
talk about this, but I think it's part of a bigger conversation: I was furious that the Donnas were getting

paid more than us on the Warped Tour. I feel embarrassed to say that because how come it didn't matter to me what all the other guy bands were being paid? It's a statement again about sexism, how there's a systematic deprivation exercise happening where there can only be a precious few females allowed through the golden gates. Well, it works. Thirteen years of being brainwashed with the same shit over and over ... you got me, patriarchy. Half of me feels total shame having fallen for it and the other half total fury because it's such a setup, and you don't have to be in a band to know what I'm talking about. I don't want to feel like I have to shy away from saying it, because we all know it's real. For women, sexism isn't the elephant in the room—it *is* the room. See: "internalized sexism." Look it up.

GINA: The irony of that! It's what everybody said about us when we got signed: "Oh, they're young girls, and that's the only reason they got a record deal." Flash forward, and there's the Donnas. They're young girls and they're getting more money and recognition. It reminded me of when we showed up on one of our European tours and found out the Vibrators were opening for us. That was really hard for me because I was such a huge Vibrators fan.

THEO: I was mortified. The Vibrators were heroes of ours.

GINA: I was like, "They're opening ... for us???" It felt wrong.

SQUID: Maybe it was all part of the burnout vibe we were experiencing. I felt the weight of the lack of opportunity and maybe respect. It's easy to be supportive of everyone around you when you're happy and feeling on top and getting what you want, and it's just as easy to lapse into pettiness and jealousy when, for whatever reason, you're not.

After kicking ass that summer on Warped, we headed into the fall of 2000 headlining a tour with Mindless Self Indulgence opening for us. We started to notice the crowds felt just a little thinner than before. Mindless Self Indulgence were from a newer (and younger) generation of up-and-coming bands who were great. Their fans made up a noticeable portion of the audience. There weren't as many people there to see us as usual, which was really hard to take. The reckoning was upon us.

GINA: We had such a great year, and I was worried that I would see our career decline. I saw it happen to other bands we were touring with that had hit a similar peak and their popularity and buzz were slipping, and they were playing to smaller crowds in smaller venues. Not that that's a problem necessarily; it's a natural occurrence, but I knew I didn't want to experience the disappointment of seeing our relevance fade. I wanted to leave Lunachicks while we were still on top. Walking away with our heads held high and feeling proud of all that we accomplished.

SQUID: During that tour, it started happening where I'd be in the van all day, just wanting to get out of the van so bad. But by the time we finally rolled into the club, after we'd been driving for hours and the sun was setting, and we were exhausted from doing nothing, I'd dread having to play and do the whole thing. One time, Theo and I went out shopping before the show. We bought some hand lotion, exfoliating scrub, or some such shit. Showtime came, and in between songs, Theo put the mic down, and we looked at each other and started whispering, like, *I can't wait to get the fuck out of here, go to the hotel and get in our pajamas, watch TV, and use my new face scrub.*

THEO: I mouthed "LOTION."

SQUID: Back to reality, "Okay, let's go, onetwothreefour!!" The writing was on the wall. Like, this is the end; it's over. That being said, I never would have pulled the plug. I was so used to being miserable—junkies are very good at that. People who live that kind of drug-addicted lifestyle have such a high tolerance for chaos and uncomfortableness. I can't imagine what shit could've gone down in the band before I would've had enough sense to get out of it.

There was never a breakup discussion. We didn't know how to break up! We didn't want to say we were through, so we never did. We also never wanted to say we quit and then have a reunion, even though that's what people think happened. By the time we got home from our last European tour, just before 2001 rang in, we each began our separate journeys but didn't have the heart to call it officially quits. It's a break, we said, a hiatus, a punk rock *Rumspringa*, if you will. The words "We're not doing this anymore" were never spoken by any one of us. It was more like, "Well, let's not book any Lunachicks tours right now. Let's walk away for a little while, and we can reconvene later. We'll be back, we just don't know when." We still talked to and saw each other practically every day. We were sisters for life and the bond we had between us was as deep as it gets, so we couldn't quite bear the thought that it would actually all be over, after all of those years, all of that work, all of that fucking glitter everywhere, still in our underwear! We'd be back someday. This couldn't be how it ends.

GINA: Life without the Lunachicks was alternately total freedom and total terror. I had creative freedom to do whatever the hell I wanted. I can sing! I can write lyrics! I can write my own dirge-y songs that Lunachicks fans might hate, but I'm doin' it anyway. It was exhilarating and at the same time terrifying because I was no longer hiding behind a tutu and gobs of makeup. And most of all I no longer had Theo and Syd at my side. I was naked and alone now. There I was standing at the mic, this is who I am, this is how I feel, and this is my art. I felt extremely exposed and simultaneously so creatively fulfilled.

SQUID: I'll never forget this Dee Dee Ramone interview I heard. He was talking about how much he hated being in the Ramones. How he wasn't allowed to cut his hair, wasn't allowed to change his clothes. How he was forced to wear this uniform of a kid who hated himself, forever. How he wasn't allowed to ever grow up and be himself and do what he wanted to do. Where's the punk rock in that? That's the thing—people want you to be what they want you to be, what works for them, not you, and when you don't obey, they call you a sellout. And what does that even mean? Granted, Dee Dee's solo band sucked so bad. We opened for them. Ugh, you can't win; such is the fucked-ness of life.

THEO: I didn't know what I was going to do next exactly, and to think of myself without this band was terrifying, but I also really wanted to do stuff on my own. I wanted to make other kinds of music. I was still modeling and acting too. I had some offers, one from a guy who wanted to make me into a tattooed pop star à la Britney Spears. I couldn't do it. I was still gonna put myself out there; it wasn't like, "I'm done with all of it." I just had to shift. It's a scary thing to do when you're known for one thing, and part of me wondered how people would react to me without the band. But I had to continue to create what was coming out of me. It's scary to put yourself out there in any way and then hope that people go along with it. Whenever people would approach me and ask about the Lunachicks, I'd say, "Oh, we're taking a break." It started to drive me nuts. No matter what type of performances I was doing, I'd get, "Hey, when are the Lunachicks gonna play?" Everybody wanted the old me, just like I had feared. I understood it, but it was still annoying! All that fan love was not really for me, it was for what I represented at a certain time. Well, why can't you love what I'm doing now? Frustrating. But I was very self-confident in my new music and I was gonna do it. That's being an artist. You create things because it comes from a need in your guts.

I kept thinking about David Bowie, one of my absolute idols, and how he kept changing. When I started doing my solo electronic music, which was all written with my partner in life and crime, Sean Pierce, I felt a little anxious performing without the band, but I also had two women who are dear friends and amazing performers in their own right, Viva Ruiz and Jaiko Suzuki, dancing with me, one on each side of me, a familiar and comforting feeling à la Syd and Gina on each side of me for all those years creating pure magic. I wasn't ready to start a new band. The Lunachicks was too fresh and too dear, in a way, for me to bring other people in like that so soon. A few years later, Sean and I found some awesome, equally tall dudes and that became Theo and the Skyscrapers. It's a VERY different experience touring with a van full of dudes, lemme tell ya.

SQUID: I started a band with my friend Tracy. That was good for me. There was something very nice about the fact that I could just write a song the way I wanted to write it without the weight of so many opinions. It was fun again to be in a room with people just playing music and not having to argue your point about everything. They were like, "You're great. We love your idea." I was like, "Really? Wow! This is easy." Maybe it sucked—who cares!? It just felt great not to be second-guessed on everything. We had all gotten so used to constantly having to negotiate on everything, I think everyone was probably feeling the same creative relief. It was good and fun just to be prolific and free without any expectations or pressure. I wrote a bunch on my four-track and played some local shows with my band. No matter how great the Lunachicks were, I never wanted to be one of those people living off the glory of the past. Once I finally had some real distance and some real direction again, I started to understand how lucky I was, that we put it down right when we did, that I had this chance to really create myself all over again from the ground up. I completely switched tracks, started my own business, and popped out a couple kids—some more things to cross off that "someday I'm gonna do this!" list. But before I was able to do any of that and really get my life going, I had to clear one more major hurdle. In 2002, I had been living in Thailand for a while ... trying to "find" myself, I guess. I had just gotten home to Brooklyn and had been feeling super-tired, like REALLY tired. I was confused; I didn't know what I was supposed to be doing with my life. Then I got a pain in my neck and then a pain in my waist. I thought it was just a pinched nerve from being stressed out, and I was right. It was a pinched nerve—caused by a two-pound tumor in my spleen that was also crushing half of my vital organs. I was thirty-three.

GINA: I'll never forget the casual phone conversation I had with Squid as she was walking in for a massage, only to get the call hours later that this was no ordinary muscle tightness, this was life and death. My heart sank. How could this be?! We were in the prime of our lives!

THEO: The news was beyond shocking. Cancer. I froze, and then all I wanted to do was run to her. None of the rest of the shit mattered. Gina and I would go to the hospital alone and together as much as we could.

GINA: It was so surreal being in the hospital by her bedside.

THEO: The two of us helped sponge-bathe Squid. I almost passed out when we were doing that, it was just beyond comprehension. My nickname for her was Tubie because she had all these tubes stuck in her. And I am a person who watched all the goriest movies possible for years. But when faced with someone I loved in this way? Nope.

SQUID: For starters, I had no health insurance, of course. I was an artist in Bush-era 2003, so I literally couldn't afford to live—or to die. I ended up doing a back-alley deal with a reputable surgeon. I showed up to this guy's office, me and my tumor, and like a drug deal, I slipped him an envelope with $12K in cash. In turn, he secretly booked a surgery room for the following week and then sneaked me into the hospital by way of the emergency room, where, by law, I couldn't be denied lifesaving medical treatment. True story. Nothing can be normal, ever. Thank god he did a great job. He saved my life. After twelve hours of surgery, I had a startling reminder of just how much I do not miss getting high. I was five years clean and woke up on a morphine drip. This is the stuff junkie dreams are made of. The big freebee get-out-of-jail-free card, get-high pass. My thumb was glued to the drip release button, squeeze, squeeze, squeeze. I was high off my face, except everyone in the room was telling me they loved me, and I was surrounded by gorgeous bouquets of flowers. Uhhh, weird. The last time I was that high, everybody hated me and was telling me to go fuck myself. At one point,

I had to go to the bathroom, and then I saw myself in the mirror. My stomach dropped. "Oh no, it's YOU again!" There she was, like no time had passed. Boring shitty junkie mess. Looking into those dead eyes, ugh, it was so depressing. It sucked. I just wanted to get off that drip and get the hell outta there.

Mentally I tapped out, I just didn't want to deal with it, which is crazy because my life was on the line, but my whole world and identity were being completely hijacked by this cancer-patient soap opera and I just wanted to be normal again already. I remember talking to Gina and I think she was asking me, like, "Did you read about this and do you know about that, have you looked into blah blah blah?" and I was like, "No. I can't." I think she got it, and she just took over—that's how she is. She took on this role where she started researching information and resources on my behalf and making sure I had all the information I needed. Maybe in retrospect to her it was relatively small, a few hours on the computer here and there, a few phone calls, but for me what lives is the feeling, like, "I can't do this," and she came in and did it for me.

GINA: We had been everywhere together, all over the globe, but we had never been in this territory before. It was harsh, and it was scary. Everything else seemed so petty.

THEO: No matter what we had been through, no matter the hurt, the anger, the pain, the worry, this was my sister/friend/bandmate and all I cared about was that she live and get better and be okay. I was there with her for the ride no matter what it would take.

SQUID: Theo, oh man. Our old friend Lee from the neighborhood had this really old family dog named Frida, like a hundred-something in dog years—cataracts, barely walking, one tooth. Sometimes we'd call Lee, like, "Hey, what are you up to?" and he'd say, "Yoooo, I gotta go. I gotta take Frida for a drag." It cracked us up every time. After my surgery, I rehabbed at my dad's place back in the old hood. Well, Theo came by every single day and took me out for my daily "drag," which was basically her holding me up and half carrying me, hobbling around the block. We were cracking up the whole time for some reason, because we thought it was funny. Because with her everything is funny.

In 2002, CBGB announced that it was closing, and a lot of bands, including us, came back to play one last time. We called it the Lunachick Fringe show: Chip's band played, Gina's band Bantam played, Theo played, and Squid's band played. Then Lunachicks played at the end of the night, and Sindi got onstage for a few songs. The next time we decided to play was two years later, 2004, at a NARAL benefit in Washington, DC, during the weekend of the March for Women's Lives. NARAL's then-president Kate Michelman joined us onstage after our set and showered us with love. We turned her into a fan for life. Theo wept.

> THEO: As soon as she walked out, I almost totally broke down and lost it. It was so incredible and special and important to be there standing up for our rights, and I felt it deeply in my heart. My knees buckled and my nose started running as I snorted back tears.

For that reason, we didn't want to say we were officially done because who knows what could come up?

Somehow, fifteen years passed. Throughout that time, we took the creative energy and unorthodox ethos that powered the Lunachicks and we transferred it to other projects—some musical, some not—all of which we approached with that same unconventional mentality. We still wanted to do what wasn't expected of us or, at the very least, keep people guessing, ourselves included. The very abbreviated version goes something like this:

Theo continued modeling and acting; made music with her hubs and partner, Sean Pierce, both on a solo album and in a band (Theo and the Skyscrapers); DJ'd and promoted Rated X/The Panty Party, a weekly rock 'n' roll dance party, with DJ Michael T and MC Peppermint Gummybear for seven years; did music and visual performance pieces with Rob Roth; wrote and toured as part of Caden Manson and Jemma Nelson's multimedia performance ensemble Big Art Group; launched a makeup line called Armour Beauty; had a daughter, Lucy; and became a pro makeup artist.

Squid retired from professional tattooing after a decade and a half; designed, built, owned, and operated a successful Brooklyn restaurant, the Roebling Tea Room in Williamsburg, for thirteen years; had two daughters; launched a coaching practice; and continues with her entrepreneurial endeavors.

In addition to releasing two Bantam albums on her label, Gina scored and coproduced a musical, composed the score for a few indie films, released a solo EP followed by several singles, made a bunch of music videos, had her first solo art show, opened up a decorative painting company, and continued to produce as much art and music as time would allow.

We also bagged some pretty fine-ass men as husbands. All three of us live in Brooklyn. This city will always be our home, and just like the cockroaches, no matter how the city changes, we will never leave.

While we were working on this book, Vans approached us to be part of a series of ads for a new sneaker collection. They chose an old photo of us playing live at CBGB in 1990, taken by Chris Boarts Larson. A full-on ad campaign was about to hit the city, including in the subway tunnels and other public areas. It was a cool thing to be part of, but we didn't give it that much thought. Then we saw it. The following is an actual text exchange:

Wednesday, February 6, 2019, 7:28 p.m. EST

Squid: Can't make this shit up.

Theo: Shut the fuck up.
Theo: Where is that???

Squid: I can't 😂

Squid: Penn Station

Theo: NO!

Squid: YES

Theo: Holy fuck

Squid: Vans has the whole tunnel

Theo: R u there now?
Theo: OMG

Squid: 😂😂😂
Squid: Yes I'm standing here like a tourist taking pictures and trying not to laugh I look insane

Theo: Omg
Theo: Gina is gonna shit

Squid: I mean I LITERALLY walked right into it 😂😂😂😂😂 😂😂😂
Squid: Someone find her a diaper quick

Theo: Hahahahah

Squid: We're up at least 3 times. It repeats.
Squid: Sorry 4 times

Gina: OMG!!! Bahhaaaaaaaaaaaaaaa!!!
Gina: Where ?????

Squid: Times Square

Gina: They cleaned the blood off my legs!!!
Gina: Pooping!!

Theo: Whoa Hahahahahahahah
Theo: Censorship!!

Gina: I know!
Gina: I have to go see this!

Theo: Yes!!
Theo: Shit
Theo: It's bonkers
Theo: So crazy you happened to see it Syd!

Gina: I know it's crazy that Syd was the one who first saw it. Perfect!

Gina: We made Times Square

Gina: We should do a photoshoot in front of it!

Squid: I went to a meeting randomly I have NEVER been to before in my life in midtown. I mean what are the fucking chances.

Squid: I just texted Sindi too

Squid: I feel like I'm on acid

Theo: Yeah I bet!!!

Squid: Like I feel weird leaving. Lolllllllll

Squid: Like maybe I should just stay here. . . . indefinitely 😂

Gina: Ha I wanna go see it!

Squid: It feels awkward just leaving us here lol

Theo: Yes!!

Gina: Syd I wish I was there with you we could start a convo for passers by

Squid: Haaaaaa

Theo: Me too!

Squid: Wait! Sorry I am on acid. I'm at 14th STREET!!!!

Theo: Hahahahahahahhahahahaha hahahahahahahah

Squid: Hah completely fucked my head up

Squid: 8th AVE

Theo: Hilarious

Squid: Squid Classic

Theo: Total

Gina: Hahaaaaa!

Squid: I need a nap

The subway posters were mind-melting, but nothing prepared us for seeing the same ad plastered on the entire side of a building in Williamsburg, Brooklyn, and another in SoHo. It was attack of the fifty-foot Lunachicks for real. The three of us met in front of the building in Williamsburg to take it all in, amazed and thrilled, the same weirdos who still recognized in each other an urgent need to be seen and heard. Any lingering feelings of lost opportunity or of being overlooked seemed to vanish. The significance of our gigantic portraits hovering over our city was not lost on us. We had made our mark and right here was a reminder of that, a really big-ass reminder. It was a great sense of recognition, however delayed it may have come, and it was satisfying *AS FUCK*.

We couldn't have predicted that several months later we'd announce our first show in fifteen years and that it'd sell out in under twenty minutes, which prompted a second show, which also sold out. Nor could we have imagined cramming into a practice space with Chip to rehearse all those old songs, trying—and failing—not to laugh, howling in hysterics the way we used to. Those thoughts wouldn't be formed for some time. At that moment, it was just the three of us standing shoulder to shoulder on a sidewalk in Brooklyn, looking up . . . at us.

THANK EWES

Thank you to everyone at Hachette Books for believing in our story, especially our editor, Ben Schafer, who supported us each step of the way. Thank you to our agent, Ryan Fischer-Harbage, for the enthusiasm and guidance. To Sindi B., our sister forever, we love you. To our drummer Chip English, we love you with all our hearts and farts. Thanks to drummers past: Becky Wreck, Kate Schellenbach, Tia Sprocket (RIP), Andrea "Big Mama Freak" Kusten, and Gus Morgan. All our love to Stormy Shepherd for so much more than just booking the tours, managing us, and always listening. Thank you to Greg Ross for working so hard and always believing in us and to whom we owe a lifetime supply of Rogaine (sorry we caused all of your hair to fall out!), and to the team at Go-Kart Records. Thanks to Loren Chodosh for handling our legal affairs and standing by with the bail money. It's impossible to name everyone who helped us along the way, so here is a very incomplete list of folks to whom we owe a lot: Ilya Chaiken, Jeanine Corbet, Katrina Del Mar, Steve Fine, Jane Friedman, Gyda Gash, G-Spot, Kim Gordon, Julie Gunther, Miss Guy, Lenny Kaye, Michael Lavine, Brad Logan, Fat Mike, Thurston Moore, BJ Papas, Louise Parnassa Staley, Andrea Purcigliotti, Howie Pyro, Hopey Rock, Paul Smith and the team at Blast First, Johnny Stiff, Richie Stotts, Wharton Tiers, Cyndy Villano, Lynne Von, and all the roadies, crew, drivers, merch sellers, and soundpeople we bled on along the way. And thanks to all the bands who took us out on tour or with whom we've had the pleasure of sharing a stage. Love to Justin Vivian Bond, Bridget Everett, Debbie Harry, Peaches, and Ann Powers for throwing their support behind our book proposal, and to Josh

Blum and Jennifer Lange for the early reads. Endless thanks to our incredible fans everywhere—we love you, you beautiful freaks. Thanks to our partners in crime, our hubs Andrew Gosselin, John Nolan, and Sean Pierce, and to our littlest Lunachicks, Rio, Pepper, and Lucy. And to our families, our sisters, and our parents, sorry, thank you, and we love you.

Annnnd . . . we could not have done this book without the brilliant, talented (and extremely patient) Jeanne Fury, who herded us feral cats and made it happen. Thank you, sorry (not sorry) for torturing you. WE LOVE YOU, JEANNE!!!!

Jeanne Fury: I'm forever grateful to my brother Paul, who introduced me to punk rock and saved my ass in the pit many times over, and to my parents, who tolerated the sweet sounds of *Jerk of All Trades* blasting from my teenage bedroom for months on end. Thanks to Ryan Fischer-Harbage for taking us on, and to Ben Schafer for being an exemplary editor and friend. Massive gratitude to my pals and confidants, especially Sandi Boerum and Stu Newman, Josh Blum, Daphne Brooks, Shawn Carney and Amy Niebel, Joss Citrone Coyle, Urcella Di Pietro, Kerry Finnegan, Donna "Mama" Gaines, Caryn Ganz, Jackson and Leah Greenblatt, Jen Lange, Ann Powers, Mike and Elizabeth Turbé, Kim Watson, the ever-awesome Evelyn McDonnell for her mentorship, and Melissa Houston, my perennial ray of light. Extra thanks to Jeanne Flavin and Nicola Pitchford for the unconditional love and communal support sessions. Love to Willie Mae Rock Camp and the Girls Rock Camp Alliance. Ultimate thank-youse to the Lunachicks for the honor of a lifetime.

In loving memory of Dean Kennedy.

Tokyo, 1993

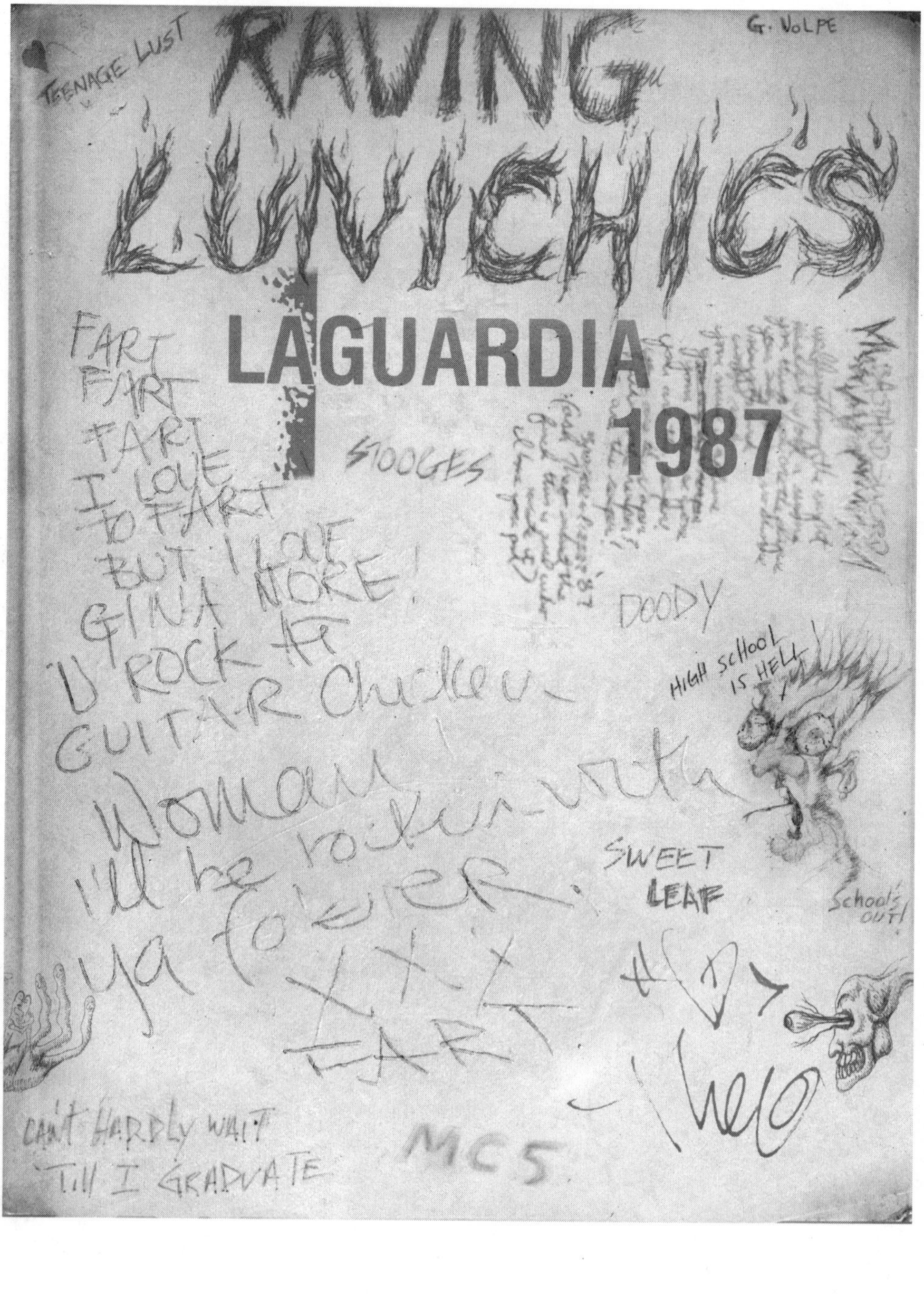
RAVING LUNATICS
TEENAGE LUST
G. VOLPE
LAGUARDIA
1987
FART FART FART I LOVE TO FART BUT I LOVE GINA MORE!
U ROCK GUITAR Chicken
STOOGES
DOODY
HIGH SCHOOL IS HELL
Woman I'll be rockin with ya forever
XXX FART
SWEET LEAF
School's out!
CAN'T HARDLY WAIT TILL I GRADUATE
MC5

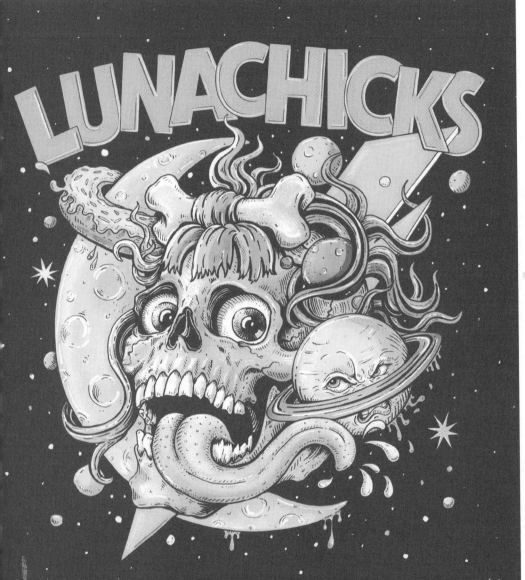